SECRETS OF THE CENTENARIANS

SECRETS

OF THE

CENTENARIANS

What is it Like to Live for a Century
and Which of Us Will Survive to Find Out?

JOHN WITHINGTON

REAKTION BOOKS

Published by Reaktion Books Ltd
Unit 32, Waterside
44–48 Wharf Road
London N1 7UX, UK
www.reaktionbooks.co.uk

First published 2017
Copyright © John Withington 2017

Printed and bound in Great Britain
by TJ International, Padstow, Cornwall

A catalogue record for this book is available from the British Library

ISBN 978 1 78023 818 0

Contents

If I'd known I was going to live this long,
I'd have taken better care of myself.

GEORGE BURNS, American comedian, aged 100

Introduction

In 1984 I spotted a small paragraph in a newspaper saying that people aged 100 and over were the fastest-growing portion of Britain's population. The story revealed that 30 years before there had been only 200 centenarians, whereas by 1984 there were well over 2,000. I was astonished. At the time, I was a reporter on *TV Eye* – then one of the ITV Network's flagship current affairs programmes – and it struck me that here was an extraordinary, intriguing and virtually unreported change going on around us that would provide the basis for a fascinating, thought-provoking programme. It was rather outside my normal staple diet of investigating the secret arrangements governing the use of U.S. military bases in the UK, exposing consultants who were cheating the NHS or reporting on the global scourge of AIDS, but I managed to persuade the series editor that we should conduct our own study of 100 centenarians to find out why there were so many more of them, how they felt about reaching this milestone and what seemed to set apart those who survived from those who died.

In addition to doing the survey, we interviewed a number of 100-year-olds on camera, including one 'celebrity', Lord Shinwell, then still an active Labour politician and probably Britain's best-known centenarian. Helped by some illuminating and moving testimony from him and the other interviewees, the programme was enthusiastically received and attracted the biggest audience for any *TV Eye* in that series. Then, as journalists do, I moved on to other stories, and, of course, all the people I interviewed gradually died off. Still, I always kept my interest in centenarians and continued to follow their story, hoarding cuttings as their numbers continue to grow remorselessly, increasing about sevenfold since 1985.

The last century has seen most of us living longer and better, and looking better for longer as well. In the 1970s, Brigitte Bardot created a sensation by still looking stunning at 40. In the 1980s, it was Joan Collins at 50. Then in the 1990s, Ursula Andress was offered $250,000 to pose nude for *Playboy* at 60. And we don't just look better. During the last decade we have seen people skiing to the South Pole in their sixties, climbing Mount Everest or appearing in professional ballet in their seventies, or editing magazines into their nineties.

And yet Professor Tom Kirkwood, a leading authority on old people and ageing, was surprised at how negatively our increased life span was often regarded:

> Just last summer, an article presenting new forecasts of even longer lifespans in the most affluent countries was published in one of the world's leading science journals. A brief editorial trailer for this report announced glumly that the situation was 'even worse than expected'. I wonder just how old was the member of the editorial team who penned that piece?

Kirkwood asked, 'Should we be pleased or depressed?', and replied, 'Surely we should be pleased.'

Despite the increase in their numbers, centenarians remain a remarkable elite. In 2014 in the UK there were about 14,500, meaning they make up about one in every 4,450 people in the population. Even so, to have about 90 times as many centenarians as there were 100 years ago surely amounts to a revolution. This is the story of that revolution and the people who made it: the centenarians.

ONE

Nasty, Brutish and Short

'Nasty, brutish and short' was how the seventeenth-century authoritarian philosopher Thomas Hobbes described human life in an imagined primitive state of nature, before government came along, with everyone at war with everyone else. And that certainly seems to have been the story for our forerunners, the Neanderthals, who began roaming the earth perhaps 200,000 years ago. An anthropologist who has examined dental records from 130,000 years ago declared of Neanderthals, 'no-one survived past 30.' This hardly seems surprising when you discover that Neanderthal remains show that nearly all of them had suffered serious wounds or broken bones, and most had been victims of malnutrition. Neanderthals died out around 40,000 years ago, but some anthropologists believe there was a dramatic increase in human lifespan while our ancestors, *Homo sapiens,* were living in the Stone Age, about 30,000 years ago, with perhaps two-thirds of those who did not die in childhood surviving past 30, and a few living beyond 50.

The story is all very different in the Book of Genesis. Methuselah, we are told in chapter 5, verse 27, lived for '969 years'. We learn little else about him, except that he was the son of Enoch (and the great-great-great-great-great-grandson of Adam) and that he 'begat Lamech'. Lamech himself did not do badly, chalking up 777 years, but the longest survivor apart from Methuselah was his grandfather, Jared, who lived to 962. We know nothing much about him, either, but the third-oldest person in the Bible is one of the most famous of all Old Testament characters, Noah, whose age when he died, according to Genesis, was 950. He was also the last of the so-called 'pluricentenarians'.

The very good old days ended with the Great Flood that floated his ark. Afterwards, longevity went, along with so much else, to the dogs: Abraham lasted only 175 years and Jacob 147, while Moses shuffled off this mortal coil at just 120. So why were these claims of extraordinary longevity made about the ancient patriarchs? For those who believe in a literal interpretation of the Bible, the answer is straightforward: in those antediluvian times, before God had to punish man's wickedness so severely, people really did survive to these amazing ages. The more sceptical offer a variety of other explanations. Perhaps an ancient translator confused months and years, or maybe someone simply multiplied the ages by, say, ten. (Both these suggestions generate some odd results, however, such as patriarchs fathering children before they were three years old.) Some thought they had detected an attempt to manipulate ages so that those of notables such as Abraham, Isaac, Jacob and Joseph were linked by complex mathematical formulae. Or maybe an ancient writer simply thought that attributing these fabulous ages to the biblical patriarchs would make them appear more important.

Still, even Methuselah's days seem like the blink of an eye when compared with the Sumerian king En-men-lu-ana, who is alleged to have ruled for 43,200 years. Indeed, stories of extreme longevity are found far and wide in the ancient world. So the Persians had a tyrannical emperor named Zahhak, who is supposed to have reigned for 1,000 years before being overthrown. Three thousand years ago in China, Peng Zu, a highly respected figure in Taoism, was said to have reached the age of 800, while the ancient Greeks had the Cretan seer Epimenides, who, when sent to look after a flock of sheep, nodded off in a cave for 57 years. His age was given variously as 154, 157 and 290. What unites all these claims of extreme longevity is that there is not a shred of evidence to support them.

From ancient Greece, though, we do start to get some clearer statistical evidence about how long individuals lived. A biological anthropologist who examined nearly 150 skeletons from Athens and Corinth concluded that the men survived to an average age of 45, and the women to 36. Until modern times, average life expectancy was dragged down by high infant mortality, and there are clear indications that some ancient Greeks did reach a ripe old age. Men were required to do military service until they were 60, while you had to have passed that age to be eligible for the senate in Sparta. We also become confident enough about the dates of birth and death of some

Methuselah stained-glass window, Canterbury Cathedral.

Sixteenth-century depiction of the tyrant Tiran Zahhak imprisoned in a cave.

notable people to say Socrates lived to 70 (and even then it took a dose of hemlock to get rid of him). His great pupil, Plato, survived until 80, while the famous playwright Sophocles reached 90, and was still creating new dramas right up until the end. The endocrinologist Professor Menelaos Batrinos has suggested that there are 83 Greek 'men of renown' of the fourth and fifth centuries BC about whose life spans we can be certain. Batrinos calculated their average age as about 70. This is strikingly similar to the life span the Bible allocates to humans in Psalm 90: 'The days of our years are threescore years and ten,' unless 'by reason of strength they be fourscore. Plainly, Batrinos's group is not representative of the ancient Greek population as a whole, and might well be expected to live longer. (Better-off people always tend to survive longer. An American study in the 1960s suggested that those listed in *Who's Who* generally had longer lives than the rest of us.) Professor Batrinos notes the factors that would have helped these early great and good: a mild climate, good sanitation and plenty of slaves to do the heavy lifting. They also had the beginnings of the Mediterranean diet – regarded today as among the most healthy in the world. Some of its modern ingredients, such as oranges, lemons and tomatoes, were not grown in Greece at that time, but other fruits and vegetables featured prominently alongside fish, olive oil, mushrooms, onions, garlic and lentils. Ancient physicians advised eating meat and sweet things only in moderation, while recommending tropical spices like pepper, ginger and cinnamon to those who could afford them. Hippocrates counselled, 'Let food be thy medicine and medicine be thy food,' but Professor Batrinos considers that the most important factor in ancient Greek longevity may have been the 'animated social life in which the aged actively participated' and the 'great respect' shown to them. Whatever the exact formula, it seems to have worked. The historian of medicine Mirko Grmek said that in ancient Greece, 'average lifespan reached heights that were not attained again until the twentieth century.'

So could the ancient Greeks provide plausible candidates for the title of first known centenarian? An expert on British centenarians, Roger Thatcher, who was Registrar General for England and Wales from 1978 to 1986, calculated it was 'unlikely' that anyone reached 100 'before about 1700'. But the American demographer John Wilmoth reckons that from around 2500 BC, the world's population was big enough for the occasional person to make the century, under the law of averages – the idea being that the more humans there are, the greater the chance that the odd one will evade the thousand natural shocks of life to attain the magic mark. And an American actuary named Kenneth Faig, who made a study of longevity in ancient times, gives cautious credence to claims that a philosopher called Gorgias may have been a centenarian. He seems to have been born around 485 BC in Sicily, to have gone to Athens in his fifties as an ambassador, and to have died around 380 BC. Faig says the idea that Gorgias reached 100 should not be 'rejected outright as implausible'. Around the same time, according to a number of ancient authorities, another philosopher, Democritus of Abdera, may have made it to 109. Democritus was one of the first people to advance the theory that the world is built of atoms. He was known as the 'laughing philosopher' and was a great advocate of 'cheerfulness', achieved when 'the soul lives peacefully and tranquilly, undisturbed by fear or superstition or any other feeling'. Sceptical about religion, he thought that people believed in the gods in order to find a way of explaining extraordinary natural phenomena such as thunderstorms and earthquakes.

It seems that when Rome took over from Greece as the centre of Western civilization, life expectancy did not improve. An analysis of inscriptions on tombstones in parts of the Roman Empire revealed

Johannes Moreelse, *Democritus*, 1630.

that men on average lived to about 45, and women only 30 – but these figures are almost certainly optimistic, since poorer people, who would tend to die younger, would not have been able to afford tombstones. A pioneer of population dynamics named E. S. Deevey gave a lower estimate, of 35, for people in ancient Greece, declining to 32 in classical Rome, but evidence is so scarce that these figures remain highly speculative. Rather than trying to come up with an average age for the whole population, a British neurophysiologist, J. D. Montagu, took a similar approach to Professor Batrinos, considering only Greek and Roman men about whose dates we can be certain. Excluding those who met a violent end, he was left with just 70 individuals, plus another 228 for whom he had reasonable approximate dates. Readily acknowledging that his subjects would have an average life span higher than that of the population as a whole, because they were more prosperous and also excluded those who died in childhood, Montagu concluded that men born before 100 BC survived for a strikingly high average span of 72 years. Intriguingly, though, for those born after that date, the figure falls dramatically, to around 62. Montagu thought this might be because the Romans used lead pipes for drinking water. He also compared his ancient life expectancy figures to those of eminent men who died between 1850 and 1899, and between 1900 and 1949, which averaged out at 71.5 and 71 years, respectively. It was only in the 40 years after 1950 that he detected a significant move up, to 78. Echoing Grmek's comments, Montagu concluded that it was only since the Second World War 'that advances in medicine have allowed us to outlive those ancients of the BC era who managed to survive the early perils'.

Even though life expectancy seems to have slipped backwards during the Roman era, centenarian candidates continued to appear, such as St Anthony of Egypt, who endured the famous temptations. Considered the father of monasticism, Anthony, during a nineteen-year retreat to a mountain, had to keep fighting off the Devil, who might appear as a monk, a soldier, a wild beast or a seductive woman. Sometimes the Satanic visions beat him to within an inch of his life, but still he was supposed to have lived to 105.

The fall of the Roman Empire was followed by the Dark Ages, and exact information about dates of birth and death generally got lost in the pervading gloom, but as the Renaissance approached things once again become a little clearer. Research on the records of aristocratic families in England in the thirteenth century suggests that men who managed to survive until the age of 21, provided they could then avoid death from violence or accidents, might expect to live on average for another 43 years, a figure that was virtually unchanged in 1745. There were one or two ups and downs on the way, with the figure falling to just 24 in the fourteenth century, when so many died from the Black Death, and reaching its highest at just over 50 between 1500 and 1550. Because this sample group is so small, it would be wrong to read too much into these fluctuations, but they do suggest that even for the privileged few there was not much significant improvement in adult life expectancy from 1200 to 1745.

At all times, overall life expectancy was dragged down by infant mortality, with around one child in ten dying at birth or within its first year, and at least one in four perishing before they reached ten. Children were carried off by a variety of diseases – apart from plague under its various names, there was dysentery, smallpox, measles, typhus and so on. And there were other, more prosaic causes: infections from unsterilized instruments used to cut the umbilical cord, parasitic worms, diarrhoea, gangrene as babies cut their teeth. There were accidents, such as drowning in streams or ponds or even in washing tubs. Lack of sanitation meant that human waste was usually dumped close to the home, spreading disease, while thatched roofs provided a habitat for insects and rodents, and the bacteria they carried. Two Cambridge historians of population, E. A Wrigley and R. S. Schofield, reckoned that life expectancy at birth in England was just over 33 in 1541, fluctuating in the thirties until 1841 when it moved to just above 40.

Still, in spite of the lack of any significant increase in general life expectancy, could medieval and early modern times have provided us with an exceptional person who made it to 100? How about Thomas Parr? A humble farmworker from Shropshire, he lies in Westminster Abbey among the kings, queens, poets, composers, statesmen and generals. His claim to fame is stated on the inscription over his grave, which says he lived during the reigns of ten monarchs. Born in 1483, while the Wars of the Roses were still raging, Parr was said to have made it right through the Tudor dynasty – Henry VII, Henry VIII, Edward VI, Mary I and Elizabeth I. Then he outlasted the first Stuart king, James I, before finally shuffling off this mortal coil during the reign of James's successor, Charles I, in 1635. When he learned of Parr's prodigious age, Charles had the old man brought up to London in

Pieter Coecke van Aelst, *The Temptation of St Anthony*, c. 1543–50.

a specially built litter, and crowds flocked to see him. He became a national celebrity, as 'the old, old, very old Thomas Parr', and was painted by Peter Paul Rubens and Anthony van Dyck, while to this day his likeness adorns bottles of Old Parr whisky. A diet of green cheese, onions, coarse bread and mild ale, or, on special occasions, cider, was his recipe for long life, along with keeping 'your head cool by temperance and your feet warm by exercise. Rise early, go soon to bed' and 'keep your eyes open and your mouth shut'. But the change of air from the purity of the countryside to the putrefaction of the capital did not agree with him, and caused his death after just a few weeks. Or at least that was the view of the great physician Sir William Harvey, who discovered the circulation of the blood, and who carried out a post-mortem at the King's instruction. Harvey pronounced Parr's organs to be in exceptionally fine fettle, especially the genitals, which led the doctor to believe the story that the old man and his second wife, whom he married at 122, had intercourse 'exactly' as other couples do. He also noted that Parr had had to do penance for adultery and fathering an illegitimate child after his 100th birthday. The old man further proved his fitness by threshing corn at the age of 130. A poetic description of him noted, 'From head to heel his body had all over/ A quick-set thick-set natural hairy cover.' It is a wonderful story, but

William Harvey dissecting the body of Thomas Parr, *c.* 1900, painting.

nowadays nobody much believes that Parr lived to 152. One possible explanation for how the story gained credence is that his birth date got mixed up with his grandfather's.

Parr's claimed feat of longevity is not unique. About the same time, in Ireland, the Countess of Desmond was said to have lived to 140, while an 1833 guide to Richmond in North Yorkshire – 'celebrated', we are told, 'for the longevity of its inhabitants' – recounts the story of Henry Jenkins, who was 'about' 169 when he died in 1670. And a churchyard at Brislington in Bristol holds a tombstone with the inscription '1542. Thomas Newman. Aged 153. The stone was new faced in the year 1771 to perpetuate the great age of the deceased.' Bizarrely, a church at Bridlington in East Yorkshire has a board carrying a virtually identical inscription. None of these claims, though, meets the standards of proof required by modern students of the oldest old. (Nor, of course, do the centenarian candidates from ancient Greece and Rome.) So who was the first person we can be sure reached the age of 100? One contender who attracted a lot of support was a Norwegian peasant, Eilif Philipsen, from a fairly prosperous rural area near Bergen. Parish records say he was christened at Kinsarvik church along with his twin sister on 21 July 1682. In 1701, in the first Norwegian census, he is recorded as being eighteen years old. As he approached 40, in 1721,

Unknown artist, *Thomas Parr*, c. 1635, oil on canvas.

he got married to a 22-year-old. In 1727 he inherited a farm which, 26 years later, he handed on to the husband of his adopted daughter. His death is recorded at Kinsarvik on 20 June 1785, shortly before he would have reached 103. It all sounds pretty well documented, and the Danish historian Thorkild Kjærgaard concluded, 'There seems to be no doubt at all that the Eilif Philipsen, who died in Kinsarvik in 1785, was the very same Eilif Philipsen, who was christened at the same place almost 103 years earlier.' But the demographer James Vaupel and the epidemiologist Bernard Jeune, who have made a special study of the oldest old, came to the conclusion that Philipsen might have been confused with another member of his family bearing the same name and that we do not have enough knowledge about his relatives to rule this possibility out. A particular problem for those trying to authenticate centenarians is that families often favour certain first names, which they use over and over again; especially problematic was namesaking: a new arrival was often given the first name of a relative who had recently died.

Another contender for first definitely established centenarian, who was favoured for a time but is now considered 'not proven', was a Dutchman, Thomas Peters, said to have been born in 1745 and to have died in 1857, just ten days short of what would have been his 112th birthday. Unfortunately, the documents to support this claim have been 'lost'. Then there was a Canadian from Quebec named Pierre Joubert, who was supposed to have passed away aged 113 in 1814. The province was noted for its excellent parish records, with 700,000 births, marriages and burials registered before 1800. To accompany the 1871 census in Canada, Joseph-Charles Taché, a top civil servant, decided to launch an investigation into claims of longevity. He began with a list of 421 people reputed to have reached 100. Of these he decided to eliminate everyone except those 'whose ages could be proved by authentic documents, examined with a rigorous scrutiny'. That whittled the list down to 82. Next, Taché examined every one of these with a leading genealogist, and their number shrank to just nine, including Joubert, who was regarded by some at this time as the oldest human being who ever lived.

In the early 1990s, however, a Quebec demographer named Hubert Charbonneau took another look at Joubert and the other eight alleged centenarians. He sought out documents about Joubert's wife and found that in 1786, parish records described her as a widow. A further check showed that Pierre Joubert had actually died in 1766, aged 65. The 'Pierre Joubert' buried in 1814 was his son, who was aged 82. Of the other eight names on the list, two were the result of confusion between relatives; another two had death certificates where the information was not precise enough to link them to the specific individuals; while in the case of two others, Charbonneau considered the supporting evidence generally weak, eliminating all but two candidates: Rosalie Lizot, who was supposed to have been born in 1738 and to have died in 1847, aged 109, and Anne-Charlotte Dumont, who lived from 1742 to 1842. Charbonneau discovered that what was thought to have been Rosalie Lizot's birth certificate actually

The Celebrated
HENRY JENKINS,
Who lived to the Surprising Age
of 169 Years.

Henry Jenkins, aged 169. Line engraving.

belonged to a cousin of the same name, but he located another that showed her as having been born in 1740, which would have meant she lived to 107. In 1999 another Canadian demographer came to the conclusion that nothing 'at this time' had been found 'to disprove the link between the 1740 birth and the 1847 death', but considered that Lizot's survival to 107 remained 'highly improbable'. This left just Anne-Charlotte Dumont, a prosperous spinster, who seems to have survived for 21 days past her 100th birthday.

This reduction of 421 potential centenarians to just one or two illustrates how hard it is to be sure about early claims of longevity. In the United States, though, there was a centenarian, born on 1 August 1728 – fourteen years before Dumont – whose claim appears to be generally accepted as authentic. Edward Augustus Holyoke was born in Marblehead, Massachusetts, the son of the president of Harvard University. We are told that in his youth 'his body was strong and agile, and fired by a vivacious disposition.' He was well behaved, and kept out of trouble 'except for one occasion after which he was fined for drinking prohibited liquors'. The young Holyoke graduated from Harvard, and then started his own medical practice in Salem in 1749. As an adult, 'his temper was hot and quick; but he was aware of this failing, and he never for a moment relaxed his control of his tongue.' Always cheerful, though 'never jovial or given to light conversation', Holyoke was sociable and enjoyed skating and dancing, 'until he decided that his advancing years made these amusements unbecoming'. A pioneer in the prevention and treatment of smallpox, he got himself inoculated during an outbreak in 1777, persuading more than 600 of his patients to undergo what was then a controversial procedure. Six years later, he was presented with an honorary MD by Harvard – the first award of its kind – and in 1814 he became president of the American Academy of Arts and Sciences. A modest man, he avoided 'parading exhibitions' of his accomplishments.

Holyoke, of course, lived through a tumultuous time, as the American colonies fought to free themselves from British rule. We are told he recognized that America would one day be free, but believed his own generation lacked the self-discipline needed to run its own affairs, and that he became so depressed at 'the violence of agitators and the mobs' he feared it would kill him. It did not, and in 1774 he was brave enough to court unpopularity by signing a letter of welcome to the new British military governor. All through the political 'violence and excitement', Holyoke remained dedicated to his patients and 'never broke his daily round of visits and study'. Indeed, he continued to practise until he was 93 years old. His wife had died twenty years earlier, after which he was looked after by his daughter, and it was a 'crushing blow' when she too passed away, when he was 96. Holyoke reached 100 at a time when, his biographer noted, 'English statisticians were denying that there was a single authenticated example of anyone living to that age.' As Holyoke's health worsened, 'he kept a careful record of his dissolution, arguing with his fellow physicians about each symptom, and trying to draw conclusions about the general nature of senility.' When he finally died on 31 March 1829, all the church bells of the town tolled, an honour that had previously been granted only to U.S. presidents. The doctor had left instructions for his body to be dissected, and he would 'have been delighted when the autopsy showed, as he had maintained and his colleagues had doubted, that a fluid had formed in his brain'.

So, if Edward Augustus Holyoke seems to be the earliest 100-year-old about whom we can be certain, who was the first authenticated British centenarian? There is surely nowhere better to look than in the works of arch-sceptic William Thoms. His treatise *Human Longevity: Its Facts and Its Fictions*, published in 1873, raised a storm of protest as it debunked the claims of many supposed centenarians, such as Thomas Parr and Henry Jenkins. But Thoms insisted his methods could be used to authenticate as well as eliminate 100-year-olds, and he set out four cases which he believed were clearly established. The earliest was a Mrs Jane Williams who died on 8 October 1841, aged 102. The widow of Robert Williams, a banker and MP for Dorchester, she was the fourth and youngest daughter of Francis Chassereau, who had fled from Niort in France because of the persecution of Protestants. Thoms acknowledges that at first he was sceptical about Mrs Williams's claims, and became involved in a 'friendly controversy' with her great-grandson. The great-grandson, says Thoms, won the argument, and the doctor recognized Mrs Williams as 'thoroughly authenticated'. She was widowed at the age of 79, and two years later had cataracts removed. At the age of 90 she was strong enough to hold her god-daughter in her arms at her christening. Then, at 93, she gave 'a not very short speech' when the 'assembled tenantry' came to Bridehead, Dorset – the grand house where she lived – to offer their congratulations on her grandson's coming of age and to drink to her health. At 95, we learn, Williams 'used to make breakfast for a large party of children and grandchildren, remembering the different tastes of each'. She also remembered the psalms and the catechism very well, and just four days before her death went out on a drive of seven or eight miles. The factor that for Thoms wiped out 'all possible doubt' about her age was the discovery, soon after her death, of an entry in the 'admirably kept register of St Martins-in-the-Fields' in London, close to where Williams's father had at the time been working. It read, '1739, Nov 14. Jane, d of Francis and Anne Chattereau – born Nov 13.' It was true that the surname did not quite tally, but Thoms was eventually satisfied: 'there can be no doubt that the entry applies to the lady in question.' For one thing, the name was so unusual there seemed no chance of confusion with any other family in the area. Nor was there any possibility that Jane had been mixed up with another member of the Chassereau family: 13 November was the day on which Mrs Williams always celebrated her birthday, and she had no doubts about her age, often referring to it. For example, when she gave each of her great-grandchildren a gold sovereign during her 102nd year, she told them, 'You will not very likely again have a sovereign given to you by an old lady of 101.' During Williams's final years a friend remarked, rather enigmatically, that she 'appeared quite unlike an ordinary being, her flesh and skin appearing so different from that of ordinary old persons'.

Those who live to 110 are known as 'supercentenarians'. There are a number of claimants to being the first. Geert Adriaans Boomgaard was supposed to have been born in what is now the Netherlands in 1788, and to have died in 1889, aged 110, having served, it is said, in Napoleon's Grande Armée. Then there was Margaret Ann Neve from Guernsey, who was also said to have lived to 110, having been born in 1792. She was married but had no children, and her mother was supposed to have lived to 99. Neve was said never to have been ill until she reached the age of 105, to have still been making marmalade at 108, and to have climbed a tree after her 110th birthday. Newspaper reports say that she got up early, would drink a glass and a half of sherry at lunchtime and a weak whisky and water at night, and that she never ate between meals. Roger Thatcher, though, was most impressed by the claims of Katherine Plunket, who was born in County Louth in Ireland on 20 November 1820 and died on 14 October 1932, at the age of 111. Thatcher believed that 1930 was 'very early for the appearance of a genuine supercentenarian', but accepted Miss Plunket, saying she had been 'most carefully validated'. We have evidence that she was baptized on 13 December 1820, and she was recorded in the census of 1821. The eldest of five daughters, she was a member of the Anglo-Irish aristocracy. Her grandfather was a Lord Chancellor of Ireland and her father was not just a baron, but a bishop. Her cousins included three titled aristocrats. Plunket never married and outlived all her sisters, spending her later years living alone, except for her servants. She was sufficiently well known to have been congratulated by King George V on her 110th birthday, and to have her obituary printed in *The Times*. It agreed with Thatcher in stating that, 'There can be no doubt about this extraordinary instance of longevity,' noting that a correspondent in 1929 had described her as 'the oldest of His Majesty's subjects'. By then, of course, Louth was part of the Irish Free State, and many of its inhabitants would not have considered themselves subjects of the king, but Plunket, we are told, was a 'very strong Loyalist and Unionist'. Life must have been very pleasant for her. Her house was 'beautifully situated on the slope of a hill overlooking Dundalk Bay'. Her gardens were famous and she often won prizes at local shows for her flowers and fruit. Plunket was a great traveller, and remained so 'even in extreme old age'. Until she was 105, she went to church every Sunday in a coach and four: 'Thereafter she kept to her room, but was able to sit up in a chair.' She still enjoyed 'excellent health' and in the summer of 1931, when she was 110, 'she insisted on being carried into the garden to enjoy the sunshine', even ordering a new hat and cape 'suitable for outdoor wear' from Dublin. Right into her final years, said *The Times*, 'Her memory was indeed remarkable, and her mind was clear and vigorous.' She 'attended to all her business affairs' and also took a 'lively interest in public affairs', especially the new regime in Ireland, which she watched 'critically'. Plunket could still reminisce about being dangled as a five-year-old on the knee of Sir Walter Scott and being 'charmed by his agreeable personality and conversation', and about how the journey from Connaught to Dublin used to take three days. Although she 'took a great interest in all the young people of the Plunket family' she continued to observe the 'social standards of a former age', so that even at 75 she would not let her sister Gertrude 'go into society unchaperoned' or travel to Dublin.

TWO

Explosion!

O n 1 July 1837, when Katherine Plunket was sixteen, a reform
was introduced in England and Wales that made the authenti-
cation of centenarians much easier – a national system for the
registration of births, marriages and deaths. Scotland followed in 1855,
and Ireland in 1863. As far back as 1538, soon after the establishment
of the Church of England, Henry VIII's chancellor, Thomas Cromwell,
had instructed the clergy to keep registers of all baptisms, weddings
and burials in their parishes. These records are still a valuable source
of information, but they miss out Roman Catholics, Nonconformists,
Jews and Quakers, and we cannot be certain that the ages attributed
to people at their deaths are accurate. In other countries, too, churches
were supposed to keep registers. A decree from the King of Denmark in
1646 required the vicar in every parish to note the dates of births, marriages and deaths, but there was no instruction on how the records were
to be kept, and their quality varies. Sweden had a similar system, but
as the nineteenth century went on, more and more countries adopted
the approach of comprehensive national registration – New Zealand
in 1855, Italy in 1865, Spain in 1871, Switzerland in 1876 and so on.

Another nineteenth-century administrative innovation that helps
us to determine who really lived to 100 is the census. Since 1801 a
census of sorts had been conducted every ten years in Britain, with
the local church minister, the overseer of the poor or 'some substantial
Householder' providing the information for 'each Parish, Township
and Place'. But it was only from 1841, when households had to start
filling in the forms themselves and giving their names and addresses,
that these surveys started to achieve modern standards of accuracy.

Even then, though, the ages attributed to people could not always be trusted. Censuses became more reliable during the nineteenth century in other countries as well. Denmark held them at regular intervals starting in 1834. From 1870, in towns and cities, it became the head of the household's responsibility to fill in the forms, but in the countryside it remained the job of the local parish council.

Censuses and compulsory registration of births and deaths not only made it possible to be more confident about which individuals really had reached the age of 100; they provided more reliable information on how many centenarians there were. This enabled Sir Cyril Clarke, director of the research unit at the Royal College of Physicians, to declare on 11 September 1984 that there were well over 2,000 in the United Kingdom, compared with just 200 only 30 years previously, making them the fastest-growing age group in the country. In reporting the announcement, newspapers noted that Clarke was a 'sprightly' 77-year-old. (These were the articles that first sparked my interest in 100-year-olds.) And in the years that followed, the total number of centenarians continued to rise inexorably. Roger Thatcher would write, 'No other demographic group has increased at anything like this rate, which has been fairly described as an "explosion".' In 2007 the Office for National Statistics (ONS) stated the number of centenarians in England and Wales (those from Scotland and Northern Ireland are counted separately) had risen from about 100 in 1911 to an estimated 9,300 nearly a century later. By 2014 the total for the UK had reached about 14,450 – a rise of 72 per cent in just ten years. So, cue champagne corks? Not exactly. Much of the press comment about this demographic explosion echoed the thoughts of *The Guardian*: this was 'another stark indication of the mounting problems facing successive governments as they struggle to finance demands on the welfare state including a rising state pension bill'. Across the Atlantic, one of the world's leading credit rating agencies, Standard & Poor's, would soon be saying that the fact we were not dying soon enough was a bigger threat to the world economy than global warming. It was left to Michelle Mitchell, then charity director for Age UK, to come up with something less gloomy: 'increasing longevity and improved health care mean many older people are able to make a very positive and important contribution to our society.'

Still, at least our monarchs seem to believe that the growing number of centenarians is a cause for celebration. For more than a

Mrs Jane Baulch of Yeovil, Somerset, with a telegram from King George v
congratulating her on her 100th birthday in April 1927.

century they have been sending out congratulations to those who
reach their 100th birthday. Back in April 1908, during Edward vii's
reign, Buckingham Palace dispatched a message to the Rev. Thomas
Lord of Horncastle, reading, 'I am commanded by the King to congratulate you on the attainment of your hundredth year, after a most
useful life.' The centenarian replied, 'I beg gratefully to acknowledge
the receipt of your Majesty's gracious congratulations. That your life

and that of our beloved Queen may be long spared to be a blessing to your people is the earnest prayer of your loyal and loving subject.' But it was only nine years later, in the reign of Edward's son, George V, that the royal tradition of sending greetings to every 100-year-old known to the palace was firmly established. In 1917 congratulations were sent to just seven men and seventeen women. One greeting from 1919 conveyed 'His Majesty's hope that the blessings of good health and prosperity may attend you during the remainder of your days.' The medium for these messages would change over the years – from telegrams to telemessages and now greetings cards. Nowadays, each centenarian gets a card on his or her 100th birthday. Those who survive to 105 get another, and from then on, they receive one every year. At first, the greetings came from a private secretary, but since 1999 the Queen has signed each one herself. The wording is not made public, so that it does not spoil the surprise for the recipient (and if twins receive congratulations, the palace makes sure each is phrased differently). The current card shows the Queen wearing a brooch she gave to the Queen Mother as a 100th birthday present. The Queen also sends out greetings to some Commonwealth centenarians. In 2011 Buckingham Palace dispatched 917 cards just for those aged over 105. Probably the most famous centenarian recipient was the Queen Mother herself, who got an official card from her daughter in 2000.

These days, the government's Department for Work and Pensions (DWP) ensures the palace gets to know about any pensioners reaching their 100th birthdays. According to its figures, the number of centenarians in England and Wales rose by 86 per cent between 2000 and 2010. The increases in Scotland – 70 per cent – and Northern Ireland – 47 per cent – were lower, but still very impressive, while the number of people aged over 105, and entitled to royal congratulations every year, had almost doubled from 360 in 2003 to 710 in 2013. Not surprisingly, more people have had to be taken on to keep information up to date, and the department now has a seven-strong 'centenarian team'. The DWP itself also sends cards to centenarians, with former Secretary of State Iain Duncan Smith saying, 'Our ageing society can only be a cause for celebration.'

That 'centenarian team' can expect to go on getting busier and busier. In 2011, using predictions from the ONS, the DWP said that twenty-year-olds were now twice as likely to reach 100 as their parents, and three times more likely than their grandparents, while a baby born now had 50 times more chance of becoming a centenarian than one entering the world 100 years before. According to some calculations, more than a quarter of the children born in the UK today can expect to celebrate their 100th birthday. The DWP estimated that by 2066, there will be at least half a million people over 100 in the UK. If the trend continues, the figure should pass the million mark around 2106. At the beginning of 2015, new projections from the ONS predicted that by 2057, average life expectancy for women would reach 100, with the figure for men being two or three years less.

The rise in the number of supercentenarians has been just as spectacular, if a little less even (as might be expected with the very small numbers involved). Roger Thatcher conducted his own study for England and Wales in 2010, applying a rigorous rule that no one would be classed as conclusively over 110 unless their birth certificate could be found, though he recognized that this might exclude some genuine cases, such as immigrants. During the years 1968–72 there were just two supercentenarians, but this rose to thirteen during 2003–6, having reached as high as seventeen between 1993 and 1997. Of the total 66 supercentenarians he identified, all but two were women. The ONS forecasts that the number of supercentenarians will rise to at least 100 in England and Wales by the mid-2030s.

Centenarians are not only the fastest growing section of the UK population: the phenomenon is being seen across the world. The United Nations estimated in 2009 that there were about 455,000 centenarians worldwide. It is hard to make firm comparisons with the past, because records are not reliable enough in many countries, but figures from fourteen European nations that reported numbers for 1946 showed they had a total of just 1,333 centenarians at that time. By 2006, more than 43,000 centenarians lived in those same countries. Many European countries have seen the number of 100-year-olds in their population double every decade since the end of the Second World War.

In 2010, globally, the country with the highest number was the United States – with more than 57,000, compared to just 4,255 in 1950. Other countries also show impressive increases over a similar period: Australia from 164 to 3,064; Belgium from 23 to 1,510; Canada from 193 to 6,000; Finland from 4 to 566; France from 195 to 8,807; Italy from 88 to 12,756; the Netherlands from 37 to 1,675; Sweden from 46 to 1,798; and Japan from 111 to a staggering 45,108. But although the United States has the highest number of centenarians, there are other countries where you have a better chance of reaching 100, such as Japan, France, Sweden and the UK. If we look only at women, the French have the best chance of reaching the century, followed by the Japanese and the Dutch, while for men, Japan is top, followed by the Dutch and the French.

While UK centenarians get congratulations from the Queen, in the U.S. it is a letter from the president, and in Ireland it is a letter from the president plus €2,540. In Japan they receive a silver cup, but some of the shine was taken off the country's spectacular longevity statistics in July 2010 when officials in Tokyo went to congratulate a man – supposed to be the city's oldest – on his 111th birthday. When they got to his home, they found a mummified corpse lying in his bed. He had in fact been dead for more than three decades. His daughter and granddaughter said he had gone into his bedroom after a family argument in the late 1970s and never come out again, shutting himself in without food or water. His granddaughter was given a suspended prison sentence for continuing to draw his pension after his death. The Ministry of Justice ordered an investigation, which discovered thousands of people who would be at least 120, and nearly 1,000 who would be 150 or older; all of them were actually dead. It is thought that a number of these passed away as long ago as the chaotic years around the end of the Second World War. One 64-year-old man told investigators that his mother had died nine years earlier, but that he had not been able to afford a funeral for her, so he did not report her death. Instead, he broke up her bones and put them in a backpack. Despite such frauds, Japan is convinced that its population of real, living centenarians is increasing rapidly, with the government announcing on 2014's Respect for the Aged Day, an annual national holiday, that the number had reached 58,820.

Just as in the UK, across the world the number of centenarians is expected to continue growing, with the United Nations predicting that there are likely to be nearly 3.25 million by 2050, and nearly 18 million by the end of this century. By far the majority of today's 100-year-olds – about 78 per cent – live in more developed countries, but the UN expects that by 2050 the proportion coming from the less developed world will have increased substantially – from about 22 per cent of the total to about 32 per cent. In numbers, that means an increase from around 40,000 to more than a million. By then, the

United States alone may have nearly a million centenarians. According to some projections, Japan will have a similar number, even though America's population is about two and a half times greater. Per head of population, the land of the rising sun is expected to continue to have more 100-year-olds than anywhere else on earth, while in France demographers have calculated that baby girls already have a one in two chance of reaching 100. Since 1971, the number of centenarians in Australia has nearly doubled every decade, so that in 2012 there were about 4,250, but by 2050, it is thought, there will be 50,000. Some of these projected increases may sound so ambitious as to be fanciful, but, as the *New York Times* observed, 'if American demographers have made one mistake consistently over the past two centuries, it's underestimating the rate at which life expectancy has grown.'

Again, as in Britain, so across the world their smaller numbers mean that supercentenarians have increased at a less even rate. America's Gerontology Research Group (GRG), which has been keeping tabs on them since 1990, said in December 2014 that it was aware of 82 validated cases worldwide. Until the mid-1970s, according to GRG figures, the number was below ten. After that it rose steadily, to reach a peak of more than 100 around the turn of the century. Since then it appears to have slipped back down, but two of the GRG's investigators warn against making too much of this, pointing out that 'missing cases, which are discovered subsequently, can bias these trends. Given that most of the missing cases are from 2000 onward, we speculate that the rise is continuing, albeit at a slower rate.' The group's standards are rigorous and it said the true total across the world at the end of 2014 was probably approaching 400. Indeed, the 2010 census in the United States reported 330 supercentenarians, though it cautioned there might be some doubt about this figure, because 'data quality generally declines as age increases.'

So why have centenarians become the fastest-growing portion of the population? Prompted by that explosion of 100-year-olds he announced in 1984, Sir Cyril Clarke decided to investigate why we were living longer, especially when, as he put it, 'we all drink too much, smoke too much and eat too much fat.' Earlier in his career, Clarke had helped save the lives of hundreds of thousands of babies by pioneering a treatment for rhesus incompatibility, in which there is a mismatch between the blood groups of mother and child. He was also an expert in the genetics of butterflies, but in his later years it was human longevity that absorbed his attention. He argued that the increase in centenarians had happened over too short a time to be caused by genetics, so it must be down to what scientists call environmental factors. And there were plenty of candidates – new drugs, the National Health Service, health education, the Clean Air Acts, better food, cleaner water, central heating. Clarke thought this 'progressive improvement in social conditions' was probably the main reason, but he also floated some less obvious ones. Had a decline in religious belief in an afterlife 'increased the urge to keep alive in this one'? He even suggested that this urge might be strengthened in England by our love of cricket, a sport in which scoring a century is a notable achievement.

Then there was 'hybrid vigour': the concept that broadening the gene pool makes for healthier offspring, while inbreeding is damaging. 'A century ago,' wrote Clarke, 'one tended to marry the girl next door but with the coming of the internal combustion engine men became more venturesome and travelled further for their mates – so there would be less inbreeding and more hybridity and therefore probably more hardiness.' Another possible explanation was improved diet. Clarke had been told that mammals at London Zoo had been living longer since keepers stopped them eating leftovers from people's picnics; but when it came to humans, he was not sure whether any worthwhile evidence could be found, because 'no one can remember what they had for breakfast yesterday.' Whatever the explanation for the growth in the number of centenarians, Clarke was confident it would continue, and that they would become commonplace. He died in 2000, aged 93.

While Clarke advanced some stimulating theories, others have gone in for a more number-crunching approach. Obviously, one of the reasons for the growth in the number of centenarians is the rise in the world's population. In 1911 it was 1.6 billion; by 2011 it had passed 7 billion – a rise of about 337 per cent – but that goes only a tiny way towards explaining the rise, for example, in the number of centenarians in the UK during that time: 9,200 per cent! So, let us develop the numbers argument. In addition to there being more human beings, if survival rates at different ages improve, that will further increase the number of centenarians. As more babies survive birth and progress into childhood, more children have the chance of surviving into adulthood, so there are more adults who might live to old age, and more of them will make it into very old age. And survival rates have been improving consistently. Until the 1840s in England and Wales, life expectancy was below 40 for men and below 42 for women. By the 1870s it was 41 for men and 44 for women. By the first decade of the twentieth century it had reached 48 for men and 52 for women; by the 1930s, 58 for men and 62 for women. Then, by 1990, the average UK man lived to 73, and the average woman 79, while by 2012 it was 79 for men and 83 for women, making an average of 81 if you combine the sexes. This was in line with a global trend that saw life expectancy in the developed world going up by around three months every year. Other developed countries had similar life expectancy figures to the UK, with a combined average for men and women of 79 in the United States; 81 in Germany; 82 in France and New Zealand; 83 in Italy and Australia; and 84 in Japan.

Experts believe that the increase in life expectancy before about 1950 was mainly produced by a big reduction in infant mortality, with smaller falls in the numbers of deaths among children and young adults. Among the factors at play were growing prosperity and more hygienic living conditions, while Robert Fogel, a Nobel Prize-winning economic historian from the University of Chicago, suggested an interesting idea: as we get bigger, we are healthier and live longer, so long as we do not become obese. Over the last 250 years, human body size in the Western world has increased by about half. Perhaps the most important factor is improved medical knowledge, and better access to health care. Vaccination has played a crucial role in the conquest of infectious diseases such as smallpox, diphtheria, polio and tuberculosis. In 1870, tuberculosis killed about one woman aged 35 to 44 in every 250. By 1960, the figure had fallen to one in every 33,000 – a drop of more than 90 per cent. In 1900, infectious diseases were reckoned to be responsible for about a quarter of all deaths in Britain. A hundred years later, despite the spread of the HIV virus, the figure had fallen to less than one in 100. But some observers felt that once we reached old age, new scourges such as heart disease and cancer had simply taken the place of the earlier killers, and up to the middle years of the twentieth century, there was little change in life expectancy for those who made it to 80. Roger Thatcher believed this was partly because 'People thought that not much could be done about deaths at such a high age and indeed there were many diseases for which people over 80 could not be treated, or it was not worthwhile to treat them.' Pneumonia, for example, was a great killer of the elderly, and became known as the 'old man's friend' because of its way of speeding the elderly to a relatively painless end.

Improvement of survival at all ages might be expected to lead to the number of centenarians growing in line with the population as a whole but, as we have seen, over the last half-century or so, their number has increased much quicker, making them the fastest-growing age group. For that to happen, people would need to be living longer in their final years of life, and indeed, the demographer-epidemiologist team of Vaupel and Jeune have calculated that two-thirds or more of the centenarian explosion can be put down to improved survival over the age of 80. The process seems to have taken off around the end of the Second World War. Again, medical advances made an important contribution. In the late 1930s, for example, new sulphonamide drugs, and after the war penicillin and other antibiotics, started to fight pneumonia with great success, until by 1950 deaths from the disease in the United States were said to have fallen by three-quarters in just over twenty years.

But the improvements seen in the 1940s and '50s were only the beginning. As time went on, there were further changes that increased the number of centenarians by improving overall life expectancy: the proportion of people who smoked fell from 45 per cent in 1974 to less than 19 per cent in 2013, and fewer people have to do heavy manual labour, which tends to shorten life. But again, there were improvements to survival specifically in very old age. In 1980 in England and Wales, the average 80-year-old man could expect to live a little less than six more years; the average 80-year-old woman another seven and a half years. Thirty years later that had gone up to another eight years for a man and nine and a half for a woman. The French demographer and gerontologist Jean-Marie Robine said that ever since the work of the pioneering British actuary Benjamin Gompertz in the early nineteenth century, demographers had believed that 'mortality increases exponentially with age, with mortality rates doubling approximately every eight years.' But in recent years, evidence seems to be emerging to suggest that the death rate actually falls over the age of 85, and that at 95 and 100 it is lower than expected. It is easier to describe these developments than to explain them. Thatcher noted, 'The big change has come above 80, but quite why – your guess is as good as mine,' while Robine noted that although mortality in old age has been falling 'drastically' in advanced countries, it has not 'been studied greatly' and 'little is still known of its causes and mechanisms.' The Office of National Statistics has attributed the fall in death rates over the age of 80 to 'improved medical treatment, hygiene and sanitation, housing and living standards and nutrition'. Among the more recent medical techniques that have helped the oldest old are developments such as pacemakers and keyhole surgery, while central heating is also considered by some to be important.

Tom Perls, whose grandmother lived to 102, founded the New England Centenarian Study at Boston University, which has followed around 2,000 people aged 100 and over in the northeastern United States since 1995. Perls had become intrigued by centenarians when he met two of them while he was doing his medical training in geriatrics. Expecting them to be frail, instead he found one who had been a tailor teaching other people how to mend clothes, while another was a still-accomplished pianist with an 85-year-old girlfriend. He compared reaching 100 to picking all the right balls in a lottery: the more balls we have to choose, the harder it is to win. The conquering of death in childhood, better public health and greater prosperity have all reduced the number of balls we have to pick, while newer developments such as better screening for high blood pressure have played a big part in reducing death rates among the very old. But if the answer to the question of why death rates among those aged over 80 have fallen so dramatically is complicated, one fact about centenarians stands out very clearly: most are women. Across the world, by the age of 100, they outnumber men by four or five to one.

THREE

It's a Woman's World

As we have seen, when the king of England first sent out congratulations to centenarians in 1917, they went to seven men and seventeen women. In the 1980s, when the explosion in the number of centenarians first began to be noticed, the women who reached 100 outnumbered the men by about seven to one. Of 66 supercentenarians identified by Roger Thatcher in 2006, only two were men. In 2012, females in the UK could expect to outlive males by four years. If there is a battle of the sexes, by the time we get to 100 women have won it hands down.

All over the world, it is the same story. A study published in 2010 showed that in Switzerland there were just over five female centenarians for every one male; in Japan and Sweden, the ratio was six to one; while in France the women outnumbered the men seven to one. In 2009 an analysis of the number of centenarians across 27 European countries found there were just over 49,000 women, compared with 8,220 men. The biggest gap ever recorded was in South Korea in 2000, where there were said to be 11.5 female centenarians for every male. In 2009, across the world, according to the United Nations, 'among centenarians women are between four and five times as numerous as men.' In less developed countries statistics are often less reliable, but it is reasonable to assume that the gap between male and female centenarians is much narrower. For a start, in these countries there are far fewer centenarians: average life expectancy in Sierra Leone, for example, is only around 46 years, compared with about 81 in the UK, and in perhaps fourteen other African countries people can expect to live on average for less than 50 years. And then in the less developed world, the life expectancy gap between the sexes is much narrower, with women having just a one-year advantage in Sierra Leone, for example. There are even a handful of countries where men live longer than women. These are all places close to the bottom of the life expectancy league, such as Botswana, Lesotho, Malawi and Swaziland.

We know it was not always like this. The scant evidence we have from ancient Greece and ancient Rome suggests that men there lived substantially longer than women. Historians estimate that in the thirteenth century girls had a 10 per cent better chance of reaching the age of ten than boys, and that after 40, a woman's life expectancy was 10 per cent better than a man's; but in the middle years, between the ages of ten and 40, a woman's life expectancy was only half that of a man, largely because of the formidable dangers of childbirth. Having children in those days was said to be more dangerous than going to war, and until 1800 it was estimated that about one woman in ten still died from the complications of childbirth.

Lack of reliable data makes it hard to be too specific about when giving birth ceased to be such a danger. As late as 1797, the proto-feminist Mary Wollstonecraft died after the delivery of her baby daughter – who would grow up to be Mary Shelley of *Frankenstein* fame – probably because the doctor who attended her did not wash his hands. Among thousands and thousands of others, childbirth also claimed the lives of George IV's only legitimate child, Princess Charlotte; Duchess Louise Charlotte of Mecklenburg-Schwerin, grandmother of Queen Victoria's husband, Prince Albert; Tsar Nicholas I of Russia's daughter, the Grand Duchess Alexandra; and Abraham Lincoln's sister, Sarah. When reliable information does start to become available, we know that at Dublin Maternity Hospital in 1849, for example, there were 2,063 births and 38 mothers died – about one in 54. In the United States, until the 1930s, the death rate for women of childbearing age was the same as that of men, before it fell off dramatically with the rise of medical innovations such as blood transfusions, better anaes-thesia and antibiotics. Northern European countries like Sweden, Denmark and the Netherlands saw earlier progress, with declines in the death rate from childbirth appearing about 1890, possibly because of conscientious use of antiseptics.

It is also difficult to pin down exactly when women's life expectancy overtook men's, but in 1998, Tom Perls and his colleague on the New England Centenarian Study, obstetrician-gynaecologist Ruth Fretts, wrote: 'It seems likely that women have been outliving men for centuries and perhaps longer.' Sweden was said to be the first country to try to keep national records of death rates, and the researchers suggest that between 1751 and 1790, average life expectancy for women was higher than that for men, at 36.6 years against 33.7. On the other hand, in Australia as recently as 1921, male centenarians outnumbered females by more than two to one, before the women moved ahead in 1933, and by 1981 they were outnumbering the men by more than five to one.

So why are there so many more women centenarians? In his paper 'Increased Longevity in Man' (1986), Sir Cyril Clarke offered a few explanations. He said that at the time about 105 boys were born for every 100 girls, but that by around the age of 30, more males had died, and the sexes were about at level pegging, remaining so until they reach their mid-fifties, after which the women began to 'nose ahead' ever more dramatically. But those twenty or so years of apparent equality led Clarke to conclude that men could not be biologically inferior, and that therefore it was 'highly likely' that the way the female of the species finally streaks away in the race of life must result from environmental factors. In other words, the gap was down to the different kinds of lives that men and women lead. Young men took more risks on the road, did more dangerous jobs, got into more fights, went to war and so on. 'Trauma' resulting from this and other dangerous habits, Clarke believed, led to that levelling out of the sex ratio by the end of people's twenties. Men also smoked and drank more, and had probably built up the health problems that killed them in greater numbers after the mid-fifties, though Clarke also noted that women began to outnumber men really significantly around retirement age, and theorized that this might be important:

> after retirement men tend to adopt an unhealthy lifestyle. They run to fat because of an excess in their calorie intake . . . they are less active, both mentally and physically – everything is in the bag, so to speak, whereas most women go on as before, cleaning the house, cooking the meals, shopping, washing etc. There is no retirement for them. So they live longer.

In support of his argument that the reasons for the centenarian gender gap were environmental and not biological, Clarke quoted two exceptions to the rule that women live longer in the developed world:

the Amish and the Hutterites, two highly traditional, selfsufficient Christian communities in North America, saying that they 'live very virtuous lives: they don't smoke or drink . . . and they generally have a fairly equable life. The men work in the fields and the women have lots of babies.' And indeed, in the early 1980s, what until then had been the only systematic comparison between the death rates of the Amish in Pennsylvania, Ohio and Indiana, and those of their non-Amish neighbours, found that middle-aged Amish men had a significantly lower death rate than non-Amish men, while the same was not true of middle-aged Amish women. (Elderly Amish women actually had a higher death rate than their non-Amish peers.) Another piece of research in 2012 came up with broadly similar findings – that while Amish men could expect to live about three years longer than the average non-Amish male, for Amish women there was virtually no difference. This might suggest that much of the longevity gap between men and women could be closed if men developed healthier lifestyles, but it would still leave females living longer, because the overall life expectancy gap in the U.S. then was about five years.

In the three decades since Clarke came up with his exploratory thoughts, many others have tried to explain why so many more women live to 100, though even the *Encyclopaedia Britannica* has had to admit that the reasons are still 'not well understood'. Dr Marianne Legato, director of America's Foundation for Gender-specific Medicine and author of a book entitled *Why Men Die First*, says, 'Men are biologically and sociologically at a disadvantage from the time they're conceived to the time they die.' For a long time it was believed that more boys are conceived than girls, with estimates varying from 120 to 200 for every 100 girls, perhaps because sperm carrying the male chromosome swim faster, but research in 2015 into millions of records from foetal screening tests, fertility and abortion clinics as well, data on miscarriages suggested that equal numbers of males and females are conceived, and that the reason a few more boys than girls are born is because more female foetuses are lost during pregnancy. But from then on for the boys, it is downhill all the way. They are 14 per cent more likely to be born prematurely, and twice as likely to suffer immature lung development. They are more prone than girls to perinatal brain damage, cerebral palsy and congenital deformities. Girls also develop faster in the womb, so that, according to the British child psychiatrist Sebastian Kraemer, 'A new-born girl is the physiological equivalent of a 4 to 6 week old boy.'

Boys are about 25 per cent more likely to die in the first year of life, and are much more at risk of finding their development hindered by problems such as hyperactivity, autism, Tourette's syndrome, stammering or being slow to pick up reading, experiencing these conditions three or four times as often as girls (though girls may be more severely affected if they do have them). 'Throughout development, girls are a little bit ahead of boys. Girls walk before boys, they talk before boys,' says Professor Joy Lawn, director of the London School of Hygiene and Tropical Medicine's Centre for Maternal, Adolescent, Reproductive and Child Health, and team leader for a major research project on gender differences. But there is one area in which boys are way ahead. They are much quicker to expose themselves to danger, and the tendency persists as they get older. Boys will indeed be boys, or, as Dr Legato says, 'A male will take risks that a female of his same age wouldn't take.'

Then, when boys reach their mid-teens, the 'testosterone storm' takes control, as hormone levels get high and volatile. This, says Tom Perls, 'can induce some pretty dangerous behaviour among young men. They don't wear their seatbelts; they drink too much alcohol; they can be aggressive with weapons and so on and so forth.' Men are three times more likely to take illegal drugs than women, according to official figures for England and Wales for 2014. Men are also much more likely to kill themselves; between 2001 and 2011, more than 38,600 males over the age of fifteen committed suicide in England and Wales – over three times the number of females. The upshot of all this is that, in England and Wales in 2013, for every four girls who died up to the age of fifteen, five boys died; from ages fifteen to 30, the death rate among men is more than twice that of women. Figures from the United States for the years 1999 to 2008 showed that up to the age of twenty, males were 44 per cent more likely to die than females, so that by the age of 25 to 30 – less than a third of the way to the century – the women are already beginning to outnumber the men.

Although Clarke believed that men and women kept pretty level pegging between the mid-thirties and the mid-fifties, if we look at mortality rates for England and Wales for years as far apart as 1963 and 2013, they show that at virtually all ages, fewer women died than men. But it is from about age 55 to 60, when mortality rates begin to pick up, that the numerical gap really starts to widen. Boys are still being boys at these ages, as the male of the species continues to be more likely to die in a car accident or from suicide. But now men also find other unhealthy features of their lifestyle catching up, as illnesses connected with drinking and smoking start to kill them off, particularly via the great modern 'plagues' of heart disease and stroke. While these claim men in significant numbers in their fifties and sixties, women do not usually suffer them for at least another ten years. According to Amy Thompson, senior cardiac nurse for the British Heart Foundation, 'For every 1,000 men who have cardiovascular problems between the age of 55 and 65, there are only 25 women in the same situation.' Men born at the start of the twentieth century smoked in very large numbers, leading to a mortality rate from lung cancer in the 1970s that was eight times worse than for women, but also playing an important role in causing the additional male deaths from heart disease. One study of data from 30 countries calculated that smoking was responsible for up to 60 per cent of the longevity gap.

So men drink and smoke too much, are too prone to violence, and take too many risks; but there is another thing about women that might give them a better chance of reaching 100: they seem to be more conscientious about seeking medical help. Figures from America suggest men are 22 per cent more likely than women to skip a cholesterol test, and 24 per cent less likely to go to the doctor. Indeed, 28 per cent do not even have a regular doctor. Dr Legato blames it on the so-called John Wayne syndrome: 'Men often deny illness; they minimize symptoms because they don't want to go to a doctor and find out something is wrong.'

Some scientists also say that women support each other better. They help to tend each other's young. They nurse each other when they are ill, they laugh and cry together, and boost each other's confidence. When things go wrong, according to Shelley Taylor, professor of psychology at the University of California, Los Angeles, 'women are much more social in the way they cope with stress.' Men are likely to respond with a 'fight or flight' mentality, adopting aggression or withdrawal. Unfortunately, both approaches can take a physiological toll, while 'friendship brings comfort that mitigates the ill effects of stress. That difference alone contributes to the gender difference in longevity.' Dr Legato takes a similar view: 'Most men tend to hold their stress and worries close to their chest, while women tend to reach out and talk to others.' Friendship certainly does seem to have an important effect on health. In 2010, researchers at Brigham Young University in Utah trawled through nearly 150 studies, concluding that having plenty of friends reduced our chances of dying early, while being lonely was as harmful as smoking fifteen cigarettes a day, and twice as bad as obesity.

Men appear to be more dependent on their spouses and partners, with married men living significantly longer than bachelors or widowers, while women gain only a marginal benefit from marriage. The ability to deal with loss is plainly crucial if you want to live to 100, because getting there means you are likely to outlive your spouse, siblings, friends, maybe children and even grandchildren. Dr Beverly Fehr from the University of Winnipeg's department of psychology says that if a relationship ends, 'a woman still has other sources of intimacy – her friends – and that provides her with another source of support,' but, according to Professor Janice Kiecolt-Glaser, director of the Ohio State Institute for Behavioural Medicine Research, 'When a man loses his primary female partner, he's in trouble.' Perls agrees: 'Any man who wants to live to 100 must be behaviourally suited to getting over the possible losses that women seem to survive more easily.' If a man's wife survives along with him, in Perls's view, it would 'improve his chances significantly', while 'the loss of a wife is usually too high a hurdle for men to clear.' On the other hand, for a woman, 'once her spouse died, she was usually able to continue the race independently.' In the UK, investigators at London's Cass Business School found in 2008 that in the year following the death of a spouse or partner, a woman's risk of death doubled, but for men it was six times higher than normal.

Clarke believed that retirement damages men's chances of reaching the century because after it, they are too prone to sitting around all day. He gained some support for this from a survey conducted in 1987 by Dunfermline College of Physical Education's Centre for Leisure Research, which interviewed more than 100 retired men. Just over half said they were enjoying more lie-ins, and relatively few had taken up any new pursuits; instead, they were watching more television. But the survey may have uncovered a more significant side-effect of retirement on men – the loss of the friendship and fellowship they had found at work. As with the loss of a wife or partner, males seemed poor at adapting to this change. Among those interviewed in the Dunfermline study, 60 per cent said that since they gave up work, they missed the 'people', and three-quarters said they had made no new friends after retiring. But a less clear picture emerged from another survey of retired people, carried out for Skipton Building Society in 2013. On the basis of interviews with nearly 800 people, the survey reported that 56 per cent of women tried to meet up regularly with friends, compared to just 33 per cent of the men, and that women were more likely to join a club or a class. On the other hand, only a fifth of the men said they felt lonely, compared with almost a third of the women.

Nearly two-thirds of the men in the Dunfermline study said work had been the most important thing in their lives, but males seem to suffer a double whammy from it. A report in 2014 from the Men's Health Forum and the Work Foundation at Lancaster University showed that unemployed men are 20 per cent more likely to die than those in work, but when they are working, men are in more danger from accidents. In the UK in 2013–14, twenty times as many men as women were killed in the workplace, while men also tend to get exposed more to hazardous substances that can damage their long-term health.

Then there is sex. In the 1990s, Professor David Gems from University College London's Institute of Healthy Ageing discovered that male worms living alone survived longer than those surrounded by other male and female worms. Gems believed that males in this latter group had shorter lives because of the stress of competing with other males as they slithered around in pursuit of females. This ties in with studies that have shown that castrated marsupial mice can live for years, while normal male specimens, who copulate for several hours every day, will die in a few weeks. Other research showed castrated tomcats were noticeably less susceptible to infections than intact males, and survived longer. Indeed, they lived as long as female cats. Castrated rams also had a longer life span. As far as humans are concerned, a study of eunuchs found they survived on average 13.5 years longer than men who are not castrated. One male American centenarian, incidentally, suggested giving up sex for one year in every three as a way of achieving long life. On the other hand, a 101-year-old Italian named Giulio Paggi credited his longevity to the fact that he still felt 'like a little boy and the secret of this youthfulness is that all my life I've put a lot into lovemaking.'

So there are plenty of differences in lifestyles that might explain why so many more women than men make it to 100, but some scientists believe that even if you strip out their effects, there is a still a gender gap. Tom Perls agreed with Sir Cyril Clarke that environmental factors were important, estimating they are responsible for 'about 70 per cent' of the difference in life expectancy, but he pointed out that this still leaves 30 per cent that is down to genetics. Are there differences in the physical make-up of men and women that help to explain the longevity gap? Dr Legato thinks there is a biological reason why boys take more risks than girls, putting it down to slower development of the frontal lobes of the brain, which deal with responsibility and evaluating risk. There is also plenty of evidence that men are, well, the weaker sex. David Goldspink, Professor of Cell and Molecular Sports Science at Liverpool John Moores University, spent two years studying 250 healthy but physically inactive volunteers up to the age of 80. He found that the male heart declines in power by about 20 to 25 per cent between the ages of eighteen and 70, while the female heart carries on merrily – the reason being that men lose about a third of the muscle in the walls of their hearts, while women lose hardly any.

Some see 'man flu' as another example of men's weakness: their alleged tendency to be rather babyish when they are ill and to make a mountain out of a molehill of sickness, or, as the *Daily Telegraph*'s science correspondent Richard Alleyne put it, 'Men's ability to turn a sniffle into flu and a headache into a migraine has long been a source of irritation to wives and girlfriends.' But Dr Amanda Ellison, a neuroscientist from Durham University, says that it may be that men really do feel worse when they are ill and have a temperature, because they have more temperature receptors in their brains. More important, though, in survival terms, is that they are actually more likely to be ill than women, because evidence is emerging to suggest that their immune systems are weaker. The inflammation that raises our temperature when we are unwell is the body's first line of defence against infection, because heat can often kill off the invading agent, but humans carry an enzyme called Caspase 12 that can block the inflammation process. Experiments on mice by researchers at Canada's McGill University in 2009 led them to conclude that the female sex hormone oestrogen prevents Caspase 12 from interfering with inflammation. Lead researcher Dr Maya Saleh said, 'These results demonstrate that women have a more powerful inflammatory response than men.'

More direct support for the idea that women have the stronger immune system comes from work by Professor Katsuiku Hirokawa of the Tokyo Medical and Dental University in 2013. His team examined blood samples from 356 healthy men and women aged between twenty and 90. They found the level of T-cells, which protect us from infection, and B-cells, which secrete antibodies, both declined faster in men than in women. Two other types of cell in the body's defence armoury, CD4 T-cells and NK- (natural killer) cells, became more numerous as subjects got older, but the increase was bigger in women. Hirokawa concluded that these findings were 'consistent with the fact that women live longer than men'. In the UK, researchers at Imperial College of Medicine in London came to a similar conclusion, which seems to fit in with their analysis of statistics from 1993 to 1998, showing that more men than women died from influenza and pneumonia. Interestingly, data from America's National Health and Nutrition Examination Survey, which followed 12,000 men and women over six years, showed that the more muscular men were, the more sexual partners they reported and the earlier their first sexual experiences were likely to have been, but also the weaker their immune systems.

Another biological difference that may give women a better chance of reaching the age of 100 is that they have a slower metabolism. This becomes apparent virtually from the moment of conception, as cells in the male embryo divide faster than those in the female. A slower metabolism may cause women to be more prone to obesity (though men may dilute this advantage by eating more); but it may also extend female life span. The idea that slower metabolism might lead to longer life seems to win support from research done on microscopic nematode worms, each about a millimetre long, which inhabit rotting vegetation and do harm to neither man nor beast. Professor Siegfried Hekimi at McGill University showed genetic mutations that produce a slower metabolic rate can enable nematodes to live five times longer than normal.

Other scientists have examined whether women's periods play a role in their superior survival. Because of menstruation, premenopausal women have about 20 per cent less blood in their bodies than men, lowering the amount of iron in the body. Iron helps in the formation of free radicals, which can damage healthy cells by oxidization, speeding up the ageing process and increasing the risk of heart and other age-related diseases. Perls has given his support to the idea, remarking that, 'One reason for that delay in onset of cardiovascular disease could be that women are relatively iron-deficient compared to men,' while studies in Finland and the United States found that men who made frequent blood donations showed greater resistance to free radicals than other males. Tom Perls also pointed to the fact that red meat is usually our main source of iron, noting research from the Netherlands which indicated that people who ate red meat had twice as much chance of having a heart attack as those who avoided it.

But at the root is something more basic. The male sex hormone testosterone not only encourages men to take all those risks when they are young. As they get older, it plays another life-shortening role: increasing levels of harmful LDL cholesterol and raising the risk of heart disease or stroke. In contrast, the female hormone oestrogen lowers harmful cholesterol and raises 'good' HDL cholesterol levels. Tom Kirkwood, Professor of Medicine at Newcastle University and an expert on ageing, has said that testosterone seems to be associated 'with heart disease and prostate cancer', noting that, as we have seen, castration appears 'partially to equalise male and female longevity'. After the menopause, women start to lose their advantage on heart disease, but their risk does not become equal to men's until extreme old age. Oestrogen may also help women live longer in other ways, because, unlike testosterone, it is an antioxidant.

Deep in our cells there are also other microscopic differences, which we have been able to examine over the last century or so. Men have an X and a Y chromosome, whereas women have two X chromosomes, and while the X contains thousands of genes, the Y is much smaller and contains just a few that are important for male development and fertility. So there is a theory that if a woman has a defective gene on one chromosome, she may be able to call on the normal gene on the other. Men do not have this luxury, so life-threatening conditions such as haemophilia and muscular dystrophy, which are caused by defective genes on the X chromosome, are far more likely to afflict men than women. But in 1985 researchers at Stanford University discovered something that may have even more significance for longevity. It was a gene on the X chromosome that is critical to the repair of DNA. Our cells constantly divide as part of the normal process of life, and as they do, sometimes a mutation appears. As we get older, we accumulate more and more mutations, and it is believed the more we accumulate, the faster we age and the more vulnerable we become to disease. So if a man has a defect in a gene that is crucial for repairing mutations, it could significantly reduce his life span, but if a woman has a faulty repair gene on one of her X chromosomes, perhaps she can get a second chance with the other. In recent years, interest has grown in the role of women's second X chromosome, with suggestions that it seems to become more active later in life. Does this mean that genes on the second chromosome increasingly kick in to take over from those on the first that have become damaged? If this were true, it would represent another considerable advantage for women. Nearly all female mammals have two X chromosomes, and the tendency for females to outlive males is found in a wide range of species. Female macaques, for example, last about eight years longer, while with sperm whales the average gap is 30 years. In birds, though, it is the males who have the two matched chromosomes, and in many bird species, males tend to outlive females.

Then there are telomeres, the sections of DNA that protect the ends of chromosomes from decay. Those belonging to men are shorter and degrade more quickly, and it may be that this too results in men ageing faster, though as yet there is no conclusive evidence. But evidence has emerged in recent years about mitochondria, tiny units to be found by the hundred or the thousand in every one of our cells, which burn oxygen to provide the energy we need to power our bodies. In 2012 at Monash University in Melbourne, Dr Damian Dowling discovered that the mitochondrial DNA of fruit flies had genetic mutations which affected the speed of ageing and the life span of male flies, but not of females. Dr Dowling said, 'the tendency for females to outlive males is common to many different species. Our results therefore suggest that the mitochondrial mutations we have uncovered will generally cause faster male ageing across the animal kingdom.' Perhaps because until recently there were relatively few very old people, our understanding of the basic biology of ageing still has many gaps, and there is speculation about yet another genetic difference between the sexes. Recent research has suggested there are particular genes, dubbed gerontogenes, that can have a big role in determining the life span of laboratory animals, such as worms, flies and mice. Experiments have hinted that these may work differently in males and females, and there is some tentative evidence to support the idea that they too may play a part in the human longevity gap.

One of the peculiarities of the gender gap, incidentally, is that just because women are better at reaching 100, it does not necessarily mean they are healthier. The giant UK financial services company Legal & General set up a Longevity Science Advisory Panel, made up of actuaries and scientists, to look at the future of long life. In 2012 it reported that in every country of the European Union, women live longer than

Ramjeet Raghav and his wife with their new baby.

men, but they also report higher levels of ill health than men at all ages. They tend to suffer more from chronic but non-fatal conditions, such as arthritis, osteoporosis and auto-immune disorders, while men have more 'killer' illnesses, like heart disease and cancer. In the words of Tom Perls: 'While men die from their diseases, women live with them.' His New England Centenarian Study found that centenarian men were generally healthier and suffered less dementia than women. Research in the UK in 2015 concluded that women centenarians were more likely to have dementia and problems with sight and hearing, while in Australia, the proportion of male centenarians still managing to live alone is nearly twice that of females, and research from Portugal in 2014 suggested women over the age of 100 were more likely to be 'frail' than men.

Another odd thing about women's longevity advantage, Sir Cyril Clarke argued, is that it appears to be the exact opposite of what Darwin's theory of evolution would suggest. After the age of about 50, women are no longer able to pass on their genes, whereas men still can until much later in life, and some are thought to have fathered children well into their ninetis, like an Indian villager and former wrestler named Ramjeet Raghav who was said to have become the world's oldest father when he sired his second child at 96 in 2012. So, should it not be men who are living longer? And that leads to another question: why has natural selection not weeded out those testosterone-fuelled males who live fast and die young?

Perls offers some answers. He argues that the life span of a species is strongly influenced by the length of time the young depend on adults to rear them. In humans, women have to be kept around to bring up children and sometimes grandchildren, while men pay the penalty for being less involved in child-rearing by becoming, in evolutionary terms, dispensable earlier in life. As to a male's ability to pass on his genes, studies of our primate relatives, such as chimpanzees and gorillas, suggest the most important consideration is 'access to females'. And is the human realm any different? Though there may be the odd exception, for most men, the ability to continue handing down their genes into old age is more theoretical than real. More important is being able to attract a suitable woman or women early in life, so if coursing testosterone facilitates this, the fact that later it makes it unlikely the man will reach 100 is, in evolutionary and perhaps other terms too, a price worth paying. Evidence to back up this idea has come from research on mice conducted by Tokyo University of Agriculture. The researchers identified a gene carried by both male and female mice but which seems to be active only in males. It allows them to grow larger, stronger bodies, helping them to compete successfully for mates. The downside is that it shortens their lives. Through genetic manipulation, the team then created mice with genetic material from two mothers, but no father. The babies' immune system worked better and they lived on average a third longer, but they were smaller and lighter, which might well be a handicap in finding a mate.

The theory that women get to live longer because of their more important role in rearing children gained support from a study of primates carried out at the California Institute of Technology in the late 1990s. Male chimpanzees take little interest in their offspring, and the researchers found that females lived about 40 per cent longer. Male gorillas are more hands-on, playing with infants and protecting them, and for them the longevity gap is just 12.5 per cent. Mammal species in which the male takes the major responsibility for child-rearing are thin on the ground, but the investigating team found two – titi monkeys and owl monkeys – in which the father is responsible for carrying the young monkeys until they can negotiate the trees alone, the young joining their mothers only for brief periods of nursing. If the father dies, the mother will abandon the infant. Among both species, the males live about 20 per cent longer than the females.

Whatever the precise reasons, women seemed to have built up an impressive and virtually universal lead in longevity, and back in 1984, as attention began to focus on this, Dr William Hazard of the Johns Hopkins University School of Medicine in Baltimore told a conference on gender differences that within two generations, the average woman could be outliving the average man by a decade. But just fifteen years later, Perls was sounding a warning. In the olden days, men used to outlive women, so that much of a woman's advantage today can 'probably be accounted for' by what Perls calls 'societal factors', such as the reduced risk of death in childbirth, and the increased availability of motor cars in which young men could kill themselves. And these factors could change more easily than differences deep in our cells.

Indeed, by the time Dr Hazard was making his prediction, perhaps they already were changing. The widest peacetime gender gap in life expectancy in England and Wales was actually seen in 1967, when it reached 6.3 years. By 2013 it was down to 4.1. The Institute and Faculty of Actuaries' Continuous Mortality Investigation looked at what had happened since 1850 in six other countries: Belgium, Denmark, France, the Netherlands, Norway and Sweden, chosen because they had the most reliable records. In all of these countries, the peak lead for women came a little later, about 1980. In Denmark, the gap was then a sliver over six years. By 2009, it had fallen back to 4.2. In the Netherlands it reduced from 6.26 to 4.11 years, while France continued to show the biggest female lead – 8.24 years in 1980 – and it also fell back less than the others, to 6.71 years in 2009. And women's lead was also being eroded in developed countries outside Europe. If you look at centenarians in Australia, the peak year for women compared with men was 1981, when they outnumbered them by more than five to one. By 2006, the ratio was down to three to one.

It is not that women were not living longer. They were. The gap was closing because female longevity was no longer improving more quickly than male longevity; instead, it was growing more slowly. An explanation favoured by some scientists was that in developed countries, women's life expectancy was getting close to the natural limits of human life span, meaning that further gains would be difficult, while men still had room for improvement. But others believed a more important factor was that women were starting to behave more like men, and not in a good way. For example, in the UK in 1971, four times as many men as women were admitted to psychiatric hospitals with alcohol-related problems, while by 1983 it was only twice as many. The number of women dying of cirrhosis of the liver rose by 37 per cent between 1979 and 1987, while the number of men increased by only 11 per cent. Some believed this might be because women were marrying later – single women were twice as likely as married women to be moderate or heavy drinkers, and alcohol does more damage to women than to men. By 2013 a study for the Organisation for Economic Co-operation and Development (OECD) was revealing that in the UK, girls now seemed more likely to get drunk than boys. According to the report, 44 per cent of British fifteen-year-old girls said they had been drunk at least twice, compared with 39 per cent of boys. Finland had a similar figure for girls, while Denmark was even higher, at 56 per cent. Professor Ian Gilmore, special adviser on alcohol to the Royal College of Physicians, said, 'We are now seeing more and more young women – in their 30s and even in their twenties – with end-stage liver disease.'

It was a similar story with smoking. In the ten years up to 1986, one in four male smokers in Britain quit, while the proportion of quitters among women was fewer than one in five, and by 1989, for the first time, teenage girls were more likely to smoke than teenage boys. This could have a big impact on the longevity gap, because data suggests that, on average, female smokers live no longer than male smokers. In the UK from 1970 to 2009, death rates from lung cancer in men fell by about 54 per cent, while the rate for women actually grew, by 72 per cent, though the disease was still killing one man in 2,000 compared with one woman in 3,200. Across the European Union, male smokers still significantly outnumber females – 31.3 per cent against 19.2 – but here also, men are giving up at a faster rate.

In another sphere, too, men appear to be upping their game. Figures for the UK for 2011 indicated that 59 per cent of men were likely to take serious exercise, against just 48 per cent of women. Obesity is perhaps the biggest health problem now facing developed countries. Its prevalence has doubled over the last twenty years, with an OECD study in 2010 indicating that just over half of all adults in EU countries are now overweight or obese. In the UK, men are more likely than women to be overweight, but obesity is about equally common among women and men, and it seems to be more damaging for women. An obese woman, for example, is 12.7 times more likely to develop type

2 diabetes than one of normal weight, while for a man, the additional risk is only 5.2. Men were also benefiting from reduction of risk in the workplace. In 1946, for example, the UK had 800,000 coal miners – one of the most hazardous of all jobs. Now there are just a few hundred.

A study in 2006 analysing the reasons for the longevity gap in the G7 club of rich countries (Canada, France, Germany, Italy, Japan, the UK and the USA) concluded that diseases of the circulatory system, such as heart attacks and hardening of the arteries, were responsible for up to half the difference, and were particularly important in the UK, Canada and the U.S., while next came violence and accidents, responsible for up to a quarter. In both cases, the study argued, the differences were beginning to narrow by 1990; medical advances subsequently helped reduce the number of deaths from coronary heart disease in England by half between 1991 and 2005. Because this kills twice as many men as women, the improvement benefits men more. Thus while the number of female centenarians in the UK rose by an impressive 58 per cent in the first decade of the twenty-first century, the number of men who reached 100 tripled. Male centenarians remained outnumbered, but whereas in 2002 for every centenarian male there were more than eight women, by 2012 the figure was down to fewer than six.

Projections suggest the gap will continue to close. According to figures from the Office for National Statistics in 2014, over the previous decade female life expectancy in the UK had been growing by 4.6 hours a day, while for males the increase was 6.3 hours a day. In the U.S., a study in 2009 predicted that over the next twenty years, men will gain three times as much benefit from giving up smoking as women. And there are signs that women are beginning to lose their lead in another area – seeking medical advice earlier than men. This seems to have happened just as women are also becoming more likely to fall victims to what used to be seen as men's illnesses. A UK Department of Health report in 2008 said that it was women who were more likely to delay seeing a doctor about possible heart disease, partly because this was regarded as a primarily male problem.

Then, in 2015, came a bit of a bombshell. Public Health England announced that for the oldest, life expectancy had actually fallen between 2011 and 2013, and that the reduction for women was bigger than for men. For women aged 75, there had been a decline of five weeks, while for men there was no change. For women aged 85, there was a reduction of two and a half months, while for men it was only five weeks. At 95, both men and women had seen their life expectancy fall by five weeks. Public Health England warned against reading too much into figures covering just two years, suggesting it might be a statistical blip, while groups campaigning for old people, such as Age UK, blamed public spending cuts: 'The most obvious likely culprit is the rapid decline of state-funded social care in recent years, which is leaving hundreds of thousands of older people to struggle on alone at home without any help.' But Professor John Ashton, president of the UK Faculty of Public Health, said the figures might reflect the way women's lifestyles have changed, 'becoming more like those of men over recent decades, with more smoking and drinking'.

Not all the signs point in one direction, though. Heart disease, for example, still accounts for about a third of all deaths in the UK. Continued improvements in combatting it might be expected to further close the longevity gap in favour of men, but there is also evidence that in some respects women have been getting less effective treatment. If this anomaly were corrected, it should lead to an increase in female longevity. And in some countries, women still seem to be extending their lead. The longevity gap in Japan grew from 5.35 years to 6.81 years between 1970 and 2009, while in Russia, where 70 per cent of men still smoke compared with about 22 per cent in the UK, it widened from 10.37 to 11.96 years over the same period.

Having considered a wide range of evidence, the Longevity Science Advisory Panel concluded in 2012 that changes in behaviour would partially close the gap between male and female longevity, but that 'there is such a significant range of genetic, endocrine, cell and molecular biology differences between men and women with impacts on longevity that we are led to the conclusion that a gender difference in longevity will persist.' According to the ONS, the gap in Britain will continue, but by 2034 it will have narrowed to just two women centenarians for every man. And as for supercentenarians, that tiny elite from the world's 7-billion population who reach the age of 110, when Roger Thatcher compiled his list in 2006, the women outnumbered the men by 32 to one, but it is predicted that by 2034, this gap, too, will not be much more than two to one.

FOUR

The Record-breakers

On 17 October 1995, a blind, deaf French grandmother in a wheelchair broke a world record. Jeanne Calment became, so far as we know, the oldest human being who has ever lived, when she reached the age of 120 years and 238 days. Mme Calment went back long enough for her to have attended Victor Hugo's funeral, and to have met Vincent van Gogh. Her family had lived for at least three centuries in Arles, and that is where she was born, on 21 February 1875. Her father, Nicolas, was a well-to-do shipbuilder, and her mother came from a family of millers. Jeanne would live in the city all her life, marrying her second cousin, a wealthy store owner, at the age of 21. For a short time, the couple stayed with the groom's mother; then they moved into the apartment above the store which would be Mme Calment's home until she was 110. Thanks to her husband's wealth, she lived a comfortable life without ever having to work, and spent a lot of time on healthy pursuits such as tennis, cycling and swimming. In 1898 she gave birth to her only child, a daughter named Yvonne, who died of pneumonia aged 36. Calment lost her husband in 1942, when she was 67, and her only grandchild, Frédéric, died aged 36 like his mother, following a road accident in 1963.

Two years later, at the age of 90, Calment sold her apartment to her lawyer in return for the right to carry on living there and be paid an annual sum for the rest of her life. The lawyer would then get ownership of the apartment on her death. In fact, Calment outlived him, too. He died aged 77, in 1995, and his widow had to carry on the payments until the supercentenarian's demise a couple of years later. It is estimated that thanks to Calment's extraordinary longevity, the buyers ended up paying out twice the market value of the apartment.

Mme Calment had taken up fencing at the age of 85, and at 100 she was still riding a bicycle, though when she travelled all over Arles to thank the people who had congratulated her on her 100th birthday, she walked. At 110, she finally moved into a nursing home, where apparently she complained that the food always tasted the same. It was here that she came to the attention of the world. In 1988, on the centenary of Van Gogh's arrival in Arles, the global press descended and were agog at coming across Calment, the last person alive who had met the painter. When she was thirteen, Van Gogh had come into her uncle's shop to buy some coloured pencils, and she had found him 'dirty, badly dressed and disagreeable'. This, of course, was pure gold for the media, and at the age of 114, Calment found herself becoming a celebrity. She put in a cameo appearance as herself in the 1990 fantasy film *Vincent and Me*, making her the oldest actress ever.

Just before her 115th birthday, Calment broke her leg and elbow in a fall, and had to start using a wheelchair. This did not seem to blunt her wit, however: 'I've only ever had one wrinkle, and I'm sitting on it,' was one of her bons mots. After she had shared those memories of Van Gogh, her birthday became an annual media event. When she could not summon up the appropriate detail to deal with one interviewer's question, she retorted, 'When you're 117, you see if you remember everything!' At her 120th, a young photographer took his leave, saying, 'Until next year, perhaps?' She looked him up and down and replied, 'I don't see why not. You don't look too bad to me,' though on the same occasion, when she was asked how she saw her future, she answered, 'very short'. Still, Calment was there a year later, releasing a CD, *Time's Mistress*, which featured her reminiscing to a score of rap and other music. The mayor of Arles noted what important occasions Calment's birthdays became: they 'were a sort of family holiday, where all the people of Arles gathered around their big sister'. But there would be only one more, her 122nd. On 4 August 1997, Jeanne Calment died, aged 122 years and 164 days. The mayor commented, 'She was the living memory of our town. She brought us comfort and hope with her liveliness, humour and tenderness. In short, we had hoped she was immortal.'

When asked about the secret of her longevity, Calment delivered a variety of responses, talking about laughter, keeping active and having

'a stomach like an ostrich's'. Then there were the two pounds of chocolate she ate every week, the port wine and the olive oil that featured
in her diet and with which she also treated her skin. But she did not
live by food alone. She thought her sense of humour was also important: 'I will die laughing,' she once predicted. At her final birthday
party, Calment described her recipe for survival: 'I dream, I think, I go
over my life. I never get bored.' On another occasion, she offered the
explanation 'God must have forgotten me.' When the British zoologist
Desmond Morris asked for her formula for long life, she answered
that it was her calmness, adding with a chuckle, 'That's why they call
me Calment.' Morris also spoke to her doctor, who told him that the
supercentenarian had never had a day's illness in her whole life. She
seemed to endorse this view, once commenting, 'I've had a beautiful
life. With good health one is happy.' Another striking thing about
Calment was that longevity ran in her family. Her mother lived until
she was 86, and her father to 93. Both were born in 1838, at a time
when average life expectancy in France was around 40. She had two
sisters who died in infancy, but her brother survived to 97. She also
smoked, taking up the habit when she got married, though she limited
herself to two cigarettes a day. She finally gave them up at the age of
119 – not, according to her doctor, because she was worried about the
health risks, but because she could no longer see well enough to light
up, and did not want to ask someone to do it for her. Looking back
over the longest stint on earth any human has experienced, Calment's
summing up was: 'I took pleasure where I could. I acted clearly and
morally and without regret. I am very lucky.'

The longevity expert Jean-Marie Robine visited Calment regularly
and wrote a book about her. His explanation for her survival was
that 'by chance' she had been 'endowed with an extraordinary genetic
makeup', adding that she had 'extraordinary resistance to sickness,
stress and depression. There's nothing exceptional about her lifestyle.
She's not athletic, not a health fanatic.' He also felt her unflappability
was a great strength, noting that she once said, 'If you can't do anything
about it, don't worry about it.'

The record Jeanne Calment broke on 17 October 1995 had been
held by a Japanese man, Shigechiyo Izumi, who was born on 29 June
1865 on the remote Japanese coral island of Tokunoshima, about 800
miles southwest of Tokyo, where he died 120 years and 237 days later.
Although he lost his record as the oldest ever human to Mme Calment,

he continued to be recognized as the oldest man ever, and Izumi was said to have established another record – for the longest working life in history, beginning at a sugar mill when he was seven and lasting for 98 years until he retired as a sugar cane farmer at the age of 105.

Like Jeanne Calment, Izumi was a great source of copy for journalists. A *Sunday Times* reporter went to see him shortly before his 120th birthday. The old man walked to meet him, 'bent almost double, with watery eyes, wispy white Confucian beard, and deeply wrinkled skin.' He was under five feet tall (1.5 m) and weighed less than seven stone (44 kg). The reporter congratulated him and gave him a woollen scarf as a present, at which point Izumi 'pulled me strongly towards him and kissed me on the forehead'. This was apparently a 'most unconventional greeting' in Japan, but the supercentenarian was indulged because of his extraordinary age. They sat on the floor and Izumi poured them a shot of shochu, 'a strong local liquor', 40 per cent proof, made from sugar cane.

Izumi's sight was still good, though one eye had been damaged in an accident half a century or so before, and his hearing was fine so long as you spoke clearly and loudly. He had lost his teeth in his eighties, and refused to wear false ones. He usually began his day with a walk around the garden, pulling up the occasional weed, but all the while, 'as recommended by the Buddhist sages, he contemplates nature.' Every afternoon, he would rest. During his lifetime, Japan had experienced tumultuous changes and traumatic events, but life on Tokunoshima had changed little, and Izumi said it had 'never ceased to be a pleasure'. As a young man, he had been very fit; a local sumo wrestling champion, he carried potatoes to market on his back. His wife died when he was 91, but he enjoyed it when women visited him and liked watching them on television, especially if they were wearing bathing costumes. The reporter's interpreter was an attractive young woman and, in a quavering voice, Izumi serenaded her with a rather risqué love song, which included the lines, 'I want to share the bed with you. If you want a child, you know what do.' The doctor who had been looking after Izumi for 30 years said that over the last half-dozen years, his health had worsened, possibly as a result of a mild heart attack. He was having trouble breathing and his legs were swollen because his heart was no longer pumping well. At the age of 117, he had suffered a bad attack of pneumonia, but had got over it with antibiotics and oxygen treatment, and even at 120 there was little cholesterol in his blood, and no sign of

Jeanne Calment, aged 122.

hardening of the arteries. The journalist reported that Izumi's mind was 'still vigorous . . . he could remember both his childhood more than 100 years ago and the people he had met the day before.'

There was little meat on the island, and Izumi consumed it only on feast days. His diet was dominated by locally grown vegetables, usually stir-fried in pork fat, but even this was said to have been nutritious and full of polyunsaturated fats, because the pigs too ate healthily.

Izumi had smoked three or four cigarettes a day, until he gave up on doctor's orders – at the age of 116. His doctor also wanted him to give up shochu, declaring that it did not 'provide a recipe for long life', but Izumi refused, saying, 'Without shochu there would be no pleasure in life. I would rather die than give up drinking.' He had started imbibing it when he was 70, and every evening he would take a slug, diluted with warm water. A local manufacturer spotted a marketing opportunity, and began selling a brand called Longevity Liquor bearing Izumi's portrait. The supercentenarian was reluctant to give reasons for his longevity, saying, 'Only God knows. God will decide how long I am here.' In response, the reporter tried another tack: did Izumi have a message for the world? The reply was a quotation from an island folk song: 'So long as we live, as far as we survive, we can do anything. Life is more precious than anything else.' Just eight months after this interview, Izumi finally died of pneumonia – on Jeanne Calment's 111th birthday, 21 February 1986.

What a wonderful story! For nine years, Izumi was the oldest human being who had ever lived, one of only two people to have survived past 120, and still the oldest man in history by a mile. Then came a sensation. Research into registration records by Toshihisa Matsuzaki, director of the Department of Epidemiology at the Tokyo Metropolitan Institute of Gerontology, indicated that Izumi had actually been 'only' 105 when he died. The error had been caused by the old bugbear of 'namesaking'. Izumi, said Matsuzaki, had been given a necronym, the name of an older brother who had died, and this had led to the mistake over his date of birth, which was actually fifteen years later than had originally been supposed. Some said that Izumi's great age should be regarded as questioned, rather than disproved, but a number of authorities on longevity disagreed, including Bernard Jeune, who wrote that Izumi's claim had 'been rejected by almost all experts who are familiar with it'. Guinness World Records also stopped recognizing Izumi as the world's oldest man.

With Izumi's claims dismissed, it meant that Jeanne Calment was the only human being known to have lived past 120, and that the title of the world's oldest man fell to Christian Mortensen, who lived to 115 years and 252 days. Born in Denmark on 16 August 1882, he moved to the United States in 1903. Unlike Calment and Izumi, who spent all their lives in the same place, Mortensen not only crossed the Atlantic but it is said that, after reaching America, he lived in 26 different states.

He worked on a farm as a child, and then became a tailor's apprentice in his teens, before leaving Europe. In the USA he went to live with relatives in Chicago, then travelled around the country for a decade from 1908, earning his living as a tailor. He came back to Chicago about 1918, working as a milkman and running a restaurant. Mortensen was married for a short time, before he and his wife divorced. They had no children. Years later, his nurse would say, 'I think his marriage was brief and not happy. After that, he didn't date women.' Mortensen spent the last 21 years of his working life in a factory, retiring to Texas in 1950, where he enjoyed sailing. At the age of 96 he moved into a retirement community in San Rafael, California. (He liked to say he rolled up there on his bicycle.) He stayed in its independent living section until he was 110, when he moved into the skilled nursing facility. In his final years, he was still able to hear if you spoke through a microphone into a set of headphones he wore. One afternoon just before his 114th birthday, the supercentenarian lit up a pungent cigar and broke into song. As he finished the cigar, he remarked, 'I don't smoke more than one cigar a day' – then reached into his neatly pressed suit pocket for another one.

When Jeanne Calment died in August 1997, less than two weeks before Mortensen's 115th birthday, he was expecting to be named the oldest person in the world. Then, two days before the celebration, Guinness World Records announced that the title had gone instead to a woman in Canada named Marie-Louise Meilleur, who was 116. Mortensen fumed, 'They did that just to ruin my party!' (Though later he is said to have remarked, 'C'est la vie.') A similar feistiness was spotted by demographer John Wilmoth, who became a frequent visitor of Mortensen's in his last three years of life. Wilmoth remarked that the supercentenarian could still speak with bitterness of his ex-wife after all those decades. But the demographer was also struck by his 'steady and practical approach to life, his strong singing voice even in his final years, and above all, his sense of humour'. By then 'he was blind and could no longer walk on his own, but he was mentally aware and could carry on an intelligent conversation (when he wanted to) almost until the end.'

Mortensen may never have been the oldest person in the world, but he did become the oldest man, and, Wilmoth said, 'he was proud of that.' As to the secret of his longevity, on his 115th birthday Mortensen declared it was 'Friends, a good cigar, drinking lots of good water, no alcohol, staying positive and lots of singing.' He avoided eating red meat, sticking to chicken, fish and vegetables. We know that smoking shortens your life, but this supercentenarian smoked cigars from the age of twenty until his death 95 years later. And that was not all: 'single men aren't supposed to live as long as married men, but Chris was single for almost all of his life,' and he led a rather solitary existence. He had 'few of the social and economic advantages that may contribute to long life and good health'. Mortensen was never rich, and 'no one could have expected' that he would become the world's oldest man. Christian Mortensen died in his sleep on 25 April 1998. A few weeks before his death, he had been under the weather with a couple of colds, but in his final month, the retirement home said, he 'started to perk up' and he had been joking, smoking and entertaining, so his passing, when it finally came, was rather a surprise.

On 28 December 2012 Mortensen's record as the oldest man who had ever lived was beaten when a Japanese man named Jiroemon Kimura took the undisputed title that had eluded his countryman Shigechiyo Izumi. Eleven days earlier, Kimura had achieved the distinction of being the oldest living human being on the death of an Iowa woman who had been born fifteen days before him (though Kimura's nephew claimed the supercentenarian was actually born a month earlier than his official date of 19 April 1897 and that an error was made when records were collated in 1955). When Kimura was born, average life expectancy in Japan was just 44 years. The third of six children, his parents were farmers who grew rice and vegetables in Kamiukawa, a fishing village sandwiched between the mountains and the sea about 40 miles from Kyoto. He left school at the age of fourteen as the second-best student in his class. After that, apart from a time in the 1920s when he was with a government communications unit in Korea (then occupied by the Japanese), Kimura worked at local post offices until his retirement in 1962 at the age of 65. He had married a local girl and had seven children, fourteen grandchildren, 25 great-grandchildren and thirteen great-great-grandchildren. His wife died when he was 74. After he finished work, Kimura liked reading newspapers and watching sumo wrestling on television. He also helped his son on his farm until he was 90.

In his final years, Kimura lived with his grandson's 60-year-old widow in a two-storey wooden house. She woke him every morning at half past seven, then took him in his wheelchair to the dining room

Christian Mortensen, aged 114.

for a breakfast of rice porridge and miso soup with potatoes and vegetables. He also liked red bean cake, pumpkins, sweet potatoes and rice.
Outside mealtimes, he spent most of his time in bed, but he was still
able to communicate. On the day he surpassed Christian Mortensen's
record, Kimura's granddaughter-in-law said that he was 'positive and
optimistic. He becomes cheerful when he has guests. He's well with
a good appetite. Even when he falls ill, I can tell he'll recover.' When
local officials came to congratulate him on passing 114, the supercentenarian is reported to have replied, 'It is a great honour, and words

alone cannot describe my feelings.' Then, when he was presented by Guinness World Records with a certificate and a copy of the book that recorded his achievement, Kimura sang out, 'Thank you very much!' in loud, clear English.

The supercentenarian was said never to have suffered from any serious illness. He never smoked and drank alcohol only in moderation. His nephew said he had 'an amazingly strong will to live' and that even as a young man, his uncle was disciplined and serious. When drinking with his brothers, he would sit up straight and keep quiet. In an interview on his 115th birthday, Kimura said he was not sure why he had lived so long: 'Maybe it's all thanks to the sun above me. I am always looking up towards the sky,' though the journalist who interviewed him said the supercentenarian had told him his secret was 'eating light to live long'. Kimura practised what is known in Japan as *hara hachi bun me*, which means stopping eating when you are 80 per cent full. There was also evidence of longevity running in the Kimura family: four of his five siblings lived to over 90, and his youngest brother survived to 100.

Only the third man known to have passed 115, Jiroemon Kimura died on 12 June 2013, aged 116 years and 54 days, and his title as the world's oldest living human being passed to another Japanese person, a woman named Misao Okawa. The titles of the world's oldest living human – man or woman – of course, change hands frequently. Those who hold them are by definition very old, and usually die soon. A 114-year-old American named Emma Tillman, for example, the daughter of slaves from the Deep South, was the world's oldest person for just four days in 2007, while the reign of 116-year-old Gertrude Weaver from Arkansas lasted five days in 2015. If you look at the last half-century or so, the average tenure of the world's oldest person has been about a year, but since 2000 it has declined to seven months, reflecting the greater number of people surviving to very old age. Jeanne Calment was a record-breaker in this respect, too: she was the world's oldest living person for nine years.

It is striking how Jeanne Calment, Shigechiyo Izumi and Jiroemon Kimura all lived virtually their whole lives in the same area, and the same is true of the oldest American and second-oldest human being who ever lived, Sarah Knauss. Knauss, who entered this world on 24 September 1880, always lived in Pennsylvania. The daughter of a mining engineer, she was born Sarah Clark in a small coal town called

Hollywood. At twenty she married, and she and her husband were together for 64 years until he died aged 86 in 1965, leaving her a widow for the last 34 years of her life. Knauss never had a full-time job, but she was a talented seamstress who made her own wedding dress and went on creating clothes and hand-sewn quilts until she was 107. Asked at the age of 115 if she enjoyed life, she said she did, 'because I have my health and I can do things'. She was a member of a local church and liked watching golf on television, as well as nibbling chocolates, cashews and potato crisps. For her last ten years she lived at an old people's home in Allentown, about 50 miles from where she was born. An administrator there described her as an 'elegant lady' who was 'worthy of all the honour and adulation she had received'. Knauss was known for always graciously thanking the staff; one said, 'I've worked here for fourteen years and she's the sweetest person I've ever known.'

A journalist who went to visit Knauss just over a year before she died reported that she was five feet tall (1.5 m) and weighed just over six-and-a-half stone (44 kg). Slight as she was, she sat 'tall and graceful' in her wheelchair. The staff said she was taking just one daily medicine, and that she never complained about aches and pains, though they thought she must suffer some. When a nurse complimented her on how nice she looked, 'she turned her head away like a school girl, smiling broadly, utterly pleased.' At lunch, she spurned chicken, carrots and mashed potato in favour of ice cream, which she ate unaided, if slowly, before wiping her chin 'like a lady'. After lunch, she was wheeled down to a craft fair at the home, where she bought a needlepoint poinsettia pin.

Knauss's daughter, who lived to be 101, credited her mother's long life to her relaxed attitude: 'She's a very tranquil person and nothing fazes her. Always calm and serene all her life, whenever there was a crisis.' So when, at the age of 117, Knauss was told that she had become the world's oldest living person, she smiled and said, 'So what?' The supercentenarian rarely got angry, and her grandson said that 'She was a jovial, lovable person to be around,' while according to her great-great-granddaughter, 'She was one of the most generous, well-meaning people you could ever meet. She was very humorous and always smiled when you came to visit her.' Knauss's own advice about living to a great age was, 'Keep busy, work hard and don't worry about how old you are.'

In the final week of her life she went to the hairdresser, just as she did every week, 'wearing a fashionable dress and her trademark smile'. A volunteer at the home said that people thought Knauss looked much younger than her formidable age. She could still talk, though her voice was very soft. The main downside of her advanced age, according to her daughter, was that she had gone 'almost totally deaf'. She also said that, as her mother approached her final year, she slept most of the time; 'She'll say, "You have on a new blouse." Or, I'll hold up needlepoint and she'll say, "That's pretty." So I know she's with it. But because of this awful deafness, there's nothing to do about it. She can't hear. We can't communicate.' Sarah Knauss died on 30 December 1999, just 33 hours before the new millennium, aged 119 years and 97 days. The executive director of the old people's home said, 'She died quietly in her room. She was not ill.' Visitors had dropped in to see her less than an hour before, but 'when the nurse went back, she had passed away,' sitting in her chair. She was survived by her daughter, a grandson, three great-granddaughters, five great-great-grandchildren and a great-great-great-grandson.

For a long time, the United States had more centenarians than any other country, so it is no great surprise that the third-oldest human being ever to have lived (and the oldest African American of all) was Lucy Hannah, born Lucy Terrell on 16 July 1875 in Linden, Alabama. Her parents had been slaves, and Lucy herself moved north to Detroit to escape the racial prejudice of the South. She got married in 1901 and had eight children, only two of whom survived her. Hannah died on 21 March 1993 at the age of 117 years, 248 days. She too is said to have had long-lived relatives, with her mother living to 99 and two sisters reaching 100.

The oldest ever Briton was a Cleveland schoolteacher, born Charlotte Milburn on 1 August 1877, the same day Alexander Graham Bell launched his first telephone company. She started teaching in her teens, and did not marry until she was 63, when she became Charlotte Hughes. 'You were not allowed to teach and marry,' she would explain, 'Teaching was the best paid job and I had no intention of giving it up in the hard times we once knew.' Later in life, she would say she always voted for the Labour Party because of the poverty she had seen when she was teaching. Even though she married so late, she enjoyed 40 happy years with her husband, a retired army captain, until he died at the age of 105. On her 108th birthday, Hughes had tea with then prime minister Margaret Thatcher. When the Iron Lady moved in for a hug, Hughes exclaimed, 'Don't cuddle me! I'm Labour.' 'Never mind, let's have a cup of tea,' was the reply. Later, the supercentenarian said that although she still did not agree with Thatcher's politics, she thought the prime minister was 'wonderful'.

Other birthday celebrations were equally memorable for Hughes. For her 109th, she took a spin around the Bay of Biscay on Concorde, and the following year she became the world's oldest air passenger when she travelled on the supersonic airliner to New York. It was the first time she had ever been to America, and as she boarded the aircraft, she declared, 'I represent all the centenarians in Britain.' She lived in her own home in the seaside village of Marske until she was 114, when she moved into a nursing home at Redcar because she was having trouble walking. On her 115th birthday she said that one of the factors in her longevity was healthy eating, with regular meals and 'not too much fatty food'. Hughes's usual breakfast was bacon and eggs, followed by a small glass of brandy, but she said she never ate or drank 'too much because it becomes bad for you'. Another factor in her long life, she said, was following the Ten Commandments and living 'a good honest life'. She expressed concern about what she saw as a fall in moral standards, but even more at the way people's command of basic English had declined: 'When I taught in an elementary school I used to go in for grammar. Do they teach it now? Many of the people I hear on the telephone don't even know how to speak the language properly.'

Charlotte Hughes was very proud of the greetings cards she received every year from the Queen, and mounted them on the wall, remarking, 'Hopefully there'll be a lot more messages from her because I think I'll go on to be at least 120.' In fact, her 115th was the last birthday she would see. She died peacefully in her sleep on 17 March 1993, aged 115 years, 228 days, having, we are told, 'maintained her faculties and sharp wit to the end'.

The person she succeeded as Britain's oldest person was Anna Williams from Swansea, who had died in 1987 aged 114 years, 210 days. And while she was the oldest woman in Britain, the oldest man also came from Swansea – John Evans. I was lucky enough to interview him in 1985 for my *TV Eye* programme on 100-year-olds, when he was 108. His long life was all the more extraordinary because he had spent 60 years as a coal miner. As *The Guardian* put it, 'he survived an occupation and a locality where chances of longevity are among the worst in Britain.' Evans first clocked on at Garngoch Colliery in 1889, and retired reluctantly in 1949. 'I was 73 when they chucked me out,' he told me, 'and I could have gone on another eight to ten years.'

Until he was 95 years old Evans looked after the vegetable patch at his home, a cottage his father had built on the edge of Garngoch Common, where he lived with his son and daughter-in-law. At 108 he made medical history by becoming the oldest person ever to be fitted with a pacemaker, and astounded doctors by being fit enough to return home three days later. In 1900 he had thought about visiting London, but decided he could not afford it. Finally, at the age of 110, he got there as a guest of British Rail, resplendent in his best suit, with a red rose in the button hole and his favourite panama hat. At 110, he testified in a dispute over a right of way, and the court relied on his recollection of its historical basis because he was the only person able to remember that far into the past.

When I asked John Evans if he was glad to have lived so long, he replied, 'Live as long as we can is the aim with us all, isn't it?' And he did seem to enjoy the publicity that came with each birthday in his final years. As to the secret of his long life, he commented, 'I've always been a teetotaller. I didn't smoke at all. My brother did smoke, and he died when he was 61. Cancer of the liver through smoking.' Another thing to avoid was 'cursing and swearing, which is disturbing to the nerves'. Singing, though, was good: 'I've been doing that since I was a little boy. Going to Sunday school, I'd sing, plenty of it.' Dieticians might raise their eyebrows at his favourite food in his younger days – bread and lard with a sprinkling of salt – but later on he set great store by eating lots of vegetables and drinking mugs of boiled water laced with a little honey. So I asked him how much longer would he like to live. 'As it please the creator, I suppose,' he told me. 'It is at his leisure I am now. In the hour that you don't expect, the Son of God will call upon.' In December 1989, the *Guinness Book of Records* declared Evans the world's oldest man, and on 10 June 1990 he died peacefully in his sleep in a chair beside his bed, aged 112 years, 295 days. He had been complaining of feeling poorly for a few days. His daughter-in-law said, 'A big gap has been left in our lives. Everyone will always have such happy memories of him.'

His record as Britain's oldest man was broken in 2009 by an even better-known supercentenarian. Evans had been too old to serve in the First World War, but Henry Allingham joined up at the age of nineteen, in 1915, and became celebrated as one of the last survivors of that terrible conflict. He was born in Clapton in east London, the son of an ironmonger; his father died of tuberculosis when he was just fourteen months old. He was brought up by his grandparents until he was seven, acknowledging that 'they rather spoiled me.' He then went to live with his mother. At his first school, there were 'a lot of rough kids', and he attended a number of others until eventually he passed the entrance exam for a 'fantastic' grammar school in south London, where 'they taught us French, science, metalwork and art.' But he had to leave at sixteen because the family was so short of money. Allingham was supposed to go into the family ironmonger's firm, but it did not appeal to him, so after a short stint working as a trainee surgical instrument maker, he took a job with a car-body builder. When war broke out, he wanted to join up, but his mother, who was ill, begged him not to. When she died in September 1915, he signed up for the Royal Naval Air Service as a mechanic, later becoming a founding member of the Royal Air Force (RAF).

After a spell maintaining sea planes at Great Yarmouth and as an anti-Zeppelin gunner, Allingham saw action at the great naval battle of Jutland in May 1916. He recalled watching shells flying across the sea, remarking, 'There were a lot of dud shells and that saved us from a lot of harm.' In 1917 he was posted for a time to the Western Front, with orders to neutralize booby-trapped bombs left behind in the trenches by retreating German soldiers. One night, he fell into a shell hole: 'It stank. So did I when I fell into it. Arms and legs, dead rats, dead everything. Rotten flesh. Human guts.' Fearing he might drown in the mud and water, he 'took a chance' and moved to the left: 'If I'd gone to the right, I don't know what would have happened.' He made several attempts to slither out of the hole. Each time he fell back into mud up to his armpits, but eventually he managed to haul himself out, though he did not dare move again until break of day. Afterwards, he 'couldn't get a bath for three or four months'. He was haunted by the sight of soldiers waiting to go over the top: 'They would just stand there in two feet of water in mud-filled trenches, waiting to go forward. They knew what was coming.'

At the end of the war, Allingham married Dorothy, a nurse he had met while he was in hospital with a cracked rib, after proposing to her on an impulse. She was, he said, the only girl he had ever kissed. They would be married for over 50 years, until she died in 1970. Allingham took a job with the Ford Motor Company, where he stayed until he retired. During the Second World War, his engineering expertise was put to use on a project aimed at combatting German magnetic mines.

Life was not always easy, and Allingham said later that he had 'two major breakdowns, one during the war and one after, but both when I was trying to do the work of three men'. After Dorothy's death, he moved to Eastbourne and looked after himself in a small flat, but it was a lonely life. As for the First World War, he took the view that, 'I'll never forget my comrades, but you can't dwell on the terrible things that happened. You couldn't go on if you did,' though he said that 'on days like Armistice Day' he would pray for them. For decades Allingham avoided reunions or talking about the war, even with his family.

As Allingham turned 100, Dennis Goodwin, founder of the First World War Veterans' Association, tried to get him to relent, but at first the supercentenarian would not even let him in the door: 'He'd say, "I want to forget the war, I don't want to talk about it."' But Goodwin started sending him letters about reunions he was organizing and, gradually, 'we got talking', though 'it was a very slow process – he's essentially a very private man.' Eventually Goodwin became Allingham's close friend and supporter, often to be seen at his side at public events and working with him on his memoirs. So in the final years of his life, the veteran discovered a new mission: to keep alive the memory of those killed in the war.

In 2003 Allingham helped launch the Poppy Appeal. He was also admitted to France's Légion d'Honneur and given the freedom of the French town of Saint Omer. Other honours followed: the freedom of British towns, doctorates, invitations to Buckingham Palace garden parties. In 2005, it is said, he became the final First World War veteran to march past the Cenotaph on Armistice Day, remarking, 'Coming here, you recall things you want to forget. But you and I owe so much to these men who gave all they could have given on my behalf and everyone's behalf. It is so important that we acknowledge them.' Apart from attending Remembrance events and writing his memoirs, Allingham gave interviews to the media and visited schools. During his 111th year, he fulfilled no fewer than 60 engagements, including meetings with Prince Charles, then prime minister Tony Blair and Chancellor Gordon Brown. On a visit to the Somme, Allingham was asked how he wanted to be remembered, and replied, 'I don't. I want to be forgotten. Remember the others.' One journalist wrote that he 'became a symbol of the sacrifice of a generation'.

Aged 109, Henry Allingham finally had to move into a care home, but he still urged others to 'hang on to your independence.' He said he was grateful for the care he received, 'but I don't like relying on other people'. Asked what the key to longevity is, his answer was, 'Cigarettes, whisky and wild, wild women – and a good sense of humour.' More philosophically, he reflected, 'You make your own happiness, whatever age you are . . . People ask me, what's the secret of a long life? I don't know,' though he admitted it was important 'to look after yourself and always know your limitations'. Max Arthur, who interviewed Allingham for *Last Post*, his book on the last survivors of the First World War, had another explanation: 'He was a very dignified, very gentle man. He was so surprised to survive the First World War that he saw whatever came next as a reward. He made the most of his life.' Allingham said he was not 'much for medicine . . . I know my mind and my body better than anyone else.' And as far as diet was concerned, 'You can't beat jellied eels from the Norfolk Broads.'

In 2009, Allingham became the world's oldest living man. Dennis Goodwin said, 'He will take it in his stride, like he does everything else.' Indeed, when asked how long he wanted to live, Allingham declared, 'I don't mind if my future is long or short, as long as I'm doing the right thing.' On 6 June 2009, the Royal Navy gave him a 113th birthday party. He died just over a month later, on 18 July. At the time of his death, he was the last surviving founder member of the RAF and the last man to have witnessed the Battle of Jutland. The chief executive of Allingham's care home said he was active right to the end. Though both his daughters died before him, he left five grandchildren, twelve great-grandchildren, fourteen great-great-grandchildren and one great-great-great-grandchild, most of whom were living in America. In the foreword to Allingham's memoirs, Prince Charles described him as 'one of our nation's historic treasures', adding, 'We should all be humbled by this quiet, genial man.' Allingham's own summary of his 113 years was, 'I've got a lot to be thankful for . . . I've had a unique sort of life. I've scraped the barrel and I've had the cream.' He admitted to only one regret: not being able to go to university.

Henry Allingham's successor as Britain's oldest man was also dubbed 'the last Tommy', as the only Briton then left alive who had fought in the trenches. Born on 17 June 1898, Harry Patch grew up in Combe Down, near Bath. His father was a stonemason and his mother a senior domestic servant. Patch was called up at the age of eighteen, and in 1917 he fought at Passchendaele, in a battle in which more than 70,000 British troops died. He saw comrades 'just blown to pieces', saying, 'it wasn't a case of seeing them with a nice bullet hole in their tunic, far from it, and there I was, only nineteen years old. I felt sick.' He said that as far as he knew, he never killed a German soldier. Instead he aimed low, trying to hit them in the legs and bring them down. On the night of 21 September, Patch was badly wounded in the groin when a shrapnel shell burst overhead. It killed three of his closest friends. A doctor cut out the jagged two-inch piece of metal while four men held Patch down. There was no anaesthetic; 'I can feel that bloody knife even now,' he would say nearly 90 years later.

Sent home to England to recuperate, Patch had been due to return to the front when the Armistice was signed. After that, it took five months for him to be demobilized. While they waited impatiently, Patch and some of his friends nearly found themselves charged with mutiny after they refused to go out on parade, even when an officer threatened to shoot them; but a brigadier defused the situation. After the war, he had a successful career in the construction industry, and during the Second World War he was a volunteer fireman during Luftwaffe attacks on Bath. Longevity ran in his family: his mother, along with her five brothers and sisters, were all said to have lived to be over 90, and his two brothers survived to 96 and 84, even though one had asthma and the other was wounded at Mons during the war. Patch himself was widowed twice, and one of his sons died aged only

First World War Veterans on Armistice Day in 2008.
Henry Allingham is on the left, Harry Patch in the centre.

45 after becoming an alcoholic. Patch's other son also died before him. Every 21 September he commemorated the three friends he lost in the shelling: 'I see their faces in my dreams,' he said. Apart from that, for a long time he wanted nothing to do with remembering the war. Then, in 2002, he relented and returned to the battlefield, finding 'near enough' the place where he had been wounded. It was now a potato patch. But when it came to laying a wreath in memory of his dead friends, he was overcome: 'the memories flooded back and I wept, and the wreath was laid on my behalf.' Two years later, he went out to meet a 107-year-old German veteran. He had been reluctant at first, but they got on well together.

Unlike Henry Allingham, Harry Patch continued to feel a burning anger against those he considered responsible for the war: 'Why should the British government call me up and take me out to a battlefield to shoot a man I never knew . . . All those lives lost for a war finished over a table.' He wrote that the 'politicians who took us to war should have been given the guns and told to settle their differences themselves, instead of organising nothing better than legalised mass murder.' Patch was also scathing about government plans in 2006 for a memorial to mark the death of the last combatant of the First World War: 'The politicians claim they want to honour the fighting men of the Great War – but there's only about three of us left. And I'm the only one who fought in the trenches. Why didn't they do more for the veterans and their widows long ago? When boys came back with lost limbs or not at all?' His views did not prevent him getting a tribute from Prime Minister Gordon Brown when he died in a care home at Wells on 25 July 2009, aged 111 years and 38 days. He was also celebrated in verse by the then Poet Laureate, Andrew Motion. His feelings did not stop him enjoying life, either; according to Patch's biographer, Richard van Emden, 'He had a sparkle about him, a dry sense of humour, he was just a lovely man. He was one of the most rewarding people to be with.' And when he was told that the newspapers had his obituary ready to be printed at the appropriate moment, Patch responded: 'all I can say is that I hope to live long enough that they will have to update it, and more than once!'

Harry Patch's death left just one living British serviceman from the First World War, Claude Choules, who was born at Pershore in Worcestershire in 1901. By the time the war broke out, his mother had left home and he was being brought up by his father. He lied about his age to try and join the army as a bugler. That ploy failed, but he managed to fool the navy, joining HMS *Revenge* and seeing action in the North Sea. He was present for the surrender and scuttling of the German fleet. After the war, he stayed in the navy, and in the 1920s he moved to Australia, transferring to the Royal Australian Navy. During the Second World War, he was chief demolition officer for the western half of Australia, and it would have been his job to blow up the strategic harbour of Fremantle if Japan had invaded.

Despite serving in two world wars, Claude Choules became a pacifist, refusing to march in the Anzac Day commemoration parades. At the age of 80 he took a creative writing course, and later compiled his autobiography. His wife, to whom he had been married for 76 years, died when he was 105. He left three children and eleven grandchildren. In his final years he was blind and partially deaf, but his mind was still lively. Choules died in his sleep in a Perth nursing home in 2011, aged 110 years, 63 days. When asked for the secret of long life, he used to reply, 'Just keep breathing,' though he added that having a happy family around him also helped. As for being the last surviving British veteran from the Great War, he said it was 'nothing to shout about'; somebody had to be the last, so 'Why not me?'

Another notable First World War veteran was the last British cavalryman, Albert Marshall. Born at Elmstead in Essex in 1897, like Claude Choules he lied about his age so he could join up. His life had been tough; his mother died of tuberculosis when he was four, and he told stories of how when motor coaches drove through the village on their way to the seaside, the local boys would get passengers to throw coins out of the windows, and would then fight over them. He had been riding horses since he was five, so Marshall was a natural for the cavalry. Some generals still believed mounted troops could win the war, but they were no match for the new technology of extermination. The horses were terrified by shells, and blinded by chlorine gas.

Marshall was wounded at the Somme. He also fought at Loos, where poison gas released by the British blew back over their own trenches. At other times the gas came from the Germans, and 90 years later it still made Marshall's skin itch, meaning he had to put on ointment twice a day. He spent his 21st birthday in a derelict farm being shelled. If one 'burst a few yards away, that made you jump for a minute, but you got used to it'. One explosion, though, buried him and two of his comrades in the mud. As he felt himself sinking he sang

Albert Marshall.

'Nearer My God to Thee', until a search party found him, but his two companions were never seen again.

Worse than the shells, he said, were the lice: 'You were smothered with them.' He had only two baths in three years at the front. He used to swap his cigarettes for other men's rum rations, which he then rubbed between his toes. This meant that when others' feet were rotting from trench foot and gangrene, his were 'as good as anything'. After

Yisrael Kristal.

the war, Marshall married his childhood sweetheart and worked as a handyman on a large estate. He did odd jobs in the greenhouses there until he was 100, and carried on riding until he was in his eighties. Like Henry Allingham and Harry Patch, for many years Marshall spoke little about the war. Then, when he was in his nineties, he joined the Veterans' Association, and when he reached 100, 'life really took off for me'. After the war, he had only ever been abroad once, on holiday (and he and his wife, who died when he was 87, had no holiday at all until their 25th wedding anniversary), but in 1997 he went to Passchendaele for the 80th anniversary of the battle. At age 101 he was invited to Downing Street with other veterans, and he was also awarded the Légion d'Honneur. Later, Marshall would meet Prince Charles, attend a Buckingham Palace garden party, lay a wreath at the Tomb of the Unknown Soldier in Paris and sing trench songs in a concert at Rochester Cathedral. He died in 2005, aged 108 years, 62 days. Incidentally, the last surviving member of the armed forces from the First World War is thought to have been a woman, Florence Green, who died just a couple of weeks short of her 111th birthday, in February 2012. She had joined the Women's Royal Air Force two months before the Armistice in 1918, and served as a mess steward at the RAF bases in Marham and Narborough.

Surviving the horrors of the First World War and making it to the age of 100 is impressive enough. But what about coming through the Holocaust, and living to be the oldest man in the world? Yisrael Kristal was born in Poland in 1903. During the First World War, his mother died and his father was captured by the Russians. At seventeen he moved to Łódź and worked in the family confectionery business. In 1940, after the Nazis conquered the country, he was sent to the ghetto with his wife and two children. Both children died there, and Kristal and his wife were sent to Auschwitz in 1944. She died, but he survived, working as a slave labourer in Auschwitz and other camps. When he was liberated, he weighed just five stone eleven (37 kg). After the war, Kristal emigrated to Israel with his second wife, where he continued to run a confectionery business, until he retired. In March 2016 he became the world's oldest man, at 112 years, 178 days. Kristal said he did not know why he had survived so long: 'There have been smarter, stronger and better looking men then me who are no longer alive.' He believed everything was 'determined from above and we shall never know the reasons why', and that we must 'keep on working as hard as we can and rebuild what is lost'. The supercentenarian lamented the 'permissiveness' he saw in the modern world, with children no longer deferring to their parents, and, he believed, getting everything too easily, but his daughter said, 'He is optimistic, wise, and he values what he has.'

Another centenarian survivor of the concentration camps was Alice Herz-Sommer. Born into a prosperous German-speaking secular Jewish family in Prague in 1903, by her late teens she was already an accomplished concert pianist, performing all over Europe and counting Gustav Mahler and Franz Kafka among her friends. In 1943, she, her husband and their five-year-old son were sent to a concentration camp in the Czech city of Terezín, which the Germans called Theresienstadt. It was promoted by the Nazis as a model institution, and many of its inmates had been among Czechoslovakia's foremost figures in the arts. Amid the squalor and the rampant disease, there was a library, and as well as doing forced labour, professors there could lecture, artists could paint and musicians could play. Herz-Sommer says that she performed in more than 100 concerts at Theresienstadt, as 'propaganda. We had to play because the Red Cross came three times a year.' Her frail mother had been sent to a death camp in 1942, and her husband was transported from Theresienstadt to Auschwitz. She never saw either of them again. Of the 140,000 prisoners sent to Terezín, 33,000 died there, while another 90,000 were moved on to the death camps. It seems Herz-Sommer's musical talent was one reason she survived the war. She told how she was stopped one day by a young Nazi officer, who said how much he treasured her concerts and added, 'You and your son will not be on any deportation lists. You will stay in Theresienstadt until the war ends.'

After the war, the pair went to Israel, but then moved on to live in London. Her son became a concert cellist, dying when Alice was 98. 'What's the secret of living to 100?' is a favourite question for any centenarian, but for Alice Herz-Sommer, it represented an even more intriguing query. One answer she gave was 'optimism and discipline', and certainly she was said to have practised the piano every day until shortly before she died at the age of 110: 'Punctually, at 10 am, I am sitting there at the piano.' As for diet, she said, 'For 30 years I have eaten the same, fish or chicken. Good soup, and this is all. I don't drink, not tea, not coffee, not alcohol. Hot water.' She found walking painful, 'but after twenty minutes it is much better. Sitting or lying is not good.' In spite of all that she had been through, she always tried to take a positive outlook: 'I am looking for the nice things in life. I know about the bad things, but I look only for the good things.' Of religious faith, she said, 'Beethoven is my religion ... He gives me the faith to live and to say: "Life is wonderful and worthwhile" even when it is difficult.'

While Alice Herz-Sommer managed to keep up her piano playing until the end of her days, the trio of war veterans – Henry Allingham, Harry Patch and Albert Marshall – had all embarked on new lives in their final years as they strove to keep alive the memory of the Great War. Perhaps the most spectacular example of this late opening of fresh chapters comes from the Japanese centenarian Yano twin sisters, who became pop stars. Born to a farming family, for their first 99 years Gin and Kin – meaning 'silver' and 'gold' in Japanese – had lived fairly quiet lives. But then the mayor of their home town, Nagoya, came to visit them in 1991 on Japan's Respect for the Aged Day, and the media picked up the story. The government designated them 'national treasures', and they appeared in a television commercial for a cleaning product. Soon they were being featured in all manner of endorsements and advertisements. They wrote advice columns in magazines, did television game shows and had a hit record called 'Granny Rap'. The song became a favourite in karaoke clubs, and one company even brought out Kin-Gin stuffed toys. The twins had to hire a publicity agent, who said the reason they were so popular was 'because it is amazing to many Japanese that the twins are still cheerful, can carry on a witty conversation and speak quite clearly'. Their success meant they had to fill in income tax forms for the first time in their lives, but they joked that at least they would be able to 'provide for their old age'.

Diminutive, dressed in identical kimonos with close-cropped snow-white hair, the twins always seemed to be laughing and giggling. Kin had eleven children, seven grandchildren and five great-grandchildren and lived with her youngest son and his family. Gin lived a few miles away with her youngest daughter, having produced five children, who gave her four grandchildren and nine great-grandchildren. At 102, they made their first trip abroad, to Taiwan, where they were greeted by 1,000 pairs of twins. Both managed to recover from illnesses when they were well over 100 – Kin from a stomach ulcer and Gin from pneumonia. At their 106th birthday party, Kin declared, 'I still feel young,' and in 1999 they became the oldest twins ever when they passed the age of 107. In keeping with their cheery image, they performed a tree planting ceremony using pink shovels. Five months later, in January 2000, Kin was the first of the pair to die. Her grandson said that she would have liked to live 'a little bit longer and become the oldest person in Japan'. Three months later, Gin became bedridden, and died peacefully just over a year after her sister. According to one of Gin's doctors, 'she possessed psychological and physical strengths that one cannot imagine a centenarian having.' The twins attributed their longevity to their walks and the simplicity of their lives. 'We never thought we would live this long,' Kin had said as they passed 100, 'We could survive because we were twins. We need each other more than anyone else in the world.'

Britain's longest-lived twins were the daughters of an Aberdeenshire farmworker. Edith and Evelyn Rennie were born on 15 November 1909, and both worked on farms from the age of thirteen until they were married. For the rest of their lives they never lived more than 50 miles apart. Each had four children. They spent their final years in the same care home, the manager of which described them as 'lovely ladies', adding, 'They spend time together through the day – they just enjoy seeing each other.' When Evelyn's eyesight failed, Edith would read to her. Edith put her impressive survival down to 'hard work, a bowl of porridge every morning and a simple life', and also 'a good husband'. She never travelled out of Scotland, while the furthest Evelyn ever went was Wales. Their mother had lived to 101, and Evelyn's husband lasted until he was 99. Edith died first, aged 104 years, 253 days in July 2014, and Evelyn just over seven months later.

As for married couples, as we saw earlier, Charlotte Hughes and her husband had clocked up a remarkable combined age of 206 when he died in 1980, but according to Guinness World Records, the oldest married couple ever by combined ages were the Norwegians Karl Dølven and Gudrun Haug. They married at Hole in the south of the country on 4 June 1927, and their marriage lasted nearly 77 years, until 24 April 2004, when Gudrun died aged 103 years and 193 days. At the time, Karl was 106 years, 237 days, making their aggregate age 210 years, 65 days. In December 2015, claims were advanced for Karam Chand, aged 110, and his wife Kartari, 103, from Bradford, West Yorkshire, as they celebrated their 90th wedding anniversary. The couple had been married in India in 1925 and moved to the UK 40 years later. They were well enough to open a shopping centre, in recognition of their achievement as the world's longest-married couple.

Centenarian twin sisters Kin (left) and Gin (right), at a big twins gathering
in Taichung, Japan, 20 May 1995.

Among other holders of the title were an extraordinary Jewish
couple from Austria. Herbert and Magda Brown were married in 1930,
when she was 26 and he was 30. According to Magda, 'We met at a
dance, and we fell in love right away.' A couple of years later, they
had a daughter. Then in 1938, the Nazis took over Austria. Soldiers
ransacked their house and Herbert, who owned two successful small
department stores, was sent to Dachau. The family sold all their
belongings and turned the proceeds, and all their life savings, over
to the Nazis. Herbert was released. 'Money talks,' explained Magda.
He managed to flee to a refugee camp in England, and Magda and
their daughter joined him just six days before Britain declared war on
Germany. Herbert had to stay in the camp, while Magda was taken in
as a companion by a wealthy woman, and their daughter went to stay
on a farm. In 1940 the family got the chance to go to America. Just
two days before they were due to set sail, word came that there was
another boat leaving a day earlier. They decided to take it, and arrived
safely in the United States. The ship they had been due to travel on
was sunk. There were no survivors. The family settled in Philadelphia,
with Magda working as a seamstress and Herbert in a clothing factory.
It was a far cry from Austria, where they had had maids: 'I'd never had
a thread and needle in my hand,' recalled Magda. Eventually they got
better jobs and scraped together enough money to buy a house. After
they retired, their main exercise was walking around shopping malls,

and Herbert carried on driving until he was 91. That was about the time his doctor suggested he should start using a cane: 'I will when I'm old,' came his reply.

In July 2005 Guinness certified them the world's oldest married couple, with Herbert aged 105, and Magda 100. A journalist who went to see them reported that Magda was meticulously dressed by half past six every morning, complete with lipstick and pearls. Herbert was impeccably smart in a crisp blue shirt that brought out the colour of his eyes, though he was frail and spoke little. Their diet gave mixed messages for those seeking the secret of long life: Herbert favoured raw carrots; Magda was a chocoholic. Perhaps the answer lay elsewhere. 'We have a happy marriage; we never fight,' said Magda. 'We have discussions, but we never fight.' Their daughter, meanwhile, believed that her father stayed alive to give her mother something to do: 'She's constantly straightening his collar.' Herbert died that December, two months after they celebrated their 75th wedding anniversary. Magda followed in October 2006, a fortnight short of her 102nd birthday.

Then there are the centenarians who did not take a spouse of their own age, or anything like it. In 2009, a Somalian named Ahmed Muhamed Dhore, who claimed to be 112 and already had thirteen children from five other wives, chose a seventeen-year-old bride. He said, 'God helped me realise my dream' – though his own charm had also done its bit: 'I used my experience to convince her of my love.' By the time he took his teenage bride, three of his wives had died, so presumably he felt the need to replenish supplies. Dhore's claim to be 112 was backed up by a birth certificate written on goatskin by his father.

In 2006, for her 21st husband, a 104-year-old Malaysian woman, Wook Kundor, chose her 33-year-old lodger, Muhammad Noor Che Musa, who was getting married for the first time. He said he had felt sorry for her because she was old and alone, saying, 'I am not after her money, as she is poor.' He added that before he met his new wife, he had 'never stayed in one place for long'. And when, three years later, he went away to a rehab centre to try to combat his drug addiction, Wook started looking for husband number 22, declaring she was afraid Muhammad was going to find a new, younger wife: 'I realise I am an aged woman . . . My intention to re-marry is to fill my forlornness, and nothing more than that.' She added, 'I'm not searching for a man as handsome as our prime minister, but someone to accompany me in my twilight years.'

We saw that Herbert Brown carried on driving until he was 91, but many centenarians have managed to stay behind the wheel well past their 100th birthday. In 2015, according to official figures, 191 people aged over 100 held licences in Britain. The RAC (Royal Automobile Club) said the oldest was a 107-year-old woman, but the oldest person in Britain known to be driving regularly was Harry Jamieson from Worthing, Sussex, who kept on motoring until shortly before his death at the age of 106, in 2014. Mr Jamieson had held a licence for 80 years, clocking up no fewer than 2 million miles without ever picking up a single penalty point or even a parking fine. He first learned to drive in the army in an armoured car. During the Second World War he worked on the development of radar, and in civvy street as an electrician until he was 70. For Jamieson, driving was much more than a means of getting from A to B; it was a 'major part' of his life: 'I just love the freedom getting into a car gives. There are no boundaries and I can go wherever and whenever I want.' It had given him 'a good life as I have seen every part of Britain because of it'. Jamieson thought it was possible that he had 'spent more time in my car then I have in my bed'. His daughter said, 'He is still a very good driver. I feel safer in the car with him then when I am in the car with a person a lot younger.' After 60 years of marriage, Jamieson's wife died aged 92. He put his own longevity down to a tipple of brandy every day, a spoonful of honey and a glass of red wine. He had lived on his own until three months before his death, when he had broken a bone in his neck and had to move into a nursing home. One of his friends described him as 'smartly dressed, polite, helpful, charming . . . never had a bad word to say about anyone'.

According to Guinness World Records, the oldest driver ever was an American, Fred Hale Sr, who kept going until his 108th birthday, in 1998. By then, it was said, he was getting irritated because other motorists were going too slowly. Hale had been a postal worker and a beekeeper, and when he died aged 113 he was the oldest man in the world. His grandson said he 'had a routine and he rarely broke it because anyone else was around', eating three meals a day, always at the same time. He also took a daily teaspoonful of honey and bee pollen, with the occasional nip of whisky, and never smoked. At 103, he was still shovelling snow off the roof of his home in New York State.

The man said to be the world's oldest cyclist was also an American, Octavio Orduno, from Long Beach, California, who would pedal along

Ocean Boulevard every day. 'He was our Superman,' said his daughter, 'he just loved life.' When he reached 100, however, his wife of 60 years insisted that he trade in his bicycle for a three-wheeler. A familiar smiling figure at local events, Orduno had run away from home during the Great Depression, hitching rides on freight trains. Later he became a gardener for stars such as Claudette Colbert, and then an aerospace mechanic. As he got older, according to his son, cycling 'gave him something to do'. Orduno had his fair share of tumbles, once having to spend two days in hospital with concussion. At 104, he could no longer get his trike up the slope to the road and had to be content with a spin around the car park by his house. After his front wheel was stolen, he finally gave up, and failing health meant he had to move into a care home. There he fell and broke his hip, dying two weeks before his 107th birthday. Octavio Orduno's formula for long life was to 'Keep moving and eat healthy,' which meant a diet based on vegetables, fruit and nuts.

Saburo Shochi from Japan had a different way of getting around. In 2012, at the age of 106, he completed a month-long, 35,000-mile round-the-world trip using only public transport – becoming the oldest person ever to achieve such a feat. A professor emeritus at Fukuoka University of Education, he travelled on trains, boats, planes and buses as he delivered lectures on education and health in North America, Europe and Africa. Shochi, who did not start globe-trotting until he was 99, told reporters on his return that he planned to live longer, and that never in his life had he complained of being tired.

Driving, cycling, snow clearing and criss-crossing the globe are impressive, but doing the 100-metre sprint or running the marathon are perhaps even more so. In 2014, a 103-year-old Japanese man, Hidekichi Miyazaki, clocked 29.83 seconds for the 100 metres – a new world record for a 100-year-old – and tottered over the line into the arms of his 73-year-old daughter with a joyful whoop. Dubbed 'the Golden Bolt' after the Jamaican sprinter Usain Bolt, whose world record stands at 9.58 seconds, the bespectacled centenarian is just five feet tall (1.5 m), weighs six and a half stone (42 kg), and only took up running at the age of 92. Miyazaki, who comes from the tea-growing prefecture of Shizuoka, about 100 miles southwest of Tokyo, said: 'My body is small so I take care of what I eat. I chew each mouthful 30 times before swallowing. That makes my tummy happy and helps my running. And I eat my tangerine jam every day.' The jam is made by his daughter. Miyazaki admitted that he might have run even faster, had it not been for the fact that he had taken a short nap before the race: 'big mistake. I felt stiff.'

The record that Miyazaki broke was 30.86 seconds, set by a 100-year-old South African, 'Flying Phil' Rabinowitz, who had knocked six seconds off the previous best time in Cape Town in 2004. Born in Lithuania, he had moved to South Africa at the age of 21. Before setting the sprint record, he was already recognized as the world's oldest competitive walker, racing regularly over distances of up to thirteen miles. Infuriatingly, he had run an even better time (and a better time than Miyazaki) of 28.7 seconds the previous week, but the record did not stand because of a fault with the official clock. His longevity recipe was fresh orange juice before breakfast, fish and chicken, 'lots of veggies', and an apple after each meal, plus walking four miles a day to his daughter's factory, where he did the accounts. He died aged 104 in 2008.

As for the marathon, the first centenarian ever to have finished one is believed to be Fauja Singh, who ran the 2011 Toronto Waterfront race in 8 hours, 25 minutes and 16 seconds. That was more than six hours slower than the winner (and two and three-quarter hours slower than his own pre-centenarian best), and by the time Singh got there, the finishing line had been removed – but friends and family were waiting to greet him. Nicknamed the 'Turbaned Torpedo', he had not taken up running until he reached 89. He thought it would help him overcome his depression following the death of his wife and then of one of his sons in a horrible accident during a storm, when a fierce wind picked up a piece of corrugated iron and decapitated him as he worked with his father in their fields. All the centenarian's other children had already left India, so he went to live with his youngest son in London. 'From a tragedy has come a lot of success and happiness,' said Singh, explaining how running had allowed an illiterate farmer to travel the world, meet dignitaries and stay in five-star hotels. The Toronto run was his eighth marathon. He eats a light vegetarian diet of mainly curry dishes with tea, and tries to stay free of stress by avoiding negative people. Singh was not able to walk until he was five, and his legs were so spindly that he was nicknamed 'stick'. At fifteen he still could not cover a mile: 'Perhaps it was the Almighty's way of preserving them for later,' he remarked.

The following year, Singh gave up competitive running, just before his 102nd birthday, though he continued to walk and jog over ten-mile

Japanese sprinter Hidekichi Miyazaki, aged 106, celebrates after competing in the
men's 100m race at the Kyoto Masters Autumn Competition, 16 October 2016.

stretches. After his last race, he said, 'I am happy that I am retiring at
the top of the game but I am sad that the time has come for me to not
be part of it. And there will always be times in the future where I will
be thinking, "Well, I used to do that."' His age has not been universally
recognized because, although his passport states he was born in India
in 1911, the country did not keep birth records at that time, so he has
no birth certificate.

But it is not only male centenarians who have performed remarkable athletic feats. In 2015 a Japanese woman named Mieko Nagaoka

Centanarian marathon runner Fauja Singh at the
London Marathon in 2004, aged 93.

became the first 100-year-old to complete a 1,500-metre swim, covering
the distance in an hour and fifteen minutes, using backstroke. Like
Fauja Singh, Nagaoka had taken up her sport late – at 82, as therapy for
her knees. Soon she was going to competitions all over the world, winning 24 titles in all. After her record-breaking swim, she told reporters,
'I want to swim until I turn 105 if I can live that long.'

Another intrepid Japanese centenarian was Teiichi Igarashi, who in
1987 became the first 100-year-old to climb Mount Fuji. A lumberjack
and then a forest ranger until his retirement at 90, he had started a

Yukichi Chuganji.

programme of annual ascents of the 12,400-foot mountain after the death of his wife aged 80 in 1975. Eight years later, at 96, Igarashi had become the oldest man ever to make the climb. In 1987 it took him three days, including two overnight stops in mountain huts. Carrying a picture of his wife and accompanied by seven of his ten children and three of his 36 grandchildren, he wore heavy socks but no shoes, and stopped every three minutes by the path to rest. When he was not climbing Mount Fuji, the centenarian was said to lead a simple life, getting up at six o'clock every morning and going to bed at eight every night, having always taken a two-hour walk in the afternoon. His standard fare was a bowl of rice with raw eggs, soybean soup and vegetables. He sometimes ate fish, but never meat. More unusually, he had started smoking at the age of 60, but gave up when he reached 96.

In recent years, we have become used to exhortations from politicians to work until much later in life, and some centenarians seem to have taken the message to heart. Yukichi Chuganji, from the island of Kyushu in southern Japan, who was for a time the oldest man in the world, was said to have carried on working as a silkworm breeder until he was 110 years old. His prescription for long life was healthy eating and being an optimist, but his views on diet were not the same as other centenarians'. His daughter said, 'He hates vegetables but loves to eat meat and drink milk.'

In Britain, Pierre Jean 'Buster' Martin was mourned as the country's oldest worker when he died in 2011 shortly after clocking off as a van washer. His age was reported to be 104, and he was quite a character. Endowed with an imposing, bushy grey beard, he fought off a gang of three teenage muggers who attacked him as he left a pub, five months after his 100th birthday, prompting a leading politician to say that Buster was 'living proof of why people should not be written off once they pass retirement age'. At 101 he ran the London Marathon, despite the fact that he liked to consume 'a beer or two and twenty cigarettes daily'. Interviewed in a 2007 television documentary, *The Oldest People in the World*, he gave an assured, if gruff, performance. One of his contributions was: 'I don't know why they make such a fuss about a man of a certain age like me working. If you want to work and you want to carry on instead of getting to be a grumpy old git, there you are. If I couldn't keep going, I'd rather snuff it.' He also played drums on a top-30 record, without any previous experience, and did a stint as an 'agony uncle' for the men's magazine *FHM*. (Harry Patch was one of three other centenarians signed up to give advice.) Buster claimed he was born in September 1906, and that his mother smuggled him into the UK from France. He said that after she died, he was raised in an orphanage in Cornwall, then worked at Brixton Market in London before serving in the army in the Second World War, marrying and fathering seventeen children.

It is another wonderful story, almost as good as Shigechiyo Izumi's, but, as with the Japanese centenarian, there are problems. Buster had no birth certificate, and there were noticeable gaps in other documentation that would have underpinned his extraordinary tale. He said he had a passport confirming his age, but according to NHS records, he was seven years younger than he claimed, which would have meant he was actually 97 when he died.

No such doubts have been raised about Connie Brown, who worked in a Pembroke fish and chip shop until a week before her death, aged 102, in 2010. She and her husband had opened the shop 82 years before. When she was 98, she was awarded an MBE for her services to the community. According to her family she had never been in hospital before she was admitted on the day she died. Then there was Mary Moody, said to be the world's oldest company chairman, who continued to attend annual board meetings of her stationer's company in Stourbridge, West Midlands, until her death aged 104 in 1985. And at age 107, David Henderson was still giving the orders on his farm at Laurencekirk in Aberdeenshire, Scotland. He said he was 'very healthy' but he lived in a nursing home, where he spent a lot of time in bed because his legs gave him 'some trouble'. Still, every day Henderson would meet his nephew, the farm manager, to make decisions and sign cheques, and once a week he would be driven around the fields. His wife had died 30 years earlier, and in his 107th year, like John Evans, he was fitted with a pacemaker, though some of his family were against it. He said, 'I worked very hard when I was young, then when I came to 65 I never thought about retiring. Retire and you lose the will. So I just carry on planning ahead, keeping my mind working.' He credited eating porridge and prunes for his long life, as well as never going to bed on a full stomach. David Henderson was Britain's oldest man by the time he died just short of his 110th birthday in 1998.

The world's oldest working author is reckoned to have been Ida Pollock from Cornwall, who died aged 105 in 2013, just before the

Author Ida Pollock with her daughter Babs.

publication of her 125th book. She used ten different pseudonyms to write romantic novels, of which she sold over a million, with titles such as *Hotel Stardust* and *The Bay of Moonlight*. Born in south London, Pollock wrote her first book at the age of fourteen, and became a full-time writer in her twenties. Over one five-year period she produced 40 titles, and said she could finish a book in six weeks. Many of her romantic heroes were said to be based on her husband, Lt-Col. Hugh Pollock, who had previously been married to Enid Blyton. He died aged 82 in 1971. Ida's marriage to Hugh produced one daughter, who also writes romantic fiction and to whom in her later years Ida would

Manoel de Oliveira in conversation in 2008.

dictate her latest work at their remote country home near Looe. Her formula was straightforward:

> a grand, dramatic setting – the Swiss Alps were always a personal favourite of mine – and a chance meeting, on a train, a cruise, or perhaps the hero and heroine find themselves shipwrecked on a desert island. The men are normally rich, well-to-do – but never vulgar with their money. Young men lack the maturity to take control so an older man is essential to provide the reassurance the heroine needs. There's always a fair amount of turbulence before he sweeps in to save the day. A happy ending is an absolute must.

Ida's daughter believed it was her mother's love of writing that had kept her living so long.

According to Guinness World Records, the oldest author to have a debut book published was Bertha Wood, whose *Fresh Air and Fun: The Story of a Blackpool Holiday Camp* came out on her 100th birthday in 2005. It was about the camp – one of Britain's first – that she founded with her husband in 1935. Renowned as an astute businesswoman, Wood died in 2007 aged 101, but she had planned and paid for her own funeral back in 1983. In the folder she left detailing the arrangements was a complaint form with instructions on claiming money back if

Hetty Bower, aged 106.

anything went wrong. Bertha's cousin, incidentally, was the inventor of the jet engine, Sir Frank Whittle, who died aged 89.

The world's oldest active film-maker, and the only one believed to have had a career that ran from silent movies to modern digital media, was Portugal's Manoel de Oliveira, who died aged 106 in 2015. The son of the country's first manufacturer of electric lamps, he was born in Oporto in 1908. In his youth he had been a keen athlete, and he worked hard at keeping fit all his life. He started acting in the twenties, then appeared in Portugal's first talkie, and made his debut as a feature film director in 1942. Oliveira became much more prolific in his later years than he had been earlier in life, averaging a film a year in his nineties, and he was certainly no less innovative. *The Satin Slipper*, which he made in his late seventies, was a seven-hour version of a verse drama, while *The Cannibals* was a very blackly comic opera about a hero whose body is mainly made up of prosthetic limbs and whose remains get eaten by his father and brothers-in-law. During his 85-year career, Oliveira won many awards, including two Golden Lions at the Venice Film Festival and a Palme d'Or at Cannes. His final feature appeared in his 104th year.

Hetty Bower was dubbed Britain's oldest campaigner. A Labour Party member for 91 years until her death aged 108 in 2013, she cut her teeth as a Suffragette, and her final protests involved marching against the 2010–2015 coalition government's policies on the NHS and the welfare state, which meant demonstrating in sub-zero temperatures outside a north London hospital. In between were many others, particularly against wars. Though Bower had had a hip replacement at 96, she asked, 'Why wouldn't I march? I've got good legs.' Just two months before her death she moved an audience to tears at a fringe event at Labour's party conference when she talked of the poverty she had seen while growing up in Hackney, where there were 'mothers having to choose between buying a loaf of bread and calling a doctor to see their sick child,' saying, 'I never want those days back.' She worked in education, fashion and business, and she was involved in setting up one of the first trade unions for women. When asked why she devoted so much energy to protesting, she replied, 'Because every individual can make a difference.'

We saw how Jeanne Calment made growing old lucrative thanks to an astute deal on the sale of her apartment. Someone else who turned becoming a centenarian into a source of income was Alec Holden from Epsom in Surrey, who placed a bet when he was 90 that he would live to see his 100th birthday. He got odds of 250 to 1, which made him £25,000 on 24 April 2007. When asked the secret of his survival, he said he ate porridge for breakfast, did as little work as possible, played chess and kept breathing, adding, 'If I saw any hooded groups from the bookmaker standing in the street, I avoided them.' Holden was another of the centenarians drafted in as an agony uncle for *FHM*.

And so to perhaps the oddest of all the record-breaker categories: the oldest criminal. In 2015, at Embu in Kenya, about 75 miles northeast of Nairobi, 100-year-old Margaret Ngima was jailed for three months for failing to pay a fine imposed over a land dispute. The incarceration of the great-grandmother caused such outrage that her fine was paid by a Nairobi senator, who got her released a week into her sentence. The charge faced by 100-year-old Bernard Heginbotham from Lancashire was murder. At Preston Crown Court in 2004, the former butcher admitted killing his wife of 67 years by slitting her throat at her care home. The court was told she was in poor health, and that Mr Heginbotham had become distressed because she had been shunted between four different homes in three months, and after just five days in the latest one, she was due to be moved again. After hearing the news, he went to the home and killed her. Then he had gone home and tried to kill himself. The judge accepted that he was a devoted husband and his plea of guilty to manslaughter on the grounds of diminished responsibility, giving him a twelve-month community rehabilitation order. He said that while Heginbotham had done 'a terrible thing', his feelings of guilt and remorse had been 'truly overwhelming'. The judge added, 'It was carried out in an effort to end her suffering while you were under intolerable pressure. It was, in truth, an act of love.' Heginbotham died just over eighteen months later, aged 102.

But possibly the most bizarre centenarian story of all concerns the 107-year-old man from Arkansas who was killed in a shoot-out with police in 2013. They were called to a house in Pine Bluff where Monroe Isadore had been rooming for a month with an 80-year-old woman, Pauline Lewis, and her granddaughter. Ms Lewis said Isadore had got angry when she told him to find new lodgings, and that he had barricaded himself in his bedroom with a pistol, threatening to fire at anyone who came near. Police said that when they announced their arrival, Isadore shot through the door. A team of negotiators tried talking to the centenarian, but when they were plainly getting nowhere, a SWAT team released tear gas into his room through a window. Then, as they tried to go in, Isadore opened fire again. They shot back and killed him. His family of three sons, seven daughters, 27 grandchildren and 66 great-grandchildren complained that the police should have contacted them before taking such drastic action. His daughter said the shooting 'didn't sit right' with her, as her father had always supported local police, while neighbours maintained he was 'very religious'. Some said Isadore's hearing was poor and suggested he may not have understood what was going on. Lewis maintained the police had no choice: 'He was very angry. He got hostile. He was gonna kill somebody.'

So, are there any clues in the lives of these record-breakers to help us detect who will survive to 100? One common factor is that they all seem to have maintained their independence until very late in life. Jeanne Calment lived at home until she was 110, while Charlotte Hughes managed it until she was 114, and most of the others seem to have done so at least until their nineties. Even when Henry Allingham had to move into a care home at 109, he urged others to 'Hang on to your independence.' A striking number of centenarians also remained active – working, driving cars, riding cycles, climbing mountains, running races or shovelling snow off roofs – while others like Calment and Shigechiyo Izumi had been very fit earlier in life. It is also noticeable how many developed new interests late in life. Calment took up fencing when she was 85; the Japanese twins became national celebrities at

99; and for Albert Marshall 'life really took off' when he reached 100, as he, Henry Allingham and Harry Patch dedicated their final years to keeping alive the memory of the First World War. But is all this just another way of saying they enjoyed good health? Calment, we are told, was never ill, while the first time Connie Brown went into hospital was on the day she died.

Most of the record-breakers had been married, although Charlotte Hughes did not tie the knot until she was 63, and Christian Mortensen's experience of matrimony was short and unhappy. Karam and Kartari Chand were said to have been together for 90 years; Karl Dølven and Gudrun Haug managed 76 years, like Claude Choules and his wife; Herbert and Magda Brown clocked up 75 years together, while Edith Rennie thought 'a good husband' was one of the reasons for her longevity. But the mutual support enjoyed in a good marriage could perhaps be found from other partnerships, too. Both sets of twins – the Rennies in Scotland and Kin and Gin in Japan – plainly derived great strength from each other.

Only Jeanne Calment and Alice Herz-Sommer came from notably prosperous backgrounds, and Herz-Sommer lost everything when the Nazis took power, while Lucy Hannah, Albert Marshall, Octavio Orduno and Hetty Bower were well acquainted with poverty, and Henry Allingham, Albert Marshall and Claude Choules all lost a parent when they were young. The First World War veterans and the concentration camp survivors had plainly had to endure extraordinary ordeals, while a number of others, such as Shigechiyo Izumi, Christian Mortensen and John Evans had had hard working lives. Edith Rennie picked out hard work as part of the recipe for her long life.

Mortensen, Orduno and Phil Rabinowitz had all left their homes to find a better life, with Mortensen and Rabinowitz crossing oceans, while Herbert and Magda Brown and Alice Herz-Sommer were forced from theirs. But it is noticeable how many of the others, such as Calment, Izumi, Sarah Knauss, Charlotte Hughes, the Japanese twins Kin and Gin, and John Evans, always lived in the same area. And is it significant that a number came from farming stock, such as Izumi, Jiroemon Kimura, and the Rennie twins? And both Izumi and Kimura talked about the importance of communing with nature, while Edith Rennie extoled the virtues of a 'simple' life.

It is perhaps surprising how many of the record-breakers smoked – Calment, Izumi, Mortensen, Teiichi Igarashi – though none of them very much. As far as alcohol is concerned, a quite varied picture emerges. John Evans was a dedicated teetotaller, and Christian Mortensen and Alice Herz-Sommer also shunned the demon drink, but Jeanne Calment liked red wine, Charlotte Hughes and Henry Jamieson brandy, Fred Hale Sr the odd nip of whisky and Shigechiyo Izumi island hooch. In spite of Sir Cyril Clarke's strictures about the difficulty of coming to any conclusion about people's diets, we have some fairly good information about these record-breakers. Most of them adopted what we would regard as healthy eating, consuming porridge, vegetables, fruit, nuts, fish, chicken and bee pollen. Most seemed to avoid red meat, and Alice Herz-Sommer even steered clear of tea and coffee, but some dieticians might raise their eyebrows at Izumi's vegetables fried in pork fat, Evans's bread and lard, or Yukichi Chuganji's shunning of vegetables in favour of meat. Jeanne Calment and Magda Brown both loved chocolate, as did Sarah Knauss, who also tucked into potato crisps. But it was not just about *what* the record-breakers ate. For Jiroemon Kimura, quantity was crucial: he always made sure he was still hungry at the end of a meal. Hidekichi Miyazaki was careful to chew each mouthful of food 30 times. For Fred Hale, the secret was regularity – a cast-iron regime of three meals a day, always at the same time – while David Henderson never went to bed on a full stomach. It is also noticeable that a number of the record-breakers were very slight, incuding Izumi, Kin and Gin, and Miyazaki.

Many of the record breakers exhibited a very philosophical attitude to life, notably Jeanne Calment, Sarah Knauss and Henry Allingham, though Christian Mortensen could be feisty. A positive approach was also common: Kin and Gin were noted for their sunny personalities, and Fauja Singh said he tried to avoid negative people because they caused stress. Both Henry Allingham and Harry Patch emphasized the importance of a good sense of humour, though Patch retained a burning anger about the First World War. Yukichi Chuganji quoted optimism as one of the reasons for his long life, while Alice Herz-Sommer linked 'optimism and discipline', and made sure she practised the piano every day. Similarly, Jiroemon Kimura's nephew noted how disciplined his uncle was.

Did faith play any part in their longevity? John Evans was deeply religious, while Charlotte Hughes talked about following the Ten Commandments. Others stressed living by a moral code: Henry Allingham spoke of the importance of doing 'the right thing', while

Jeanne Calment said she had tried to act 'morally'. For Herz-Sommer, her 'religion' was Beethoven, and some of the other record-breakers had passionate interests, whether it was driving in the case of Henry Jamieson, or writing for Ida Pollock. There is also a suggestion that a crucial factor may be their genes. The twins are the most obvious example of a genetic link to longevity, but we also know that Sarah Knauss's daughter lived to be 101, and among the others with close relatives living to a ripe old age were Jeanne Calment, Jiroemon Kimura, Lucy Hannah and Harry Patch. So, what of famous people who have lived to be 100, the celebrity centenarians: do they share the same characteristics as the record-breakers?

FIVE

Celebrity Centenarians

The most famous centenarian from the UK is almost certainly Queen Elizabeth, the Queen Mother. Born Elizabeth Bowes-Lyon on 4 August 1900 (in the back of a horse-drawn ambulance, according to some accounts) she was the ninth of ten children of the Earl and Countess of Strathmore and Kinghorne. She spent her childhood in her parents' Hertfordshire stately home, St Paul's Walden Bury, and acquired a love of the countryside and of horses. She was educated at home by a governess, and her aristocratic parents were said to have been warm and loving 'for the times'. As one of the babies of the family, she was indulged, and became known as 'Merry Mischief' because of her charm and sense of fun, allied to considerable determination. Once, when she wanted money, she sent a telegram to her father, reading 'SOS. LSD. RSVP'. (LSD, in those pre-decimal currency days, stood for pounds (*l*), shillings (*s*) and pence (*d*).) These characteristics survived in Bowes-Lyon; decades later, the writer and historian Sir Roy Strong would say her 'beguiling mask of humorous charm' could not disguise the 'determined set of the lips'. The family's Scottish home was Glamis Castle, the medieval seat of Macbeth and also reputed to be the abode of a mysterious monster. When the First World War broke out, the castle was turned into a military hospital. The young Elizabeth did what she could to help, talking to the patients, mopping their brows, running errands and writing letters for them. One of her brothers was killed at the Battle of Loos, in which Arthur Marshall also fought.

After the war, Elizabeth became one of the most admired girls in polite society. Though not a conventional beauty, she was very attractive, with a fine complexion, gentle curves, sparkling blue eyes and a quiet assurance enlivened by that mischievous twinkle. The Bowes-Lyons were well connected. Occasionally members of the royal family would stay at Glamis, and Elizabeth was a bridesmaid at the wedding of King George v's daughter, Princess Mary. The rumour mill lined her up with a series of prospective husbands – a war hero, a royal equerry, even the Prince of Wales, later King Edward viii. In fact, it was not the Prince of Wales's heart that Elizabeth had won, but that of his younger brother, Albert, the Duke of York, known as Bertie. Painfully shy and hampered by a terrible stammer, he tried at first to propose through an intermediary. Worried that a royal marriage might lock her in a gilded cage, condemning her 'never again to be free to think, speak and act as I feel I really ought to', Elizabeth turned him down. Eventually, Albert plucked up the courage to put the question himself and, at the age of 22, Elizabeth said yes. Three months later, they were married.

For thirteen years, life was rather idyllic. The couple lived in a big house in Piccadilly, and had two daughters, Elizabeth and Margaret. They did undertake some royal duties, but they could spend much of the time together as a happy, well-heeled family. His wife gave Bertie more confidence and helped him overcome his stammer. Visitors said there was an easy informality about them not usually found in royal or aristocratic circles at the time. Elizabeth's charm made her popular, as she became the first modern royal to smile in public, and she even won over crusty old King George v, who had terrified his sons. But the couple's delightful home life came under attack from an unexpected quarter.

George v died in January 1936, and Bertie's elder brother succeeded him, as Edward viii. Within a year, his determination to marry the twice-divorced American Wallis Simpson led to his abdication, and in December 1936 the Duke of York suddenly found himself King George vi. It is said that he wept when he heard the news, and Elizabeth, who had already had a few run-ins with Simpson, was furious because of her apprehension about the strain that would now be heaped on her husband. Soon, though, her characteristic determination took over. It is said that it was thanks to Elizabeth that when Simpson married the former king, now the Duke of Windsor, she was not given the title Her Royal Highness – a slight the Duke never forgave. And after her husband's coronation, she wrote to the Archbishop of Canterbury that she and the king were 'leaning on each other', adding, 'I can hardly believe that we have been called to this tremendous task, and the curious thing is that we are not afraid. I feel that God has enabled us to face the situation calmly.'

The new queen's charm helped get the reign off to a promising start, with successful visits to France, the United States and Canada, where she pioneered the royal walkabout. Then came the Second World War. At first, the impeccably turned-out Elizabeth ran into some hostility when she visited working-class areas that had been bombed, but bombs also fell in the grounds of Buckingham Palace, and when it was suggested that she and the children should take refuge in Canada, she famously replied, 'The children won't go without me. I won't leave the King; and the King will never leave.' Instead, she learned to fire a revolver in case the Germans should invade, and although the royal family did not share all the privations of their subjects, visitors to Buckingham Palace noted how meagre the food seemed, and how little bath water there was. Soon the King and Queen had become so popular and such a symbol of national resistance that Hitler dubbed Elizabeth 'the most dangerous woman in Europe', while Churchill wrote, 'This war has drawn the throne and the people more closely together than ever before was recorded, and your Majesties are more beloved by all classes than any of the princes of the past.'

So 1945 saw perhaps the monarchy's finest hour of modern times, as the country celebrated victory against formidable odds after such a long, hard road. But the ordeal, and his smoking, had taken a terrible toll on George vi's health, and in February 1952 he died of lung cancer. Though resolutely dry-eyed at his funeral, his widow was broken-hearted; but while Queen Victoria had largely retired from public life after the death of her beloved Albert (to such an extent that a wag put up a 'For Sale' sign on Buckingham Palace), Elizabeth threw herself into a round of public engagements. Resplendent in her trademark crinolines of chiffon and lace, she became consistently the most popular member of the royal family. Prince Charles said she had the 'ability to enhance life for others through her own effervescent enthusiasm'.

Early on in her relationship with her husband, she had got into hot water with King George v by giving an interview to a newspaper. She learned her lesson, and for the next 80 years she remained resolutely reticent. Still, the odd glimpse of her private life did emerge. The Queen Mother was interested in spiritualism and alternative medicine. She

HM Queen Elizabeth, the Queen Mother.

was fond of rather rowdy house parties featuring games like Sardines, in which leading politicians, exhibiting varying degrees of enthusiasm, were invited to participate. She also had ways of getting away from it all, going fly fishing and staying at a castle bolt-hole in the far northeast of Scotland. She was famously extravagant, spending on clothes, jewellery, fine wines and racehorses – more than 450 winners came home in her colours. When it was revealed in 1998 that she had run up a £4 million overdraft, as ever in the face of royal revelations, publicly she did not bat an eyelid.

Elizabeth was decidedly not teetotal. The icing on her 100th birthday cake contained a splash of gin, and when at the party the Archbishop of Canterbury inadvertently reached for her wine glass, she raised a laugh by exclaiming, 'that's mine!' Her secret, she said, was 'I love life.' But her hedonism was allied to a powerful sense of duty – the idea that every privilege brings with it a responsibility. Well into her nineties she carried out official engagements, and served as patron or president of more than 300 organizations. She believed that if you found someone boring, it was your fault: you were not trying hard enough to draw them out.

The Queen Mother was not one of those centenarians who never had a day's illness. At the age of 66, she underwent surgery for colon cancer. At 93 she was rushed to hospital when a fishbone stuck in her throat, but that same year she fulfilled 90 engagements. During her nineties she also had two hip replacements, and a cataract was removed from her eye. In her last few years she used a golf buggy, which became known as the Queen Mum Mobile, to help her get around. At the age of 100 she had an emergency blood transfusion for anaemia. She was three months past her 101st birthday when she performed her final public engagement – the recommissioning of the aircraft carrier *Ark Royal* – and she insisted on walking the length of an aircraft hangar, and standing for much of the ceremony. The following February, while the Queen Mother was convalescing at Sandringham after a chest infection, she received news that her younger daughter, Princess Margaret, had died, aged 71. To the great concern of her loved ones, she insisted on attending the funeral at Windsor in a wheelchair, taking care that no photographs were taken of her. She died on 30 March 2002, aged 101.

At the time of her death, she was the longest-lived royal in British history, but within three years her record was beaten by her sister-in-law, Princess Alice, Duchess of Gloucester, who died two months

Princess Alice, Duchess of Gloucester.

before her 103rd birthday, in October 2004. Like the Queen Mother, Alice came from Scottish stock. Her father was the great landowner the 7th Duke of Buccleuch, who had served in the navy with George v. She was educated at home until she was twelve and was said to have been rather starved of affection as a girl. In her twenties she fell in love with Africa, and described herself as 'a kind of pre-beatnik'. During her travels there she caught cerebral malaria, which she was lucky to survive. At the age of 34 she married George v's third son, the Duke of Gloucester. After a series of miscarriages, she did not give birth to her first child, Prince William, until she was nearly 40. When she was 64, she was almost killed in a serious road accident. Then her husband suffered a series of strokes, which left him paralysed and unable to speak, and William died aged 30, when the light aircraft he was piloting crashed during an air race. Alice admitted, 'I was completely stunned and have never been quite the same since.' Two years later, the Duke died. A small, elegant figure, who was nervous and shy in public, Alice was the patron or president of about 100 organizations and had particularly strong links with the Armed Forces. She carried on public engagements until she was almost 100 years old, and also gained some happiness in her private life when her younger son made her a grandmother.

If the Queen Mother had an American equivalent, it might be Rose Fitzgerald Kennedy, so-called 'founding mother' of the Kennedy clan, but her life was touched by more tragedy than that of either of the British centenarian royals. Rose was the eldest of six children, born in July 1890 to a rising politician who would go on to become Boston's first Irish American mayor. At the time, her parents were living quite modestly, and Irish Catholics still faced discrimination in the city. She graduated with good marks from high school and was also voted the most beautiful girl in her class. In 1914 she married Joe Kennedy, whom she had first met when she was five years old and who was now on the way to making a fortune from his business empire. She would have nine children, but the marriage was not happy – first because of Joe's philandering, which Rose studiously ignored, and then because of his anger and disappointment when his dream of becoming president faded after he backed Hitler to win the Second World War.

Another source of heartache was the discovery that one of her daughters had severe learning difficulties, made worse by a botched lobotomy. A worse blow came in 1944, when her eldest son was killed in the war. Four years later her daughter Kathleen, from whom she had become estranged, died in an aeroplane crash. Triumph followed tragedy in 1960, when her son John F. Kennedy was elected president of the United States, but just a year later her husband suffered a debilitating stroke. Then, after less than three years in office, John fell to an

SECRETS OF THE CENTENARIANS

assassin's bullet; extraordinarily, his younger brother Robert suffered the same fate as he emerged as a leading candidate for the presidency five years later. The year after Bobby's death, Rose's husband finally died, after eight years during which he was fully conscious but unable to speak or move. Then, when Rose was 93, one of her grandsons lost his life through a drug overdose.

The founding mother bore it all – just as the Queen Mother had borne the death of her husband – with stoic fortitude. One of her grandsons said she had been 'a source of enormous strength through all the good, fun times that we had growing up, as well as through many of the sad times our family has faced'. On the inside, though, things may have been different, as Rose confided: 'it has been said that time heals all wounds. I don't agree. The wounds remain. Time – the mind protecting its sanity – covers them with some scar tissue and the pain lessens, but it is never gone.' She saw the cultivation of her family as the main aim of her life, regarding child-rearing 'not only as a work of love and a duty, but as a profession' as interesting as any in the world, and declared she would rather raise a great son or daughter than create a great book or work of art. In this important task she had the help of servants, and admitted she 'did little diaper changing', but she made sure she had breakfast with her children and got them off to school. She also read to them and took them out on educational trips, but she was strict, and spanked them if they offended one of her many rules. And even when the children were growing up, she spent a lot of time travelling alone, missing her father's funeral because she was away in Paris when he died, and could not get back in time. John F. Kennedy once told an aide that he could not remember ever hearing his mother say, 'I love you.'

Discipline was one of the pillars of Rose Kennedy's long life. Until she was well into her eighties she would swim in the ocean near her Cape Cod home, even on chilly days. She was slight – barely five feet (1.5 m) tall, and worked at staying slim. The other great pillar was her religious faith. At eighteen she had been sent, rather against her will, to spend time in a convent. She emerged a devout young woman, and for the rest of her life she would attend Mass every Sunday – though later in life, after she had had a series of strokes, the priest would come to her home. She also had her own private retreat for prayer and contemplation. Rose declared, 'I have come to the conclusion that the most important element in human life is faith,' while one her grandsons said,

Rose Kennedy.

'You got a very, very profound feeling that she was working with God on a daily basis!' But perhaps there was also a third pillar – her genes. Rose's father had lived to 87, and her mother to 98.

Even at the age of 100 Rose would go around the grounds of her house in her wheelchair, keeping up with the news on television and jotting down points for a speech, or sometimes joining guests in a singalong. She continued to support the Kennedy clan, which now included 28 grandchildren and 22 great-grandchildren, and the Kennedy Foundation, which helped people with mental disabilities. More than 370 friends and relatives came to celebrate Rose's 100th birthday, but when one of her grandsons asked if she was excited at reaching her century, she replied, 'No. I wish I was sixteen.' In January 1905, surrounded by members of her family, Rose Kennedy died of complications from pneumonia, aged 104.

Irving Berlin.

Whatever tribulations they faced, the Queen Mother, Princess Alice and Rose Kennedy all lived privileged lives, but some of the world's best-known centenarians came up the hard way. Irving Berlin, perhaps America's most famous songwriter, was born Israel Baline in a Siberian village in May 1888, one of eight children of a Jewish cantor. When he was five, their house was burned down in a pogrom, which persuaded Israel's father to take his family to New York, where they settled among the poor, overcrowded tenements of the Lower East Side. Three years later, the father died, and Israel had to drop out of school to get a job. On his first day as a newspaper seller, he fell into the river, and had just gone under for the third time when he was hauled out, still clutching the five cents he had made for the family budget.

He found his first steady job in the down-at-heel Bowery district, with its bars, brothels and pawn shops, working for a busker named Blind Sol, guiding him through saloons and looking after his money. Israel began contributing the odd singing performance himself, and soon he was striking out on his own, carrying beer and waiting tables. At fourteen he ran away from home, sleeping in dosshouses, and graduated to become a singing waiter at an establishment in Chinatown known as Nigger Mike's. After closing time, he would sit at the piano and pick out tunes. When the restaurant boss heard that a rival eatery had a singing waiter who wrote his own songs, he got the young man, now aged nineteen, to change his name to Irving Berlin and to start composing. The result was a ditty entitled 'Marie from Sunny Italy' – not generally regarded as one of Berlin's best – but it earned him 37 cents, and the rest is musical history.

The songwriter's first big hit came with 'Alexander's Ragtime Band', released when Berlin was 23. It is said that four different versions of the song occupied the top four places in the record charts. There followed 'White Christmas', 'Let's Face the Music and Dance', 'There's No Business Like Show Business', 'Always', 'How Deep is the Ocean', 'Blue Skies', 'Cheek to Cheek', 'God Bless America' and more than 1,000 others, including the scores for nineteen Broadway shows – all despite the fact that Berlin never learned to read music. Sammy Cahn, who wrote the lyrics to many hit songs, including 'Come Fly With Me', declared, 'If a man, in a lifetime of 50 years, can point to six songs that are immediately identifiable, he has achieved something. Irving Berlin can sing 60 that are immediately identifiable', while Jerome Kern, composer of classics such as 'Ol' Man River', would say of Berlin, 'He *is* American music.' 'White Christmas' alone sold more than 50 million records. But the Jewish immigrant never forgot his humble beginnings and the part they had played in making him who he was, observing, 'Everybody ought to have a Lower East Side in their life.'

In 1912 Berlin married Dorothy Goetz. They went to Havana for their honeymoon, and six months later she died of typhoid fever, contracted while they were there. Berlin's grief inspired a song called 'When I Lost You', which sold a million copies. It would be thirteen years before he fell in love again. In 1925 he met the young heiress Ellin Mackay, daughter of the telegraph company magnate Clarence

SECRETS OF THE CENTENARIANS

Hungerford Mackay, an Irish Catholic. He was dead set against the romance, and whisked his daughter off to Europe. Berlin wooed Ellin across the airwaves with his songs 'Always' and 'Remember', and when the Mackays returned to New York, the couple married. It was a scandal and a sensation. Mackay threatened to disown his daughter, and for years he refused to speak to Berlin. Then came the Great Crash of 1929. The magnate lost all his money. Berlin, an astute businessman who had set up his own publishing house, bailed him out with a gift of a million dollars, even though he had lost ten million in the Wall Street wipe-out himself. Mackay still hated him.

Ellin and Irving, though, were a devoted couple for more than 60 years, producing three daughters as well as a son who died in infancy. They remained inseparable until Ellin's death in 1988 at the age of 85, just two months after Berlin's 100th birthday. A small, slender man who kept his good looks after most of his contemporaries had died, the composer virtually gave up songwriting at the age of 74, when his last show got a disappointing reception. He continued to manage his business interests from his opulent home on the Upper East Side, just a few miles from where he had started in New York in desperate poverty, but as he got older he became more and more reclusive, and did not attend the concert to celebrate his 100th birthday. He died aged 101 in September 1989.

'If I'd taken my doctor's advice and quit smoking when he advised me to, I wouldn't have lived to go to his funeral.' So said another American show business centenarian, George Burns. Like Irving Berlin, he came up the hard way. He too was Jewish and grew up on the Lower East Side, and, also like Berlin, lost his father when he was young – aged just seven. Born in 1896, the ninth of twelve children, George had to start doing odd jobs to help support the family – selling newspapers, shining shoes, running errands. While he was working in the basement of a shop, he started singing with the other boys. People began throwing down coins, so the youngsters took up performing as a quartet in saloons, on street corners and on the Staten Island Ferry. Never stuck for a quip, Burns said they particularly liked this venue, because the only way people could avoid their act was by jumping overboard.

At thirteen, he and a friend opened a school of dance: 'We got most of our clients right off the immigration boats at Ellis Island. We told them one of the first requirements of becoming a United States citizen was a $5 course of dancing lessons.' When asked if this was not dishonest, Burns replied, 'Have you ever been hungry?' At fourteen, he started smoking cigars and carried on doing so for the rest of his life, getting up to about fifteen a day, though he said he'd never smoked a cigarette. Soon he was appearing in vaudeville shows as a dancer or a trick roller-skater, or performing with a seal. He said his acts were so bad he had to keep changing his name. At 26, he met a young Irish Catholic vaudeville performer, Gracie Allen. Burns said he never knew how old she was, because her birth certificate had been lost in the great San Francisco earthquake of 1906. They started to work together, with Gracie acting as George's straight person, but as it became clear how funny she was, he started giving her the best lines. She developed her character as the 'dizziest dame in the world'. When George asked why she put straw in the pan when she was boiling eggs, for example, Gracie would say it was to make the eggs feel at home. By the time the couple married in 1926, they were already big vaudeville stars. They went on to excel on radio and television, and in films. Their success made them both rich. Diminutive, gravel-voiced and always drawing on a big cigar, George became one of the best-known figures in show business.

George Burns's marriage to Gracie turned out to be as devoted as Irving Berlin's to Ellin, successfully crossing the religious divide. Burns said his religion was to 'always treat other people nicely', and he was unfailingly generous about his wife's talents, declaring, 'Gracie was the whole act.' They adopted two children, but Gracie was plagued by heart disease, and in 1959 she retired. Five years later, she was dead. George was heartbroken: 'My life was Gracie,' he said. He found solace through work, though he would still visit her grave regularly, to bring flowers and talk to her: 'I tell her what I'm doing.' He continued to perform on television and in nightclubs. In 1976, at the age of 80 and after undergoing major heart surgery, Burns became the oldest actor ever to win an Oscar for his portrayal of an ageing comedian in the film *The Sunshine Boys*. He went on to appear in a number of other pictures playing, among other parts, both God and the Devil. He said that at first he was nervous about portraying God, because he did not know what kind of make-up he used, but in the end he agreed: 'Why shouldn't I play God? Anything I do at my age is a miracle.' Often to be seen with a beautiful younger woman on his arm, he would say, 'I'd go out with women my age, but there aren't any.'

Burns was generous, giving millions away to charity. When he was 98, he said, 'The happiest people I know are the ones that are still

George Burns.

working. The saddest are the ones who are retired.' On another occasion he said, 'When I'm out in front of an audience, all that love and vitality sweeps over me and I forget my age.' He got himself booked to play the London Palladium to celebrate his 100th birthday; his opening line was going to be: 'It's nice to be here. When you're 100 years old, it's nice to be anywhere.' But eighteen months before the event, he fell in his bath, and never fully recovered. Instead of treading the boards, he spent the landmark birthday quietly with his family. Six weeks later, he died. He was buried next to Gracie, in his best suit with three cigars in the breast pocket. The epitaph on their tomb reads: 'Gracie Allen. George Burns. Together Again.' George said he always wanted Gracie to have top billing.

The third great American show business personality to see his 100th birthday was Bob Hope. Like Berlin, he had been born far away from the United States – in Eltham, south London, in 1903, the fifth of seven sons. His father was a hard-up stonemason and his mother a light opera singer who had had to work as a cleaner. The family emigrated to Cleveland, Ohio, when Bob was four. Things did not get much easier in the New World and, like Berlin and Burns, the young Hope was soon having to do odd jobs to help eke out the family budget. At the age of eleven he won a talent contest with an impersonation of Charlie Chaplin, before dropping out of school at sixteen and trying his hand at a variety of trades, such as newspaper reporting and boxing. At eighteen he went into vaudeville, appearing at one time as a dance partner for a pair of Siamese twins. Vaudeville was a ferociously competitive business, with ticket prices as low as ten cents, and Hope would often do four shows a day followed by a gig in a nightclub. When he was 24 he was discovered by the famous film comedian Fatty Arbuckle, and over the next five years he became a star. Like Burns, Hope graduated from vaudeville to radio, then musical comedy and films, making the highly successful *Road* series with his golf partner, Bing Crosby. Hope produced and helped finance the pictures, as well as starring in them, enabling him to amass a fortune that was once estimated at $500 million, and to become the biggest private landowner in California.

A good deal of mystery surrounds Hope's personal life. It appears that when he was 29 he married his vaudeville partner, Grace Troxell, and then divorced her the following year (though he was said to have quietly sent her money until her death 40 years later). The same year he split from Grace, Hope embarked on 69 years of happy marriage to the singer Dolores Reade, living in the same house for 60 of those years. But since Hope's death, claims have emerged that he was an incorrigible philanderer who had affairs with a string of women, including Jane Russell and Doris Day. It was also claimed that Hope and Dolores may never really have been married, because of the absence of wedding photos or a marriage licence. A devout Catholic, Dolores once said of Hope, 'He's a rover by nature and there were times when I wanted to pack it in.' They performed together for a time, with Dolores remarking that Hope was a perfectionist who did not suffer fools gladly. She then gave up her career to look after the four children they adopted when they found they could not have any themselves.

During the Second World War, Hope embarked on a series of tours to entertain U.S. forces overseas; these would go on for more than half a century. Sometimes the shows were alarmingly close to the front line.

Even though he hated flying, the comedian would go all over the world, covering two million miles – to Berlin during the Airlift, to Korea and Vietnam, and to Beirut and Saudi Arabia during the first Gulf War. In 1943 John Steinbeck, then a war reporter, wrote:

> When the time for recognition of service to the nation in wartime comes to be considered, Bob Hope should be high on the list . . . He works month after month at a pace that would kill most people. Moving about the country in camps, airfields, billets, supply depots, and hospitals, you hear one thing consistently. Bob Hope is coming, or Bob Hope has been there.

Hope himself said laughter at the front line was 'a very precious thing', adding, 'There's a lump the size of Grant's Tomb in your throat when they come up to you and shake your hand and mumble "Thanks." Imagine those guys thanking me! Look what they're doing for me. And for you.' When their children grew up, Dolores joined him on some of the tours, though he once sent her home from Vietnam when her singing moved the troops to tears. She finally produced her first album when she was in her eighties.

In recognition of his services, in 1997 Hope became the only man in u.s. history to be named an honorary veteran of the Armed Forces by Congress. He received more than 50 honorary degrees and the freedom of more than 500 towns and cities, becoming a friend of presidents, and once even playing golf with presidents Bill Clinton, Gerald Ford and George Bush Senior. Hope wisecracked, 'I have performed for twelve Presidents and entertained six.' For years, there was no bigger name in show business, and some u.s. senators even wanted him to run for president. Hope responded, 'The money's not right, and anyway I don't want to move into a smaller house.' Despite having a reputation for meanness, he gave millions of dollars of his own money away, and built a hospital as well as the biggest youth centre in the United States. He was still playing golf into his nineties, and is said to have joked to his family, 'I'm so old, they've cancelled my blood type.' During the last decade of his life, he became a Catholic. His health faded, and he was too frail to attend celebrations for his 100th birthday, dying of pneumonia two months later. Dolores survived him by eight years, living to 102.

Bob Hope.

Leni Riefenstahl was also in show business. She was Adolf Hitler's favourite film-maker. Born to comfortably-off parents in Berlin in 1902, she grew up loving the outdoor life, but she soon exhibited a talent for painting and dancing, which was encouraged by her mother, who enrolled Riefenstahl in Berlin's most prestigious ballet company. Her father, who owned a heating and ventilation company, was outraged at the idea of his daughter becoming a dancer. But that is exactly what she did, and she was soon performing professionally, designing her own costumes and doing her own choreography. Her blossoming career, though, began to be blighted by a series of injuries. Then, when she was 22 and on the way to an appointment with her doctor, Riefenstahl saw a movie called *The Mountain of Destiny* (1924), directed by Arnold Fanck, an example of the 'mountain film' genre – in which Fanck excelled – with its stories of humans pitted against dreadful dangers in high places.

Through a mutual friend, Riefenstahl managed to engineer a meeting with the director. Fanck was enchanted by the glamorous young dancer, and cast her in his next seven films, showing her fearlessly climbing rock faces barefoot, crossing perilous crevasses or almost being swept away by avalanches. Though slight of stature, Riefenstahl stood up to the very tough conditions in which much of the shooting was done. Women directors at that time were rare, but at the age of 30 Riefenstahl directed and co-wrote *The Blue Light*, in which she also appears as a peasant girl protecting a mountain grotto. It was around this time she first saw Hitler speak. She admitted that he made such a strong impression on her that she 'felt paralysed', and wrote to him asking if they could meet. Hitler was said to have loved *The Blue Light*, seeing Riefenstahl as the epitome of the perfect Aryan woman. When they met, he told her, 'Once we come to power, you must make my films.' Riefenstahl also recorded that the future Führer was sexually attracted to her, though she always emphatically denied that he had been her lover. Plenty of men were, but she was married only briefly, to an army officer for a couple of years in the 1940s.

When Hitler became Chancellor, he did indeed commission Riefenstahl, to film the Nuremberg Rally of 1933. Deploying a battery of innovative ideas – moving cameras (including one that could be raised up a flagpole behind the speaker's podium), telephoto lenses, distorted perspectives, aerial photography and alternating stark close-ups with wide panoramas – she created *Triumph of the Will*. Was it a landmark in cinematic art, or a shameful piece of Nazi propaganda – or both? David Hinton, author of *The Films of Leni Riefenstahl*, said, 'The film was out and out propaganda, and yet it's impossible not to be stirred by the imagery.' Riefenstahl herself claimed she was never a Nazi, and that she was simply trying to create a work of art. In 1936, Hitler turned the Berlin Olympic Games into Nazi propaganda, and once more Riefenstahl was commissioned to record it. Again she pulled out all the stops, hiring 170 cameramen and technicians. Cameras were placed underwater as divers plunged into the pool, or in sandpits as long jumpers and pole vaulters landed. They raced along with sprinters, and soared on balloons. Dramatic close-ups from the longest lenses then available captured

Leni Riefenstahl and Adolf Hitler in Nuremberg, 1934.

the concentration on an athlete's face or the exhaustion of a marathon runner completing his last painful steps. Riefenstahl ended up with 250 miles of film, which it took her two years to edit, selecting every shot herself, frame by frame. Her *Olympia* won the Grand Prize at Venice's International Film Festival in 1938. The American film critic Pauline Kael would describe it and *Triumph of the Will* as 'the two greatest films ever directed by a woman', while *TIME* magazine's Richard Corliss said that all modern-day televised sport was indebted to the techniques Riefenstahl pioneered. In response to criticism, Riefenstahl pointed out how she highlighted the four gold medals won by the black athlete Jesse Owens that so infuriated Hitler. But the film opened on the Führer's birthday at a premiere bedecked with swastikas, and Hitler was delighted with it, presenting the director with a bouquet.

When Germany invaded Poland in 1939, Riefenstahl went to the front as a war correspondent but soon left, in disgust at Nazi brutalities, she claimed. The following year, however, she sent congratulations to Hitler when he occupied Paris. She saw him on a number of occasions during the war, the last in March 1944, when she wrote that, although he had aged noticeably, 'he still cast the same magical spell.' That same year, she made a feature film, *Lowlands*, which used gypsies from a con-centration camp as extras. After Germany's defeat in 1945, Riefenstahl was arrested by the Americans. Over the next few years, she was held and interrogated in a variety of camps and prisons, escaping a number of times. In 1949 she was released, but found it impossible to resume her career as a film-maker because of her association with Nazism. She reckoned she made about fifteen attempts. During one of them, she was looking for possible locations in Africa when she was injured in a serious motor accident that left her with broken ribs, a collapsed lung and severe head injuries.

Barred from making films, as she got into her sixties Riefenstahl took up photography, winning acclaim for her pictures of the Nuba people of Sudan. At the age of 71 she began scuba diving, pretending she was twenty years younger so she could get a licence. This led to the publication of more acclaimed photographs and eventually her first movie in half a century, released on her 100th birthday. She carried on diving into her nineties, but when she was 97 she was seriously injured in a helicopter crash in the Sudan, suffering two broken ribs. With her, and also injured, was her constant companion and assistant for nearly 40 years, Horst Kettner, who was 42 years younger than her. He was still by her side when she died in 2003 aged 101. Controversy over Riefenstahl's past dogged her to the end. She never denied that she had believed Hitler could save Germany, nor that it took her too long to withdraw her admi-ration of him, but she continued to maintain that she had never been a Nazi and that 'no anti-Semitic word' had ever passed her lips. Critics, though, pointed out that the name of her co-writer on *The Blue Light*, who was Jewish, had been removed from the film's credits. And even in her last months, she was being taken to court over allegations that she had failed to protect the gypsies she had used as extras in *Lowlands*, and that some had later been murdered in the concentration camps.

Albert Hofmann, probably the most famous Swiss centenarian, lived a pretty quiet life – but he did discover LSD. He was born in 1906, the son of a factory worker, and at university studied the gastro-intestinal juices of the vineyard snail. He then went to work for a pharmaceutical company in Basel, where his job was to examine the medicinal properties of plants. His discoveries included treatments to improve poor circulation and stabilize blood pressure. In 1938, while investigating ergot, a fungus that forms on rye, Hofmann synthesized lysergic acid diethylamide – LSD – but when it was tested on animals, it seemed to have no significant effects, and he lost interest in it. Five years later, he decided to take another look at the compound. As he got into the final stages of synthesizing it, he experienced 'a remarkable restlessness, combined with a slight dizziness'. When Hofmann got home, he lay down and sank into 'a not unpleasant intoxicated-like condition, characterized by an extremely stimulated imagination. In a dreamlike state, with eyes closed, I perceived an uninterrupted stream of fantastic pictures, extraordinary shapes with intense, kaleidoscopic play of colours.' After two hours, the sensations faded away. Hofmann had just experienced the world's first LSD trip. It had transported him back to a mystical experience he had had as a child on a forest path, when he had glimpsed 'a miraculous, powerful, unfathomable reality'.

The chemist concluded that he must have inadvertently ingested some LSD, and a couple of days later decided to put his theory to the test by swallowing a tiny amount. After 40 minutes, he experienced 'dizziness, feeling of anxiety, visual distortions, symptoms of paralysis, desire to laugh'. Carrying on with work as normal was out of the question, so Hofmann asked his laboratory assistant to take him home. On the way, his visions began to take more threatening forms. Everything was 'distorted as if seen in a curved mirror', and he had the illusion of being unable to move, even though he and his assistant were travelling 'very rapidly'. When Hofmann reached his home, a kindly neighbour bringing round some milk appeared instead to be a 'malevolent' witch wearing 'a lurid mask'. Hofmann lay on the sofa, writhing and screaming, thinking he was going to die. Then, five hours after he took the drug, uplifting images emerged again, 'opening and then closing themselves in circles and spirals, exploding in coloured fountains'. An hour later, the effects had passed. Doctors found nothing physically wrong with him, noting only that the pupils of his eyes were extremely dilated.

After that occasion, Hofmann took LSD dozens of times. The pharmaceutical company sent out samples of it to psychiatric researchers, and over the next twenty or so years more than 2,000 papers were published on the drug's potential use in treating various mental illnesses and drug and alcohol addiction. In mid-1960s America, the counter-culture adopted it as a recreational drug. It was taken in high doses and impure forms, from sugar cubes and blotting paper, and was blamed for incidents in which people jumped off tall buildings in the belief they could fly, and for other accidents and murders. A moral panic ensued, and governments around the world began to ban the drug, while Hofmann's company stopped producing it. The scientist was disappointed. He agreed that LSD could be dangerous, but he believed that if used properly, it was 'medicine for the soul'. In his autobiography, he described the drug as his 'problem child', arguing that its use could combat the widespread psychological problems caused by our alienation from nature through materialism, urbanization and industrialization, and our lack of satisfaction 'in a mechanised, lifeless working world'. However, he also suggested that people could achieve the same result by getting out and enjoying nature: 'Go to the meadow, go to the garden, go to the woods. Open your eyes!'

Hofmann went on working for the same company, being promoted to director of research for the Department of Natural Products, and working on hallucinogenic chemicals found in so-called magic mushrooms and the morning glory flower. He retired in 1971, after which he served as a member of the Nobel Prize Committee. For the final 38 years of his life, he lived with his wife in a house they had built on an Alpine hilltop. She died in December 2007, when he was 101; three months later he was due to speak at the World Psychedelic Forum, but had to pull out because of poor health. A month later, Albert Hofmann died, aged 102.

One man who went on making speeches well past his century was Lord 'Manny' Shinwell, the oldest person ever to address the British Parliament. On his 100th birthday, in 1985, colleagues from all parties in the House of Lords paid tribute to him. In return, Lord Shinwell praised the 'dignity' of the House, but acknowledged he had often fallen short of its high standards: 'Many times my behaviour has been shocking.' Shinwell was born in east London in 1884, the eldest of thirteen children, to a Jewish tailor from Poland. When Manny was still a child, the family moved to Glasgow, and at eleven he left school to take up an apprenticeship in the clothing industry, while in his spare time he tried to educate himself in the public library. He joined his first trade union at seventeen, and became a noted left-wing fire-brand, playing an important role in a national docks strike in 1911 and spending five months in jail in 1919 after being convicted of inciting strikers to riot.

In 1922 Shinwell was elected to Parliament, and became a minister in Britain's first Labour government, but he fell out with its prime minister, Ramsay MacDonald, when he formed an emergency coalition with the Conservatives in 1931. In the general election four years later, Shinwell stood against his former boss in his County Durham constituency, and defeated him. Then, in 1938 during a Commons debate, he punched a Tory MP. The centenarian saw these early trials and tribulations as one of the reasons for his longevity: 'I think I had rather a struggle in my life. If you get it easy, you soften very rapidly.' He had had it hard, 'living amid the squalor of the East End of London, and then going to Glasgow where you had more squalor, unemployment, and then getting into trouble politically.'

When Labour came to power in 1945, Shinwell was appointed to the Cabinet as Minister of Fuel and Power, and piloted through the nationalization of the coal mines, but he was heavily criticized over a fuel crisis during the exceptionally severe winter of 1946–7. After a spell outside the Cabinet, he returned as a pugnacious – some said jingoistic – Minister of Defence during wars in Korea and Malaysia, and was keen to send British troops to Iran when its government nationalized the oil refineries, but his colleagues stopped him. After Labour's election defeat in 1951, Shinwell's political star declined, though in 1964 Harold Wilson appointed him chairman of the Parliamentary Labour Party, and six years later he became a life peer. In the speech on his 100th birthday, Shinwell told the House of Lords, 'As we grow older, we lose the need for aggression, for attack. We want to listen more and learn more, and play our part in a civilised society.' But some would question whether the centenarian ever mellowed much. In 1982, the former agitator resigned the Labour whip in protest at left-wing militancy, and he once told Labour leader Neil Kinnock in front of television cameras, 'take that grin off your face . . . You can grin like a Cheshire cat – but it's not going to get you anywhere.'

In his personal life, Shinwell had his fair share of sadness. He was married three times, and widowed three times. His third wife died

Lord 'Manny' Shinwell.

when he was 92. Interviewing him when he was 101, I asked him if he was lonely. 'In what particular sense?' he replied. 'Do I need a woman? I don't know whether I ought to say this, but I have really no sex desire at all, but that's a bad thing. Perhaps I ought not to have said that. It rather shows a sense of decay.' I also asked him for his thoughts on death. 'Sometimes at two o'clock in the morning I feel terrible,' he said, '"Oh My God, it's come now at last," I say. I really say that, if I go to sleep now I won't wake up. Then I shake myself up. No, I won't have it . . . I'm not afraid of it – that's the one thing I can say. I don't know what it would be like. I would like to know. I would like to see what's on the other side of the hill.' Lord Shinwell finally did discover what was on the other side of the hill, on 8 May 1986, when he died aged 101, just three weeks after his final speech in the House of Lords, on the importance of parliamentary question time.

One of the most famous Japanese centenarians, the novelist Fumio Niwa, also had a rebellious streak, and at the age of 43 wrote a novel attacking his county's veneration for old people. Entitled *The Hateful Age* (1947), it tells the story of a married couple saddled with their 86-year-old grandmother. The wife thinks she is 'like some sort of disease visited permanently upon their family', while the husband spits out that 'in that little body of hers the spite, hypocrisy and dishonesty of 86 years have coagulated into a solid core of wickedness.' The couple manage to unload the old lady onto other relatives, who live in a cramped house on a remote hilltop. Niwa was born in Yokkaichi, about 180 miles west of Tokyo, in 1904. His father was a Buddhist priest who expected his son to follow the same calling. After taking a degree in literature, the young man tried it for two years, but found the life too oppressive and left for Tokyo. Although he was allergic to alcohol, he soon became a familiar figure in the capital's bars. His mother obviously found temple life a bit stifling too, because she ran off with an actor when Niwa was eight years old. The young writer had film-star looks, and clocked up a series of conquests; the first stories he wrote were explicit erotic fantasies that fell foul of the authorities. At the age of 29 he published his first novel, based on one of his love affairs.

During the Second World War, Niwa was wounded while accompanying the Japanese navy as a correspondent, and wrote a highly praised documentary novel, *Naval Engagement* (1942). Then came *The Hateful Age*, which established his reputation. He was prolific, turning out more than 80 novels as well as many essays and short stories, and winning a number of literary prizes. In his fifties he turned again to Buddhism, writing novels about the religion, including *The Buddha Tree* – probably his best-known work in the West – as well as biographies of saints and priests. As head of the Japan Professional Writers' Guild, he worked hard to improve life for his fellow authors, organizing a health insurance scheme and buying land for a graveyard, as well as urging them to improve their health by joining him on the golf course. In his eighties he started to suffer from Alzheimer's disease. When his wife took him to task about his past love affairs, he tried to strangle her, and she took refuge in a care home. Five months after his 100th birthday, Niwa died of pneumonia.

Perhaps the most famous artist to reach 100 was the self-taught American primitive painter Grandma Moses, whose life might be an illustration of the saying 'it's never too late'. She was born Anna Mary Robertson in a small community in upstate New York in 1860, just before the Civil War. Her father was a farmer. She received little education, and at the age of twelve she was sent to be a domestic help, doing chores on a neighbouring farm. She would work there for fifteen years, until she married Thomas Moses, who also worked on the farm. Her husband was offered a better job in North Carolina, but on the way there the couple saw a farm in Virginia, and took it on as tenants. Anna loved the Shenandoah Valley, though life was hard. They had ten children, five of whom died in infancy.

Eventually, the couple made enough money to purchase their own farm, but Anna's husband did not share her affection for Virginia, and after eighteen years in the Old Dominion State, they went back north, buying a farm not far from where Anna was born. They called it Mount Nebo, after the place in the Bible where God shows Moses the Promised Land. It was there, when Anna was 67, that Thomas died of a heart attack. Five years later, Anna went to Bennington, Vermont, to look after her daughter – also called Anna – who was suffering from tuberculosis. Anna showed her mother a picture embroidered in yarn, and challenged her to copy it. This motivated the older Anna to start creating pictures in worsted wool for friends. When she reached 76, her arthritis made it too painful to hold a needle, and her sister suggested she should try painting instead.

Anna sent some or her efforts to a country fair, where, she later noted, she won prizes for her jams and bottled fruits, but none for her pictures. After the fair they sat, carrying price tags of $3 to $5, gathering dust in a local drugstore window. Then one day they were spotted by an engineer and amateur art collector, Louis Caldor. He was entranced by the brightly coloured, cheerful, naive portrayals of country life, which ignored normal rules of perspective, and snapped up the lot, then drove to the painter's home, which was about 5 miles away, and bought another ten pictures from her. Caldor told Anna she was going to be famous, and sent her her first set of professional paints and canvasses. He then embarked on the thankless task of trying to interest art dealers in the works. Even those who liked them were put off when they found out the artist was in her late seventies. But in 1939, Caldor managed to get three of Anna's pictures into a private exhibition at New York's Museum of Modern Art. Then, just after she turned 80, she had a one-woman show in the city, entitled 'What a Farmwife Painted', put on by an art dealer with a particular interest in self-taught painters – whose work was sometimes regarded as more original and authentic than that of trained artists.

Soon after, 'Grandma Moses' was born, as a journalist doing a story about Anna discovered her local nickname, and the painter got a crucial breakthrough when a New York department store organized a special Thanksgiving exhibition of her pictures. She was invited up to the Big Apple, and in her little black hat and lace-collared dress, she charmed the press corps. Soon, her paintings were being shown all around the United States and in Europe, as well as appearing on Christmas cards. The painter, who had never heard of artists such as Pieter Breugel or Henri Rousseau until she heard herself being compared to them, was awarded honorary degrees by august academic institutions. When she was 89, she went for tea with President Harry S. Truman, who presented her with a special award and played the piano for her. Her 100th birthday was declared Grandma Moses Day by New York's governor.

Drawing on her memories of farm life, Moses would begin the creative process by sitting quietly: 'Then I'll get an inspiration and start painting; then I'll forget everything, everything except how things used to be and how to paint it so people will know how we used to live.' She would work for five or six hours, sitting on a battered old swivel chair, laying her painting flat on a table rather than on an easel. She worked from the top down: 'First the sky, then the mountains, then the hills, then the trees, then the houses, then the cattle and then the people.' Her tiny figures cast no shadows. She was prolific, turning out more

Grandma Moses.

than 1,000 pictures – 25 of them after she had passed 100 – her work-room cluttered with domestic appliances, such as a washing machine and a dryer, that had spilled over from the kitchen. For relaxation in the evenings, she would watch westerns on television, because she liked to see the horses.

Noted for her mischievous grey eyes and quick wit, Grandma Moses died three months after her 101st birthday. Her doctor said that while the official cause of death was hardening of the arteries, it would be truer to say, 'she just wore out.' She had survived all her children, but she left nine grandchildren and more than 30 great-grandchildren. President Kennedy said, 'The death of Grandma Moses removed a beloved figure from American life. The directness and vividness of her paintings restored a primitive freshness to our perception of the

American scene. Both her work and her life helped our nation renew its pioneer heritage.' Moses's own take was that her life was 'like a good day's work, it was done and I feel satisfied with it. I was happy and contented, I knew nothing better and made the best out of what life offered.' Her stock continued to rise after her death; in 2006, for the first time, one of her paintings sold for more than $1 million.

While Bob Hope was entertaining American troops fighting the North Vietnamese, the enemy was being led by a commander who would also reach his century. General Vo Nguyen Giap had not been trained as a soldier. He was a lawyer. Then he taught history, and once claimed that his only military instruction had come from an encyclopedia entry about hand grenades. He had grown up on the land, though his father was an intellectual as well as a farmer, and Giap went to the same French lycée that Ho Chi Minh had attended twenty years earlier. At fourteen, Giap joined a secret group dedicated to overthrowing the French colonial regime. Later, he would throw in his lot with the Communist Party, and when he was 27, as the Japanese prepared to invade Vietnam, he fled to China. So did Ho, and there Giap fell under his spell, calling him 'uncle', while Ho thought the young revolutionary was as 'beautiful as a girl'. In 1944, under Ho's leadership, Giap founded the Armed Propaganda Brigade for the Liberation of Vietnam with 31 men, three women, and a collection of antique firearms. By the end of the war, the organization had grown enough to hold power briefly after the Japanese left, but the French were in no mood to concede independence, and as guerrillas the group made little progress, until Mao Zedong's Communists took power in China in 1949 and began to channel weapons and supplies to them. Even so, Giap's first confrontation with the French in 1950 was a disaster, and he lost 20,000 men. By that time, his wife had been tortured and had died in a French prison. His father also died in French custody.

After another four years of fighting, Giap pulled off a major coup. The French had built what they considered an impregnable position at Dien Bien Phu, protected by heavily forested hills which they believed were impassable. But Giap followed the maxim of his hero Napoleon: 'If a goat can get through, so can a man; if a man can get through, so can a battalion.' Quietly, in single file, 55,000 guerrillas took up their positions. But Giap also had another army, perhaps more important – more than a quarter of a million peasants, who carried supplies in baskets and dragged up artillery piece by piece. Stealthily, the guerrillas dug tunnels and trenches until they were almost within touching distance of the enemy, before opening fire. After a siege lasting 55 days, the French surrendered. It was one of the most famous of all anti-colonial victories, but it had been very costly, with Giap's forces suffering far more casualties than the enemy.

It did not produce an independent, united Vietnam, either. Instead, the Communists won the North, while in the South the French, and later the Americans, helped maintain an anti-Communist regime. A small, dapper figure sometimes in a white suit, a trilby and a club tie, and proud of his impeccable if slightly archaic French, Giap never looked like a completely authentic Communist, and scorned the puritanical lifestyle that some of his colleagues at least pretended to adopt. Instead, he had a curtained Russian limousine and lived in a grand French villa. He could also be frosty and imperious and had a fierce temper, which earned him the nickname the 'Snow-covered Volcano'. He was appointed defence minister in the new North Vietnam government, which began a brutal campaign of Maoist land reform in which thousands of people were killed after being condemned as landlords. The government sent Giap out to calm the angry crowds, and he was able to pull it off, thanks to his prestige as the victor at Dien Bien Phu. Later he would say 'sorry' for the regime's excesses, admitting they 'executed too many honest people . . . and, seeing enemies everywhere, resorted to terror'.

When the United States took over as the enemy, Giap showed his skill in logistics and diplomacy as he kept open the Ho Chi Minh Trail to supply the Communist rebels in the South, but militarily he enjoyed only modest success. He found it hard to combat the Americans' mobility, and his forces suffered heavy losses. Though he apologized for some of the regime's political failures, he remained haughtily unrepentant when taken to task over the number of military casualties his side sustained, dismissing the figures as small compared to the number of people who died from natural causes every day. The Tet Offensive that he masterminded in 1968 was particularly costly, but although it looked like a defeat, it played an important role in undermining support in America for the war. It would take another seven years to overthrow the u.s.-backed regime in the South, but Giap was patient, and anyway, he had expected it to take even longer. After the victory of 1975, the general was gradually sidelined. He was critical of what he considered the new government's extreme economic policies, and of its decision to invade Cambodia. Twice his many admirers in the army urged him to seize power, but the old guerrilla preferred a

General Vo Nguyen Giap.

comfortable retirement with his second wife and their two sons and two daughters. He died aged 102 in 2013. In response to flattering comments from admirers, Giap would often say, 'It wasn't me who won the Vietnam War, it was the Vietnamese people.'

Among other well-known people who have lived to the age of 100 is Sir Thomas Sopwith, creator of the famous First World War biplane the Sopwith Camel. It was a Camel that shot down Germany's most celebrated flying ace, the 'Red Baron' Manfred von Richthofen. Sopwith had raised the money to manufacture aircraft by stunt flying. During the Second World War he was involved in making the Hurricane fighter plane. He lived to 101, dying in 1989.

Charles Warrell, better known as Big Chief I-Spy, died in 1995, aged 106. A former headmaster, he published a series of highly successful children's spotter books over 38 years. Readers would get points

Luise Rainer receiving a star on Berlin's Boulevard of Stars in September 2011.

Sir Nicholas Winton.

for noting items of interest, such as a Victorian pillar box or a four-leafed clover. A real Big Chief, Joe Medicine Crow, the last war chief of Montana's Crow Nation, lived to 102, dying in 2016. As the first member of his tribe to gain a master's degree, he became its historian. He was awarded the Presidential Medal of Freedom, and continued lecturing into his nineties.

Lord Denning – described by Margaret Thatcher as 'probably the greatest English judge of modern times' and by Lord Bingham, the Lord Chief Justice, as 'the best loved judge of this, or perhaps, any generation' – had a reputation for championing the underdog. He died in March 1999, aged 100.

Dame Ninette de Valois, founder of the Royal Ballet, lived to 102, dying in 2001. She was born in Ireland, and at the age of 23 joined Sergei Diaghilev's Ballets Russes as a soloist, later becoming a leading choreographer. She continued to teach ballet until late in life, despite the pain she suffered from arthritis and undiagnosed childhood polio.

Born in Trinidad, the bandleader Edmundo Ros was credited with popularizing Latin American music in Britain. He sold millions of records, and plenty of top people would frequent his club. The Queen is said to have danced for the first time in public to Ros's music, and he was often invited to play at Buckingham Palace. After retiring to Spain, he died aged 100 in 2011.

The Brazilian architect Oscar Niemeyer, famous for designing the United Nations building in New York and Brazil's futuristic capital, Brasilia, lived to 104, dying in 2012. Many of his creations featured long, sweeping curves, inspired, he said, by the shape of Brazilian women. He was still working on new projects until shortly before his death.

Luise Rainer, the first Hollywood star to win consecutive Oscars, died in 2014, also aged 104. Born in Germany, her first award for best actress came in 1936 for *The Great Ziegfeld*, followed the next year by *The Good Earth*, in which she portrayed a Chinese peasant. Her last film role came when she was 87, playing a gambling-addicted granny.

Oscar Niemeyer's Juscelino Kubitschek Bridge in Brasilia.

Olivia de Havilland, photographed in the 1940s.

Sir Nicholas Winton, dubbed the British Schindler, was a Jewish stockbroker who organized the rescue of more than 660 Jewish children in Prague who were about to be sent to concentration camps. He kept quiet about his exploits for half a century. Sir Nicholas died in 2015, aged 106.

Perhaps best known for portraying Melanie Hamilton in *Gone with the Wind* (1939), a rather goody-goody contrast to Vivien Leigh's tempestuous Scarlett O'Hara, Olivia de Havilland passed 100 in 2016. But her private life demonstrated butter did melt in her mouth, as she fell in love with Errol Flynn and James Stewart, clocked up two broken marriages, and feuded for years with her sister, Joan Fontaine.

Kirk Douglas.

Later the same year, it was the turn of another Hollywood icon, Kirk Douglas, to pass the 100 mark. The son of Russian Jews who had fled the pogroms, he grew up in poverty in New York State. It is said he did more than 40 different jobs before becoming an actor and playing celebrated screen roles such as Spartacus and Vincent van Gogh. When Dame Vera Lynn turned 100 in 2017, her image was projected onto the white cliffs of Dover, commemorating one of the songs that had seen her dubbed the 'forces' sweetheart' as she travelled the globe during the Second World War performing for British troops. She said the secret to a long life was to 'Be active to your full capabilities.'

So what insights do these centenarian celebrities give us into the recipe for living to 100? As with the record-breakers, many remained active until very late in life – with Grandma Moses still painting, the Queen Mother performing public engagements, Leni Riefenstahl charging around the African bush, Lord Shinwell speaking in Parliament and George Burns planning to play the London Palladium on his 100th birthday (though Fumio Niwa had Alzheimer's, and Irving Berlin became something of a recluse in his final years).

Some had long and happy marriages – Albert Hofmann for more than 70 years, while Irving Berlin was with his wife for more than 60, and Leni Riefenstahl found her first long-lasting relationship for the last 40 years of her life. But others had long periods as widows or widowers – the Queen Mother for half a century, Moses and Burns for more than 30 years – while Shinwell was widowed three times and Rose Kennedy's marriage was not happy. Many, like Kennedy and Princess Alice, had their share of tragedy.

The Queen Mother, Princess Alice and, to a lesser extent, Riefenstahl all emerged from privileged backgrounds, but many of the others had come up the hard way – notably Irving Berlin, George Burns, Bob Hope, Manny Shinwell and Grandma Moses. Albert Hofmann had the most strikingly quiet and stable life – in spite of his experimentation with LSD – while Grandma Moses and, when she could, the Queen Mother enjoyed the tranquillity of the countryside. Leni Riefenstahl, Manny Shinwell, Fumio Niwa and General Giap, on the other hand, all had pretty turbulent lives. George Burns was proud to be a smoker, though of cigars, not cigarettes, and the Queen Mother was fond of a drink. As with the record-breakers, a number of the centenarian celebrities were noticeably slight in build: Princess Alice, Rose Kennedy, Irving Berlin, George Burns, Leni Riefenstahl and General Giap.

Faith was probably most important to Rose Kennedy, but the Queen Mother and Bob Hope too were religious. The philosophical attitude to life found among so many of the record-breakers is less evident among the celebrities, though both the Queen Mother and Rose Kennedy were noticeably stoic in public when faced with misfortune. More striking is a steely and determined sense of mission – the Queen Mother in her royal duties, Rose Kennedy towards her family, Bob Hope in his dedication to perfection and serving his audience, General Giap to freeing his country and Leni Riefenstahl to her art.

SIX

Who Will Survive to 100?

In the old joke, a doctor tells a patient, 'You need to give up smoking, drinking, and rich foods, and take more exercise.' The patient asks, 'Will that make me live longer?' 'I can't promise that,' replies the doctor, 'but it will certainly seem longer.'

So what about the people most successful at living longer – the centenarians? Have they had to shun life's pleasures? Or is having fun crucial to survival? In this chapter we examine what the factors are that determine which of us will get to 100, and which of us will fall by the wayside.

It is worth repeating that, in spite of their growing numbers, centenarians remain a very select group. In the UK they make up just one in every 4,470 people. The record-breakers and the celebrity centenarians suggest some pointers as to who will find their way into the elite. A sensible and moderate diet; a positive and, when necessary, philosophical attitude to life; a touch of determination; a happy marriage; keeping active; discovering new interests late in life; and inheriting the right genes might all play a part. But scientists and statisticians would dismiss the evidence we have seen so far as anecdotal, so what do they have to say on the subject? We already know one very important factor: women have a much better chance than men of living to 100. Now it is time to delve deeper.

In 1974 Marjorie Bucke, vice-chair of the British Association for Service to the Elderly, got together with a community physician named Morag Insley to do a pioneering study of British centenarians. They interviewed 38, spread between rural and urban areas, and immediately recognized that they were 'dealing with a physiologically elite group'.

The women in particular had kept their subcutaneous fat and 'seemed rosy cheeked', looking much younger than their age. The medical histories of those in the sample showed a 'striking' absence of illness, though a number said they had been 'delicate' in childhood, and several had had major surgery in the previous ten years. Obesity was 'totally absent', and none of the centenarians were 'excessively tall'. They did not seem to have followed special diets, but they were all 'frugal' in their eating habits. There were no vegetarians, nor were there any teetotallers, but none drank much. One or two had been heavy smokers earlier in life, but of those still smoking, none now indulged much. As far as exercise was concerned, the majority said they had been keen walkers.

Another conspicuous feature of this admittedly small sample was that per head of population, there were about twice as many centenarians in rural as in urban areas. Another was that many had lived in the same place for a long time, exhibiting 'a remarkably settled mode of existence'. In terms of social class, they were 'certainly not wealthy', and they had 'modest expectations from life'. Bucke and Insley considered that 'all had worked hard', and all those asked for their recipe for longevity said they felt that 'hard work had probably helped'. Another factor the researchers picked out was 'a philosophical attitude to life, and towards its adversities and changes'. They were a group characterized by 'a sense of humour . . . coupled with a tolerant but active interest in all that has gone on and is still going on around them in the lives of others, but with the ability to be untouched by it all'.

A decade later, in 1985, for my *TV Eye* programme on 100-year-olds, we surveyed 100 centenarians – a big sample amounting to about one in every 30 then alive in the UK. We also interviewed a few on camera. As expected, the women heavily outnumbered the men, by 81 to 19. And they were certainly an elite: of women born 100 years before, about 700 had died for each one who survived, while for men the survival rate was just one in 5,000. Michael Bury, a medical sociologist from the University of London, helped us analyse the results. As far as social class was concerned, a clear picture emerged. People from 'the upper end' of the spectrum were more likely to reach 100. Half of our sample were from professional, managerial or non-manual occupations, while only sixteen were unskilled manual workers, including just one man.

A third of the women, but only one of the men, had never married, leading Bury to observe that marriage was 'better in terms of survival for men than it is for women'. There was also an indication that the centenarians had received some help from their genes. The parents of those in the sample had lived about 30 per cent longer than the average for their generation. Nearly 40 of those interviewed said they had never drunk alcohol, while 44 described themselves as drinking a little; only four admitted to drinking more, with a 100-year-old man from the Isle of Mull remarking, 'I never refused a dram, but I never got drunk.' Questions about diet revealed little, with 67 centenarians describing theirs as 'normal', though five said they now ate very little. One man extolled the virtues of oatmeal porridge, milk, potatoes, salted herring and 'lots of spring water'.

Some of the most unequivocal figures emerged on smoking: 79 had never smoked, another fourteen had smoked but had given it up, and five were still smoking, though only three had ever got through more than ten cigarettes a day. One of those who had given up was the Mull centenarian, who said, 'I smoked all my life until two years ago I stopped. It didn't agree with me.' The results on smoking were confirmed by America's New England Centenarian Study, which found that few centenarians had smoked much, though when the head of the study, Tom Perls, remonstrated with a 110-year-old woman who lit a cigarette, she replied, 'My last doctor who told me to stop smoking is dead.' And, of course, there is a long list of exceptions – George Burns; Shigechiyo Izumi; Alfie Grant, once the oldest man in Britain, who had smoked ten a day; the American actress Estelle Winwood, reputed to have got through 60 a day until she died aged 101; Winnie Langley from Croydon, who lived to 102 after consuming an estimated 170,000 cigarettes, and only gave up when she could not see clearly enough to light up; not to mention the woman who gave up smoking when she got to 103 and then promptly died. But we are talking here about the broad picture, and it seems clear.

Further evidence that smoking severely damages your chance of reaching 100 came from a survey of 157 centenarians in Rome in 2004, which found that nearly 84 per cent had never smoked, 13.5 per cent had smoked but had given up, and fewer than 3 per cent were still smoking. In America, Lynn Peters Adler, founder of the National Centenarian Awareness Project, conducted interviews with 500 centenarians. Nearly three-quarters had never smoked, while most of the others had 'stopped between the ages of 40 and 70'. A study of 34,000 Seventh-day Adventists, whose faith frowns on smoking, showed that the men could expect to live seven years longer than an

Estelle Winwood.

average white Californian male, while for women the advantage was four years. Perhaps even more impressive was research that followed 35,000 British doctors over a period of 50 years. In 2004, the study reported that the smokers died on average ten years earlier than the non-smokers.

So, everything was going swimmingly until 2011, when researchers at Albert Einstein College of Medicine of Yeshiva University in New York City produced their findings on 477 Ashkenazi Jews aged 95 and over, who had been asked questions about what their lifestyles had been like when they were 70. Surprisingly, 60 per cent of the men said they had smoked, as did 30 per cent of the women. Commenting on the results, Dr Nir Barzilai wondered whether it meant the centenarians had special genes that made them less susceptible to the harmful effects of smoking: 'it's not that if you want to live to be 100, you can smoke . . . It's that there are rare people who are going to be 100, and for them it doesn't matter – they get there anyhow.' And we know that our genetic inheritance does have an important effect on our survival; identical twins, who share all their genes, have life spans that are more similar than those of non-identical twins, who have just half their genes in common. Sceptics, though, sounded a note of caution about the Yeshiva results, questioning how accurately people could remember their habits of three decades earlier.

Overall, there is not much medical opinion to the effect that smoking will help you live longer, but with drinking alcohol it is a bit different. Although most comment dwells on the harm it can do, we are also used to seeing stories about how, in moderation, it can be beneficial, perhaps in preventing heart attacks, or reducing the risk of breast cancer and diabetes, or even preventing the common cold. And as the *TV Eye* study hinted, with centenarians too, the alcohol story seems less clear-cut than the tobacco story. Among the record-breakers, we saw that John Evans, Christian Mortensen and Alice Herz-Sommer were all teetotallers, but Jeanne Calment liked red wine, Charlotte Hughes and Henry Jamieson brandy, Fred Hale Senior whisky and Shigechiyo Izumi a redoutable local brew. And a number of centenarians are known to have had special tipples: Vinson Gulliver, once Britain's oldest man, would take a glass of whisky mixed with orange and honey every day, while Harry Williams, a former Church of England priest, would always have a glass of wine with his lunch, and said he also liked 'a good brandy'. On the other hand, María Capovilla, an Ecuadorian who was the oldest person in the world when she died aged 116, never drank or smoked. Neither did two African Americans who were both also for a time the oldest living human beings – Gertrude Baines, who survived to 115, and Emma Tillman, who made it to 114.

From her 500 centenarian interviews in the United States, Lynn Adler found that 'while some never drank, most said they enjoyed only an occasional cocktail or a glass of wine; some still do.' This time, the Yeshiva study had not dissimilar results. A slightly higher proportion of men in the centenarian group than in a comparison group of people aged around 70 said they had drunk some alcohol, while fewer of the centenarian women drank. Also in America, the Georgia Centenarian

Study, which followed centenarians over a period of nearly twenty years, concluded that 'few . . . consumed excessive alcohol', while an analysis of 34 studies, covering a million people, calculated that the death rate among heavy drinkers was 18 per cent higher than among light drinkers. A similar picture emerged in Asia, where a national survey of South Korean centenarians, which began in 2001, found that three-quarters did not drink at all, but that just over one in twenty drank a little each day. Okinawa, at Japan's southern tip, boasts one of the highest average life expectancies on earth, with about three and a half times as many centenarians per head of population as America. A study of 900 of its centenarians that has been running since 1975 found they often drank 'moderate' amounts of alcohol.

No one has to smoke or drink alcohol, but we all need to eat. So, does diet influence our chances of living to 100? As we saw, many of the record-breakers practised what you might call 'healthy eating'. Some avoided red meat – though Yukichi Chuganji was quite a carnivore, and 117-year-old Misao Okawa from Japan, another who was for a time the world's oldest human, loved beef stew and ramen noodles, telling a reporter, 'Eating delicious things is a key to my longevity.' Maria Gomes Valentim, the first Brazilian to be named the oldest person in the world, when she was 114, sang the praises of her national dish *feijoada*, a meat and bean stew, though she also swore by 'healthy' breakfasts of a bread roll, fruit and coffee. Then there is the question of sweet things. Jeanne Calment, Magda Brown and Sarah Knauss all loved to eat chocolate, a taste also shared by a centenarian from Devon named Peggy Griffiths, who ate 30 chocolate bars a week. We are often warned about the dangers to our health of sweet, fizzy drinks, but a 104-year-old Texan, Elizabeth Sullivan, said she drank three cans of Dr Pepper every day. In a now familiar refrain, she noted, 'Every doctor that sees me says they'll kill you. But they die and I don't.'

As we have seen, research from the Netherlands indicated that people who eat red meat have twice as much chance of having a heart attack as those who shun it, and a study in 2009 that followed the eating habits of nearly 550,000 Americans concluded that those who ate the most red meat increased their chances of death over a ten-year period by about a third. Meanwhile, the survey of Seventh-day Adventists showed that vegetarians could expect an extra two years of life compared with meat-eaters. As for processed meats, such as bacon, sausages and burgers, a study in 2013 that looked at nearly half a million Europeans found that those who ate a lot of them were 44 per cent more likely to die prematurely than those who ate little. But bacon was a favourite with Pearl Cantrell, a 105-year-old from Texas, as it was with Gertrude Baines, who said, 'I eat bacon, toast, I like all kinds of food. If it tastes good, I eat it. If it doesn't taste good, I don't eat it.' Bacon also featured in the diet of 116-year-old African American Susannah Mushatt Jones, who became the world's oldest living person in 2015. She started every day with bacon, eggs and grits. This was very different from the diet of another one-time holder of the 'oldest person in the world' title, Hendrikje van Andel-Schipper from the Netherlands, who lived to 115 and attributed her longevity to a slice of pickled herring and a tumbler of orange juice every day; while a 104-year-old former nurse from California, Marge Jetton, was a vegetarian, eating oatmeal and flaxseed for breakfast, green salad for lunch, and soup and a vegetable sandwich for dinner. For some, such as Fred Hale, the world's oldest driver, routine was the crucial thing, with three meals a day, always at the same time, while for Walter Breuning, the world's oldest man when he died at 114, the regime was a strict two meals a day.

In Europe, a study from 2005 gave participants points for each kind of healthy food they ate, such as vegetables, fruit, beans, fish,

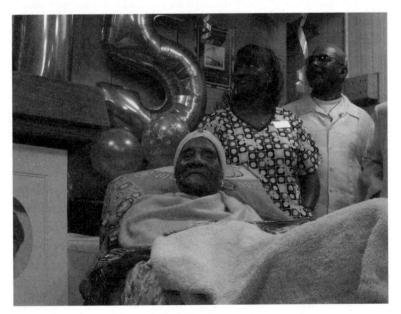

Gertrude Baines turns 115.

whole grains and unsaturated fats like olive oil. Those who scored six or more points saw their risk of early death reduced by 17 per cent compared with those who scored zero to three. Many of the foods that earned points feature in what has become known and admired as the Mediterranean diet. A survey of five villages in the Sicani Mountains of western Sicily, where sweet drinks, tinned vegetables, white bread and processed foods are shunned, found they had nineteen centenarians in a population of fewer than 19,000 – five times as many per head as you would find in the United States. Similarly, the Georgia Centenarian study found that 100-year-olds had diets rich in carotenoids, present in vegetables such as carrots, sweet potatoes and spinach, which seem to reduce the risk of heart disease and of some cancers. The centenarians also tended to make sure they ate breakfast, and had avoided diets designed to lose weight. The American company UnitedHealthcare carries out an annual survey of centenarians. In 2013, 86 per cent of those it questioned said they regularly ate nutritionally balanced meals, while a study in South Korea revealed that 87 per cent of the food in the diets of female centenarians was coming from plant sources.

But as Bucke and Insley found back in the 1970s, it may not be what 100-year-olds are eating that matters, but how much. 'Frugal' was their word for the centenarian diet. First World War veteran Fred Lloyd, who lived to 107, might have declared that he had a 'terrific appetite . . . I clear my plate every day', but, as we saw, Jiroemon Kimura, the only man known to have lived to 116, stressed the importance of leaving the table when you are only 80 per cent full. In 2004, a 40-year study of 5,800 Japanese American men on Hawaii concluded that those who ate fewer calories lived longer, with the optimum figure being about 15 per cent fewer calories than average. And the Okinawa Centenarian Study (ocs) said that people there 'have traditionally kept eating a low-calorie' diet, following the '80 per cent full' rule. One of the benefits of fruit and vegetables beyond their nutrients is that they contain plenty of fibre and water, filling people up and making it more difficult for them to over-eat. Among the 500 American centenarians interviewed by Lynn Adler and her colleagues, only about a fifth said they had ever tried specialized diets, but many were critical of 'supersize' portions.

We are used to the idea that to be healthy, as well as not eating too much, we have to make sure we exercise. Centenarian athletes such as 'Flying Phil' Rabinowitz and Fauja Singh took this to remarkable lengths, while at a less competitive level, Jeanne Calment was still cycling aged 100, and at 103 Fred Hale was shovelling snow off his roof. There are plenty of other examples, too. Marge Jetton, the 104-year-old former nurse with the healthy diet, walked a mile every day at her retirement home, as well as using an exercise bike and doing a bit of light weight training. Among Lynn Adler's 500 centenarians was 101-year-old Louise Caulder, who said she did half an hour of stretches every day, as well as making sure she walked a mile, while at 100, George Blevins was still bowling, and Joe Meyser won a medal for golf at America's National Senior Games.

In 1998, a Finnish study that had followed 16,000 twins for seventeen years reported that those who were inactive were more than twice as likely to have died as those who exercised. Similarly, a survey of 5,000 Danes in 2006 suggested regular exercise got you about six extra years of life. 'Regular exercise' has also been identified as one of the features of the lifestyle of Okinawan centenarians, as it was among the people who survived better in a University of Cambridge study of 20,000 middle-aged men and women. The 2015 UnitedHealthcare survey found that 46 per cent of centenarians said they walked or hiked, while 34 per cent reported that they did exercises to strengthen their muscles. Once again, the Yeshiva study is a bit of an outlier. Only 43 per cent of the male centenarians reported that they had exercised regularly when they were 70, which is 14 per cent fewer than in the comparison group, while 47 per cent of the centenarian women said they had taken regular exercise – slightly higher than the figure for the control group; but again, there are questions about how accurate people's memories were.

So, what about build – fat, thin, short, tall? It is striking how many of the record-breakers and the celebrity centenarians were noticeably slight – Princess Alice, Rose Kennedy, Irving Berlin, George Burns, Leni Riefenstahl, General Giap, Jeanne Calment, Shigechiyo Izumi and so on. And they were not alone. The Rev. Peter Humphrey, for a time Britain's oldest working priest, was described as a 'small, spritely man', and the Italian Nobel Prize-winning biologist Rita Levi-Montalcini, who still sat in the Italian senate when she passed 100, was said to be 'tiny and bird-like'. But not all centenarians come from this mould. Manohar Aich from Calcutta won the Mr Universe title at the age of 40. With 18-inch (46-cm) biceps, a 47-inch (120-cm) chest, a 14-inch (36-cm) forearm and a 6 1/2-inch (16.5-cm) wrist, 'slight' he was not, though he was short, at less than five feet (152 cm) tall. He worked out in the gym until he was 98, and in 2012 he passed his 100th birthday, declaring, 'I have given maximum importance to my body. I have regularly exercised and led a disciplined life.' Another well-known strongman centenarian was New Yorker Joe Rollino, who once shifted 3,200 pounds (1,450 kg), even though he weighed just 150 pounds (68 kg). Still able to bend coins between his fingers, he died in 2010 aged 104 after being run over by a car near his Brooklyn home.

As for what science and statistics have to say, the analysis of centenarians in Sicily's Sicani Mountains found that while they were 'non-obese' and tended to be 'small in stature', they had a 'regular' rather than a lean body mass index (BMI). (People with a BMI higher than 30 are considered 'obese'; those with an index of 25 to 29 are 'overweight'; 'lean' is a BMI lower than 23. BMI is calculated by dividing a person's weight in kilograms by the square of their height in metres.) In 2008, Natalia Gavrilova and her husband Leonid Gavrilov from the Center on Aging at the University of Chicago compared the build at age 30 of 171 men who went on to live to 100, with 171 others randomly chosen from those who had not made the century. Taking men born in 1887, the researchers were able to use the data about their physiques recorded on their draft cards for the U.S. Armed Forces in 1917. The most arresting finding of the study was that there were twice as many 'stout' people among those who had died earlier in life than among the centenarians. In the words of the investigators, 'obesity at young adult age (30 years) is harmful for attaining exceptional longevity.' The men with the best chance of making it to 100 in the Gavrilovs' study were of 'medium' build, and they found no evidence that being 'slender' helped. When it came to height, those in the 'medium' category had a better chance of surviving, too, while the tallest and the shortest did worse.

Obesity is linked with diabetes, heart disease and some cancers, and the Gavrilovs' findings regarding being too heavy chime with most other studies on the issue. According to a report in the *Journal of the American Medical Association* in 2003, the most severely obese young adults can expect to lose up to thirteen years of life. But just being overweight also increased your chances of death over a decade by 20 to 40 per cent, according to a study published in 2006 by America's National Cancer Institute looking at the lifestyles of 527,000 people aged 50 to 71. 'Even carrying a few extra pounds is associated with increased risk of dying prematurely,' said Michael Leitzmann, senior author of the study. The lowest death rates occurred towards the upper end of 'normal' weight, rather than among the very thin, and there is evidence that thin women can be more vulnerable to hip fractures and lung diseases such as pneumonia. In the UK, the Academy of Medical Royal Colleges reported in 2013 that having a BMI of 30 to 35 reduced life expectancy by an average of three years, while a BMI of over 40 cut it by eight to ten years. The New England survey also noted that 'few centenarians are obese,' though it added that male centenarians are 'nearly always lean'. Support for the slender also comes from the Okinawa study, which found that its centenarians had generally been 'lean' throughout their lives.

The often renegade Yeshiva study found that centenarians were 'just as likely' to be overweight as anyone else, but when it came to obesity, it too fell into line with the general conclusion. Fewer than one in twenty of the centenarian men said they had been obese at 70 – about one-third the rate among the general population – while in women the difference was not so pronounced, but it was clear and significant. Another factor was lobbed into the debate about build and longevity by results in 2015 from a study of nearly 200,000 people conducted by scientists at the University of Leicester. They found that taller people were less likely to suffer from heart disease, the leading cause of death in the UK. Every two and a half inches of height cut the risk by 13.5 per cent. On the other hand, an American study of 144,000 women showed that being tall was associated with greater risk of cancer.

So there are few clear answers on build, except that obesity is likely to be bad for your chances of reaching 100, and obesity is linked with social class. In 2013 Dr Alison Tedstone, Director of Diet and Obesity at Public Health England, warned, 'Children in poor communities are far more likely to be obese.' And, as we saw in the *TV Eye* study, people's chances of reaching 100 do appear to be affected by class. As in many aspects of life, being better off gives you an advantage. That is not to say that centenarians cannot come from very poor backgrounds; we know that several of the record-breakers and the celebrity centenarians managed it. And then there was Jessie Gallan, who lived to 109 and was for a time the oldest woman in Scotland. She was born in a tiny two-room farm cottage, where she slept on a straw mattress with her brother and five sisters, before leaving home at thirteen to become a milkmaid; while Bill Proctor, the oldest man in Britain when he died at 109, had also known hard times, walking 100 miles as a teenager from the Cumbrian coast to the Wirral looking for work.

But the statistical evidence tends to support the *TV Eye* survey. As we saw, an early attempt to test the hypothesis that those higher up the social scale live longer than those lower down came in the 1950s and '60s, when two actuaries compared the death rate over twelve years of 5,800 eminent people listed in *Who's Who in America* with that of the general population. Only seven people in 100 died among the *Who's Who* entries, compared with ten in every 100 among the huddled masses. In 2014, the UK health research organization the King's Fund said, 'Men and women from the richest social class can, on average, expect to live more than seven years longer than those in the poorest.' The University of Gothenburg followed 50 men born in 1913 for 50 years, from 1963 to 2013, and concluded that longevity was closely linked with 'high social class'. Even more graphically, a famous report in 2006 showed male life expectancy in Calton, a deprived area of Glasgow, was 28 years lower than it was in the affluent district of Lenzie, just eight miles away, while the Gavrilovs' study suggested that a black man born in America in 1887 was only about half as likely as a white man to survive to 100.

Having money, then, appears to help your chance of reaching 100. Perhaps less predictable, however, was Bucke and Insley's finding that centenarians seemed to be twice as common in rural than in urban areas. Christian Mortensen, Shigechiyo Izumi, Jiroemon Kimura, Grandma Moses, the Japanese twins Gin and Kin, and the Scottish Rennie twins were all raised on farms. Another example was Lancastrian Nicholas Swarbrick. After dodging U-boats as a merchant seaman during the First World War, he went to work on his father's farm, and stayed there until he retired, dying aged 107 in a nursing home overlooking the fields. In 2014 the photographer David Bailey took portraits of nine centenarians; three of them came from farming stock. (At least another four left school at age fourteen, and two others, born in India and Cyprus, seem also to have had pretty hard lives.) In South Korea, a study of 961 centenarians in 2005 found that 'most' had worked in farming.

Between 1977 and 1980, the pioneering British social scientist Mark Abrams followed 432 people in their late sixties. He concluded that living 'in the heart of a very large metropolitan conurbation' was bad for your longevity. Similarly, the Gavrilovs discovered that being a farmer doubled the chances of the men in their sample reaching 100, offering the explanation that 'people in the past had poor sanitation in towns,' putting them at higher risk of disease. And in 2015, urban living still appeared to have its longevity drawbacks: a study by Imperial College and the London School of Hygiene and Tropical Medicine suggested that the death rate among people living by noisy roads is about 4 per cent higher than average. (In London, 1.6 million people live in areas where traffic noise is above the maximum considered safe by the World Health Organization.) Old people in particular suffer badly, with the number of strokes they experienced going up by 9 per cent. The theory is that noise raises blood pressure, increases stress and makes it harder to sleep. It may also be a factor that people in cities tend to be more mobile than those in the country, undermining the 'settled' way of life that Bucke and Insley had identified among centenarians, which also seemed to apply to record-breakers such as Jeanne Calment, Shigechiyo Izumi, John Evans, Charlotte Hughes and the Japanese twins Kin and Gin.

The biggest decision most people make in their lives is when or if they marry. And as we saw in the *TV Eye* survey, marriage does seem to help people, especially men, reach 100. Among the celebrity centenarians, Albert Hofmann and his wife were together for more than 70 years, a figure equalled by a number of couples among the record-breakers, while Edith Rennie thought 'a good husband' was one of the reasons for her longevity. On the other hand, Christian Mortensen's experience of matrimony was short and unhappy, and there are a number of centenarians who see no longevity benefits in tying the knot. At her sister Sophia's 100th birthday party in Neath, Glamorgan, 104-year-old Margaret Lacy said, 'We were both far too busy ever to get married and it certainly hasn't done us any harm.' Jessie Gallan went even further: 'My secret for a long life has been staying away from men. They're just more trouble than they're worth.' Marie Bremont, a 115-year-old Frenchwoman who was once the oldest woman in the world, seemed closer to the Edith Rennie view, declaring, 'I had two good husbands. I have always been happy'; but she was widowed for the second time 44 years before she died.

So, which of these positions is right? Back in 1858, a British epidemiologist named William Farr produced a study showing unmarried people died 'in undue proportion' compared to those enjoying the delights of matrimony. Since then, the opinion that marriage is good for you has become widely held, with the rider that while it seems to be good for women, it is even better for men (as the *TV*

Eye survey suggested). But overall, the relationship between marriage and longevity seems to be best summed up in the title of the romantic comedy in which a couple who divorced ten years before embark on an affair: *It's Complicated*. Research in 1973 by Vanderbilt University in Tennessee found that married people 'have lower mortality rates than the single, the widowed, or the divorced and that the differences between the married and unmarried statuses are much greater for men than for women'. In 1992, figures from the UK's Office of Population Censuses and Surveys showed that in all age groups, married women had lower death rates than single, widowed or divorced women, while in every age group below 80, married men had lower rates than single, widowed or divorced men. Three years later, a pro-marriage charity, One plus One, sifted through a pile of studies from Europe and America. Using official UK figures on people aged 45 to 49, it found divorced men had a 76 per cent greater risk of premature death than married men, while for divorced women the additional risk was 39 per cent. Well, what do you expect a pro-marriage pressure group to say? But after One plus One's report appeared, plenty of other surveys seemed to show that marriage contributes to longevity. The UK's Office for National Statistics (successor to the Office of Population Censuses and Surveys) declared in 2001, for example, that divorced men aged 45 and over are 30 per cent more likely to die prematurely, with single men 23 per cent more at risk and widowed men 20 per cent more, while remarriage improves survival chances.

Similarly, a study of 67,000 Americans by researchers at the University of California, Los Angeles, published in 2006, found bachelors aged 19 to 44 were more than twice as likely to die as married men. And never marrying was worse for survival chances than marrying and then getting divorced or separated. The beneficial effects of marriage were also affirmed by the Terman Life-cycle Study, initiated by Lewis Terman, psychologist at Stanford University, in 1921, which followed 1,500 American children for 80 years in what became known as the Longevity Project. Terman died in 1956, but others continued his work, and findings released in 2011 suggested men from the sample who remained in long-term marriages were likely to live beyond 70 – an age that fewer than one in three divorced males would live to see. The project found that married men lived longest, but that those who never married did better than those who married and divorced. Divorce was much less harmful to women, with female divorcees living nearly as long as those who remained married. One of those who carried the

Generalissimo and Madame Chiang Kai-shek
with Lieutenant General Joseph W. Stilwell in Burma, 1942.

Terman torch after the project's originator died was psychology professor Howard Friedman. He said, 'Women who got divorced often
thrived,' especially if in doing so they were getting rid of 'troublesome
husbands'. Acknowledging that there was much more work to do on
the data, Friedman also noted, 'the overall marital satisfaction of the
man is more important to the future health of both the men and the
women than is the marital happiness of the woman.'

Although there seems to be doubt about whether never marrying
or getting married and then divorcing is worse, the figures do appear to
support the idea that being married improves your chance of reaching
100, especially if you are a man. So why should that be? Is it the sex?
Aristotle thought that every time a person made love, it shortened their
life, and as we have seen, a study in 1969 found that eunuchs lived an
average thirteen years longer than uncastrated men, while a 103-year-
old American man extolled the benefits of giving up sex for one year
in every ten. It was also said that Madame Chiang Kai-shek, widow of
the Chinese Nationalist leader, who lived to 105, never had sex with her
husband at all. On the other hand, the 101-year-old Italian man Guilio
Paggi believed having sex had helped him reach his ripe old age, and
his views seem to be supported by a study from the Caerphilly area

of Wales. From 1979 to 1983, it questioned more than 900 men aged 45 to 59 about how many orgasms they had. In 1997 the subjects were followed up, and those who had fewest were found to have been twice as likely to die as those who had at least two a week. An earlier Swedish study had also found that men who give up sex earlier seem to die earlier. And good sex seems to help women, too: research in America in the 1970s suggested that those who were sexually dissatisfied were more likely to have heart attacks, while Howard Friedman said, 'we know that married women with a great sex life live longer, but we don't know why.' When the centenarians themselves were questioned in the UnitedHealthcare survey of 2013, nearly a third said maintaining a sex life had been crucial for healthy ageing.

One plus One did not major on the sex. The pro-marriage charity suggested wedlock's main contribution to longevity was to act as a buffer against stress and anxiety. The Vanderbilt study also considered that marriage might help, by improving psychological well-being and reducing mental illness. Possible confirmation of this mechanism came in 1989 when researchers in the Ohio State University department of psychiatry found that men and women who were separated or divorced suffered greater depression and loneliness and had weaker immune systems than those who were happily married. One plus One picked out other factors, too, suggesting that marriage break-up leads to risky, life-shortening behaviour such as smoking, drinking and having unsafe sex. Deaths from heart disease, cancer, suicide and accidents were all higher among the unmarried. But the 2006 Los Angeles study found that single men were only slightly more likely to smoke than husbands, and were less likely to drink regularly. They also exercised more and were less overweight, but it did look as though risky behaviour might still be a damaging factor for the younger ones, for whom accidents, suicides, murders and AIDS were the main causes of death, while for the older ones it was heart or chronic disease. But overall the authors concluded it was really 'social isolation' that was increasing the risk of premature death for single men, who often lack the support networks married males enjoy. Unmarried women appeared less at risk. The authors also conceded that the chain of causation might run in the opposite direction: maybe it is not that marriage makes you live longer, but that healthier people are more likely to get married.

In 2014 researchers at the Universitat Autònoma de Barcelona examined data for thousands of Americans to try and settle the question of whether marriage helps you live longer. They concluded there was no significant gap between the health of married and single people between the ages of twenty and 39, but that once people got into their fifties, those who were married had opened up a significant advantage, which was indeed because of the 'protective effects of marriage on health'. An additional possible mechanism the researchers identify is that married people are more likely to take preventive action to look after their health, such as having checks for high cholesterol or cancer. Other people's marriages – or, to be more precise, those of our parents – also seem able to affect our chances of reaching 100. In the Terman Life-cycle Study, children of divorced parents lived on average five years fewer than the offspring of those who stayed together, with deaths coming from a mixture of natural causes, accidents and violence, while the early demise of a parent seemed to have no measurable effect on life span. It was noticeable that among the nine centenarians photographed and interviewed by David Bailey, three said they were either not close to or positively disliked their fathers, while the same number specifically drew attention to how close they were to their mothers: 'My mother was just wonderful,' said former model Eileen Symonds. Though perhaps this is just a reflection on the times in which they were brought up.

Of course, the benefits of marriage are not confined to having a spouse. It can bring children, grandchildren, great-grandchildren – even great-great-grandchildren. George Francis, the oldest man in America when he died aged 112 in 2009, left a son, three daughters, eighteen grandchildren, 32 great-grandchildren and eighteen great-great grandchildren. Lynn Peters Adler's interviews with 500 centenarians convinced her that family was 'universally important' to them. Centenarians 'enjoyed their roles as matriarchs or patriarchs and many spoke of the pleasure of watching younger generations grow and flourish'. One credited her longevity to 'a wonderful and loving family, the good Lord and a rum and Coke every afternoon'. Looking at their sample of men born in 1887, the Gavrilovs found no statistical difference in the survival rates of those who were married at 30 and those who were not, but having four or more children by that age did significantly increase the chance of reaching 100. The investigators mused on two potential explanations: that high fertility might be an indicator of good health, and that having a lot of children might ensure that there are plenty of carers around later in life. The Korean centenarian study of 2005 found 100-year-olds tended to live with two or three generations of their family under the same roof, and in 2013 centenarians in the UnitedHealthcare survey said friends and family provided them with the most support and had the biggest impact on their lives. No fewer than 97 per cent maintained that staying close to loved ones was one of the secrets of healthy ageing.

Help in reaching 100 can come from friends as well as family. A 102-year-old woman in a Maryland retirement community made a round of visits every day to see friends and favourite staff members, while another played bridge regularly. A 107-year-old in the same community said, 'I'm always interested in other people. I think that makes a difference.' And the UnitedHealthcare study of 2013 said more than one in three of its centenarians had kept up a friendship for more than 75 years. Across the Atlantic in Britain, Lady McFadyean, widow of the diplomat Sir Andrew McFadyean, maintained the reason she had survived to 100 was, 'I've always been busy.'

The importance of meeting other people and having what he called 'a fully engaged life' was identified by the Scottish medical sociologist Rex Taylor in the 1980s as a key to longevity. A five-year study of old people's lifestyles led him to conclude that those who survived had 'much fuller diaries. They have extensions into the future as well as present involvement. They're looking forward to things happening.' Around the same time, Mark Abrams's British longevity study found those who were most socially isolated were most likely to die young, and that if people started dropping out of the organizations to which they belonged, that could also be a predictor of earlier death. In the u.s., a study from 1979 revealed that over a nine-year period, men with small social networks were more than twice as likely to die as those with large networks, while for women the risk was almost three times as great. There is plenty of other evidence that friendship helps. Research from California, for example, shows that women with breast cancer are four times more likely to pull through if they have a good social circle, while 50-year-old men with lots of friends are less prone to heart attacks; and Professor John Rowe from Mount Sinai School of Medicine in New York City has said that older people who regularly mix with others stay young for their age.

An analysis of the results of 148 studies on loneliness and health, following more than 300,000 people, concluded in 2011 that gregarious folk have a 50 per cent better chance of avoiding early death than lonely ones, and in the UnitedHealthcare survey of 2013, more than a third of the centenarians said they attended a social event every day. As we saw, some centenarians took social engagement even further – with the Japanese twins becoming celebrities and Henry Allingham completing 60 speaking engagements in his 111th year. Another centenarian who was still finding new interests and new directions was Holocaust survivor Frieda Lefeber from Pennsylvania, who had her first solo exhibition of paintings when she reached the age of 100 in 2015. Once again, though, we must sound a note of caution. Is it that having a busy life helps you live longer, or is it just that if you are healthy, you are more likely to have a busy life?

As far as health is concerned, some centenarians seem never to have had a day's illness, like chip shop owner Connie Brown, who was first admitted to hospital on the day she died. Others have run into serious health problems, but have overcome them. Ex-miner John Evans had a pacemaker fitted. So did Winnie Langley, when she was 98. She had already recovered from cancer a decade earlier. In 2015, 112-year-old Gladys Hooper from Ryde on the Isle of Wight became the oldest person in Britain to have a hip replacement. Joe Britton, a 103-year-old Chelsea pensioner, spent three months in hospital after a serious motorcycle accident when he was 33, being told – wrongly – that he would never walk again, while First World War veteran Cecil Withers said he still suffered from coughs and phlegm caused by the poison gas he had been subjected to nearly 90 years before. At the age of 88, he underwent three serious operations. The surgeon told him he had never known anyone else who survived them all.

A study by King's College London concluded that centenarians have found a way of beating the common scourges of old age, such as cancer and heart disease. After analysing 36,000 death certificates, they said that among 80- to 84-year-olds, cancer was responsible for a quarter of all deaths and heart disease nearly a fifth, while for 100- to 115-year-olds, cancer claimed the lives of fewer than one in twenty, and heart disease fewer than one in eleven. The centenarians were more likely to die of infections such as pneumonia, which took one in five, while the deaths of more than a quarter were simply put down to 'old age'. A team of American researchers identified three groups among centenarians: escapers, delayers and survivors. Escapers avoid the main fatal diseases that come with old age. Delayers are able to push back the date at which they suffer the illnesses, while survivors contract them, but survive. The New England Centenarian Study reckoned that among men, 32 per cent were escapers, 44 per cent delayers, and 24 per cent survivors, while among women it was 15 per cent escapers, 42 per cent delayers and 43 per cent survivors. According to analysis of 244 centenarians from the Georgia study, 80 per cent had suffered some kind of heart disease, but just 30 per cent had had cancer, while a Danish study suggested that most centenarians were 'survivors', with three-quarters of them having been treated for serious conditions like heart attacks, strokes and pneumonia.

But perhaps what goes on in the mind is as significant as what happens in the body. A number of centenarians have stressed the importance of having a positive outlook. Aged 103, Ella Scotchmer from London said, 'I don't sit back and moan, moan, moan. People in their 70s and 80s, they sicken me, many of them. They've given up and it's such a pity. They've no interest in life . . . they expect to be waited on, hand and foot.' Positive thinking was also part of Lady McFadyean's make-up: 'I've had a wonderful life,' she declared; while a 100-year-old woman in a nursing home in west London said, 'If I make myself happy, naturally I will be, but if I make myself miserable, natu-rally I shall be miserable.' In Abrams's study, the death rate was higher among people who had low morale or who got little satisfaction from life, while according to the UnitedHealthcare survey of 2015, more than 60 per cent of centenarians said they were positive people, almost half said it got easier to feel positive as they got older, and a quarter said a positive outlook was the most important thing for a long, healthy life. In the company's survey from 2013, half the centenarians said they would not change a thing about the way they had lived their lives, compared with just 29 per cent of interviewees aged 60 to 65. Nearly three-quarters believed it was crucial to look forward to each day and more than half stressed the need to maintain a sense of purpose. As for what was the best time of their lives, while nearly half answered that it was when they were young adults, 12 per cent said it was when they were approaching their 100th birthdays. This would seem to fit with George Francis's outlook. His granddaughter said he always stressed the importance of 'living life to the fullest', making sure you 'cherish each day'. First World War veteran Alfred Anderson, who lived to 109, said, 'We lived for each day during the war – and even at my age now, I do the same thing.' Meanwhile, Misao Okawa, who died aged 117, complained that life seemed too short.

If positive thinking keeps you going, feeling hopeless can kill you. A study of more than 940 men in Finland in 1997 found it was as bad for your heart as smoking twenty cigarettes a day, leading to a 20 per cent increase in hardening of the blood vessels. Howard Friedman said if you do not feel you are able to do anything worthwhile in your job, and you do not like your fellow workers, that can blight your chances of longevity. Scientists talk about 'allostatic load' – the cumulative physiological toll exacted on our bodies by the trials and tribulations of life. It is arrived at by measuring such things as blood pressure and levels of stress hormones. Dr Teresa Seeman of the University of California, Los Angeles, found that elderly people with a high degree of social engagement had lower allostatic loads. (They were also likely to be better educated and to come from a higher social class.) The notion that stress is a killer also gained support from a study of more than 2,450 bus drivers in Denmark, published in 1997. It revealed that those on the busiest routes were twice as likely to be admitted to hospital with heart attacks as those on the quietest. In Abrams's sample, the people who showed the highest levels of anxiety were the ones most likely to die, but other students of centenarians do not believe that avoiding stress is necessarily the issue. Leslie Martin, another psychology professor, who worked with Howard Friedman on the Longevity Project, said that when study participants who had stressful jobs 'found meaning in those jobs and they were committed to them, stress really didn't hurt them'. Indeed, she maintained, 'some degree of worrying actually is good.' According to Friedman,

> working hard to overcome adversity or biting off more than you can chew – and then chewing it – does not generally pose a health risk. Striving to accomplish your goals, setting new aims when milestones are reached, and staying engaged and productive are exactly what those heading to a long life tend to do.

Jessie Gallan remembered, 'I always worked hard and seldom would I ever take a holiday,' but she added that she had always worked with 'very nice people'. On the other hand, London centenarian David Arkush spent his working life until he was 70 as a dentist, even though, he said, he 'never liked' the work. Tom Perls believes that 100-year-olds often have 'an ability to manage their stress very, very well', partly because they tend to be 'gregarious and very interesting people'. Incidentally, in the UnitedHealthcare survey of 2015, nearly a third of the centenarians reported that they meditated or took some other action to relieve stress.

Using data from China on more than 3,400 centenarians and nearly 4,600 people in their nineties, a study by American and Chinese experts in 2010 set out to discover whether 'resilience', defined as 'the ability to adapt positively to adversity', was an important factor in reaching 100. Through questions such as 'Do you feel the older you get, the more useless you are?' and 'Do you always look on the bright side of things?', the subjects' resilience was assessed. The researchers discovered that those aged 94 to 98 who were 'resilient' had a 43 per cent better chance of reaching 100 than those who were not. From the experience of his New England study, Perls stressed the importance of the ability of centenarians to adapt when things went wrong, describing how a woman who found her sight was getting worse bought 'some dentist's visors, these magnifying lenses with bright lights, and found that increased markedly her ability to read'.

Vinson Gulliver, aged 109, was for a time the oldest man in Britain. The woman who looked after him said he was fully aware of this, 'and he just loved it.' So, how far is a simple will to live a factor in deciding who makes it to 100? Determination is certainly a trait visible in centenarians such as the Queen Mother, Madame Chiang Kai-shek and Rita Levi-Montalcini, the Italian Jewish biologist who had to carry on her work underground during the 1930s and '40s, and then saw her discoveries sniffed at by scientists in the 1950s and '60s, but went on to win the Nobel Prize in 1986. Winnie Langley, who survived smoking 170,000 cigarettes, was described by her great niece as 'feisty and stubborn', while Joe Britton admitted, 'I was a little sod as a boy, always fighting.' As a centenarian at the Royal Hospital, he said, 'When breakfast is late, I get hold of my spoon and go bang! bang! I'm a stirrer, and I can't get out of the habit.'

Sir Cyril Clarke pointed out how life expectancy for children with Down's syndrome had increased from about nine in the 1920s to around 50 in the 1980s. He put this down to their being given a stronger urge to live: 'They're dressed decently, a lot's made of them and they're encouraged to do things.' And there is evidence to suggest willpower can keep people going. At 119, Sarah Knauss may have ended her long innings just 33 hours before the new millennium, but in the UK, 65 per cent more people died in the week after 1 January 2000 than in the week before. While in New York City, 46 per cent more people passed away in the week following the millennium than during the last week of 1999. In both cases, the number of deaths in the first week of 2000 was way ahead of the normal number for the first seven days of a year. Robert Butler, founder of the International Longevity Centre, thought that people did seem to be hanging on to see the new millennium: 'It does look significant. The will to live can be pretty powerful.' The view of Richard Suzman, associate director of America's National Institute on Aging, was: 'It's pretty well established that people who are seriously ill will hang on to reach significant events, whether they be birthdays, anniversaries or religious holidays. The mechanisms are something of a mystery but the phenomenon is very real.'

So what about religious festivals, for example? Do people really have the ability to stay alive for them? In 1988, researchers at the University of California studied what happened to the death rates of Jewish men in the 24 weeks around the time of Passover, when they take the main role in rituals. For a month before the festival, the death rate for men declined, reaching its lowest level the week before. The highest rate came in the week after. There was no significant change in the rates for women and children. Two years later, researchers examined the death rate among Chinese people in California around the time of the Harvest Moon festival, in which women play the main role. Female deaths fell by a third before the festival and rose by a third after. No effect was seen on men. A different kind of determination to keep on living was perhaps demonstrated by Rosalind Strover of Colchester, Essex, who for her 90th birthday in November 1994 was given the present of a £150 bet made by her daughter-in-law that the nonagenarian would live to 100. Strover continued to exercise every morning and play the violin. Sure enough, ten years later, in 2004, the bet paid out. She blew her winnings on a spectacular party for 200 friends and relatives.

When it came to summing up the kind of personality that helps people survive, Friedman and Martin arrived at some surprising conclusions. Positive thinking might be important, but, Martin said,

> One of the findings that really astounds people, including us, is that the Longevity Project participants who were the most cheerful and had the best sense of humour as kids lived shorter lives, on average, than those who were less cheerful and joking.

It was the most prudent and persistent individuals who stayed healthiest and lived the longest.

Being prudent, persistent and planning things, said Friedman, was the strongest 'personality predictor' of long life. He explained that the happy-go-lucky ones tended to take more risks, and while an optimistic approach could be helpful in a crisis, 'too much of a sense that "everything will be just fine" can be dangerous', because it can lead to carelessness, especially about health. The two psychologists concluded that what they called 'conscientious' people were likely to live longest. These people might worry quite a bit, but they avoided risky behaviour such as drinking, smoking or driving too fast, and they tended to gravitate to happier marriages, better friendships and healthier workplaces. Friedman and Martin also speculated that the conscientious might have different levels of certain chemicals in their brains from the unconscientious, also making them less susceptible to a number of other illnesses not connected with risky behaviour.

Professor Leonard Poon of the Georgia Centenarian Study called centenarians 'expert survivors' and identified in them a number of specific coping mechanisms. They were 'dominant. They want to have their way,' he stated, but on the other hand they were relaxed and flexible. Many were 'suspicious' – refusing to accept things at face value, but questioning them and thinking them through carefully. They were good at problem-solving and tended to be practical rather than idealistic. Ella Scotchmer's advice on the temperament a centenarian needs was, 'never allow yourself to get angry. As soon as you get angry, your body is at tension and you start being ill.'

As we saw earlier, Sir Cyril Clarke believed a decline in faith in an afterlife might mean more people are motivated to live to 100, but Lynn Adler reported that 'almost all' the centenarians in her American sample said they had been supported by their religious faith, and that 'most' believed they would live as long as God had a purpose for them. Many also stressed the importance of 'doing what you know is right and following your conscience'. A 101-year-old woman whose house had twice been destroyed by a lightning strike said, 'Perhaps we are here to be an example to others in hard times.' In Britain, First World War veteran Cecil Withers, who lived to 106, remarked: 'For all the suffering and death I saw in the trenches I never lost my faith. I still pray, and I still believe. The fact that I'm still here is because of some power above.' A similar view was expressed by a 113-year-old Portuguese woman who told an interviewer that she was 'very sick' and did not know what to do with her life, but added, 'God is up there seeing us. He's the one who knows.' On the other hand, another veteran of the First World War, Alfred Finnigan, who lived to the age of 108, said he had 'no time' for 'any form of religion', adding that when he got married, he 'made a conscious decision that we would not have any children – I was not prepared to produce cannon fodder for the army, nor fodder for industry.'

Faced with the growing mountain of data on centenarians, one observer started to feel a little defeatist, remarking that for every healthy eater, there will be an enthusiastic carnivore; for every one who pursues the quiet life, there will be a daredevil; and that for everyone who is religious, there will be a militant atheist. To every rule, of course, there will be exceptions, but the scientific and statistical research can give us some pointers on the kind of lifestyle we need to follow to give us the best chance of getting to 100, such as avoiding smoking and getting angry, eating and drinking sensibly, taking plenty of exercise, making sure you lead a socially active life and having a positive attitude. But suppose none of that matters, and that the factors that determine which of us survive and which of us die are actually beyond our control?

We have already seen that if you are born female, you have a much better chance of reaching 100. Less obviously, there is whether you are right- or left-handed. The Queen Mother and George Burns were both said to be left-handed, but a study of Californians in 1991 suggested that left-handers have a much lower chance of reaching 100 than right-handers. Analysing the records of 987 people, it found right-handers survived on average to 75, while for left-handers the average age at death was only 66. The authors found hardly any left-handers among those who survived beyond 80. One obvious explanation is that left-handers have to survive in a world designed for right-handers, and so face more risk when using machines, for example, and an examination of 19,000 accidents needing hospital treatment did suggest that left-handers had a higher chance of being injured. But one of the authors of the California study, Professor Stanley Coren, argued the reasons went beyond this, saying there was evidence that left-handers weighed less at birth, and were more likely to suffer from allergies and weaker immune systems. Other scientists were sceptical, and suggested that if there was a difference in life expectancy, it was more likely to have resulted from the stress the left-handers in Coren's sample endured while they were growing up, as some adults tried to force them to become right-handed, and that left-handers were rarely now put under such pressures. A range of studies on whether left-handers die first was examined by two British statisticians in 2005. They concluded, 'left-handedness is associated with a small increase in the risk of death.'

It also seems that the month in which you are born can have an important effect. A study looking at Americans born in 1885, 1889 and 1891 examined how much longer they could expect to live when they got to the age of 80. Those with birthdays in April, May and June survived less well than those born in January and February. The authors acknowledged the reason was a matter of speculation. Was it because the worst weather might be expected in November and December, so people born earlier in the year got a longer run before they hit these hazardous months? The short answer is that we do not know, but the researchers did discover that after the age of 100, the effect disappears, 'indicating', they say, 'that centenarians indeed represent a selected population'.

Another unexpected indicator of longevity, at least for women, could be the age at which they have children. Elisabeth Bing, a pioneer of natural childbirth who died aged 100 in 2015, did not produce her first child until she was 40, and Princess Alice's younger son was born when she was 42. In 1997, Tom Perls and Ruth Fretts from Harvard Medical School studied a group of 132 women born in 1896, and concluded that those who survived to 100 were four times more likely to have had children in their forties than those who died in their seventies. A number of other studies have come to a similar conclusion. Perls and Fretts stressed that this does not mean that putting off childcare duties until later in life makes women live longer; more probably, it is genetics at work: 'the factors that allow certain older women naturally to conceive and bear children – a slow rate of aging and perhaps also a decreased susceptibility to the diseases associated with aging – also improve these women's chances of living a long time.'

So how much is our chance of reaching 100 determined by our genes? As we saw, the parents of the centenarians in the *TV Eye* sample lived about 30 per cent longer than the average for their generation, and a study of 365 people aged 90 by an American biostatistician suggested their parents and grandparents all had longer lives than average. Individual examples, though, can be a bit baffling. A 110-year-old

Boston woman named Rubye Cox had two sisters who also passed 100. Cecil Withers had one sister who lived to be over 100, and another who made it to 90, but her twin died young from tuberculosis, which also claimed one of Withers's brothers during the First World War. Another sister was killed by a flying bomb in 1944, while another brother died of bronchitis aged just seven. To try to answer the question of whether becoming a centenarian depends on your genes, in 2002 Tom Perls, along with the demographer John Wilmoth, studied 444 American families in which at least one person had lived to 100. They found that sisters of centenarians had an eight times better than average chance of reaching 100, while brothers of centenarians were seventeen times as likely to reach the milestone. A study of 360 Ashkenazi Jews by New York's Yeshiva University in 2015 produced less dramatic results, but it still showed that mothers of centenarians lived about five years longer than average, while there was also a tendency for centenarians' fathers to have longer lives. In the 1990s Swedish scientists studied identical twins who had been separated at birth and reared apart. If genes were the dominant factor, you would expect each pair to die at about the same age, but in fact there were variations big enough to lead the researchers to conclude that only about 20 to 30 per cent of our life span is determined genetically. Howard Friedman came to a similar conclusion: 'Genes constitute about one-third of the factors leading to long life. The other two-thirds have to do with lifestyles and chance.'

Still, 30 per cent is a sizeable portion, and as our knowledge of the human genome has advanced, so the search has intensified for specific genes that might give people a better chance of reaching 100. In 2001 Perls discovered an area on one of the 23 pairs of human chromosomes that was present in centenarians, but not in those who died younger. One of the odd things he had come across while studying more than 2,000 centenarians was that some people did 'horrendous damage to themselves over time with smoking and drinking' but still reached 100 (though that was 'very, very rare'), while others did 'everything right' but only made it into their eighties. In 2008 Perls speculated that this might be because the ones who died off had 'what we call "disease genes", some genetic variations that are relatively bad for them', while the survivors had the 'right combination of some really special genetic variations that we call "longevity enabling genes"'. Perls and his colleagues were on a 'mad hunt' for them, but it was proving 'a very complicated puzzle to tease out'. Two years later, the team reported they had discovered 150 variants in the genes of centenarians. As we saw, in the New England survey, just over 40 per cent of the centenarians appeared to have mechanisms that could delay the onset of diseases. The average age of diagnosis for centenarians in the study who had had cancer was just over 80, compared to 63 for the general population, and certain cancers were very rare among centenarians. And of the 244 centenarians in the Georgia study, only 9 per cent had ever suffered from diabetes. In 2013, Perls summed up what his team had learned so far:

> we've found a number of these variations that are potentially very interesting for how and why some people can live to such a very old age. We've also seen that longevity isn't just because you have one or two of these rare variants, but probably many. What makes these people rare is that you have to get the right combination of these variants. It's kind of like winning the lottery.

Other scientists have also been on the trail of longevity genes. Some have uncovered different genes related to long life in different populations – some in French, German and Italian centenarians, some in Japanese from Okinawa – which seemed to protect them against autoimmune diseases such as rheumatoid arthritis and multiple sclerosis. Nir Barzilai from the Albert Einstein College of Medicine found that 24 per cent of Ashkenazi Jewish centenarians had a genetic variation that was linked to lower prevalence of high blood pressure and heart disease. Researchers investigating Japanese American men in Hawaii discovered that a variation in the gene FOXO3A seemed to double or triple the chance of reaching 100. Dutch researchers pieced together the complete DNA sequence of Hendrikje van Andel-Schipper, who had left her body to medical science. They discovered that her body showed no sign of furring of the arteries, and her brain no trace of dementia. Indeed, when her mental skills were tested at the age of 113, she had produced the performance you would normally expect from someone in their sixties or seventies. The researchers surmised that her genes had protected her. Van Andel-Schipper had been born prematurely and had not been expected to survive. At the age of 100, she beat breast cancer.

Scientists from the University of Southern Denmark took a different tack. In 2009 they showed pictures of 387 pairs of twins in their seventies, eighties and nineties to volunteers and asked them to guess their ages. Thirty-five years earlier, Bucke and Insley had noted how centenarians looked young for their age, and when Gertrude Baines became the world's oldest human at the age of 114, another woman at the same nursing home said she looked 'wonderful, and with hardly any wrinkles'. Now the Danes found that the twins who were considered younger-looking in their survey tended to outlive their siblings. The researchers, led by Professor Kaare Christensen, said it could be that those who had had the hardest lives looked older, but they also considered a genetic explanation, involving our telomeres – the sections of DNA that protect the ends of our chromosomes from decay. The shorter they are, the older we look, and the poorer our cells are at replicating, which means we tend to die earlier. The twins in the study who looked younger had longer telomeres.

But finding the factors in our genetic make-up that might help us live to 100 is proving anything but straightforward. Research on 153 centenarians in four different regions of Italy, for example, showed that in three of the areas, centenarians had high levels of vitamin A and vitamin E, but the same did not apply to the 100-year-olds from Sardinia. So, if the scientists are still not sure, to what do the 100-year-olds themselves attribute their long lives? When the question was put to van Andel-Schipper, she replied tartly, 'breathing'; but others offered different answers. George Burns credited dancing close to young girls and 'smoking fifteen cheap cigars a day'. Quite a number swore by particular foods or drinks. Sydney Platt, a 101-year-old Briton, paid tribute to porridge and sherry – his 'one and only tipple'. Luke Dolan, once Ireland's oldest man, said the secret was a boiled egg every day, plenty of sugar in his tea and a devoted wife. For the Rev. Peter Humphrey, it was not a specific food, but 'moderation in all things. I do not over-eat or over-drink or over-smoke.' And the American Marge Jetton said her formula was taking 'care of my body as well as I know how'.

Others, like Ella Scotchmer, cited attitude: 'I endeavour to forget everything that's unpleasant . . . You must forgive and have no resentment. I make the best of things. I have no regrets.' The recipe according to Maud Ford, a 100-year-old former hospital administrator from London, was 'taking things lightly, not worrying too much. Everyone has worries, but some people make theirs bigger.' The American Besse Cooper, at one time the world's oldest human, said it was down to minding her own business. Some were more fatalistic. Gertrude Baines referred the question to God, saying, 'Ask Him', while a 105-year-old

British woman, who survived a serious road accident when she was 89, put it in a more secular way: 'There's no secret. I think your lifespan is decided immediately you're conceived. You don't go before your time.' An American couple aged 101 and 102 attributed their longevity to good genes, while Lucy d'Abreu, the oldest person in Britain when she died aged 113 in 2005, claimed bafflement: 'God alone knows why I have been given such a long life. I have done nothing useful.'

Several surveys have asked centenarians for their recipe for long life. In the Korean centenarian study of 2005, the favourite explanation, given by 40 per cent of the sample, was eating moderately. Six years later, in the Yeshiva University study of Ashkenazi Jewish centenarians, a third said longevity ran in their family, while a fifth mentioned physical activity, just ahead of the 19 per cent who put it down to having a positive attitude. In its survey from 2013, UnitedHealthcare asked what the secret of healthy ageing was, allowing the centenarians to choose more than one answer. At the top, with 98 per cent, was keeping an active mind, while staying mobile and exercising came next, with 96 per cent.

Back in 1985, we asked the 100 centenarians in the *TV Eye* survey for their answers. The favourite, chosen by fourteen, was 'absence of stress'. By contrast, thirteen centenarians attributed their survival to hard work. A woman who had toiled in domestic service for 40 years reminisced, 'I was here, there and everywhere. They used to call me Lightning.' Some were still active. A former suffragette who said she had specialized in 'smashing windows' and had served time in prison was still a school governor and had taken part in a campaign to save her local post office. Her prescription was: 'I eat well, and I'm busy. I use my brain. You could fade if you don't use it.' Other explanations offered were 'leading a good life', from nine respondents, and 'God's will', from six. Mary Gray from Glasgow, who had never married (she described herself as 'an unclaimed jewel'), seemed to subscribe to both. She spent much of her time visiting people, almost always younger than her, who were housebound. On the day we filmed her, she was going to see a 77-year-old. Gray said the most important thing was 'to be kind to each other', adding that you also had 'to do right for the Heavenly Father . . . That's the secret. And God is with me all the time.'

SEVEN

The Lives of 100-year-olds

I n Jonas Jonasson's best-selling Swedish novel *The Hundred-year-old Man Who Climbed Out of the Window and Disappeared* (2009), the hero, among other things, escapes from a retirement home, steals a suitcase containing a fortune, kills a homicidal thug who is pursuing him by getting an elephant to sit on him, marries, and agrees to help Indonesia make an atomic bomb. It is fair to assume that not many real centenarians have lives like this. So what do they do all day? How many are able to live on their own? Are they healthy? Are they happy? Are they glad to have lived to 100?

At 103, Ella Scotchmer from Fulham in London was for a time believed to be the oldest person in Britain still living alone. A reporter who met her described her scurrying around 'like a squirrel – agile, lively, and robust'. She could still make it to the shops, although, she said, 'I have to stop if I've walked too far', and though Meals on Wheels brought food for her during the week, she cooked for herself at weekends. Also aged 103, Arthur Boylin from Deptford in south London was living in the same flat that had been his home for nearly 40 years. He had diabetes, but said he was able to keep his independence thanks to an emergency communications system run by his local council. The centenarian wore an alarm around his neck that enabled him to call for help at any time of the day or night. He said that once he fell in the bath, and an ambulance was there in ten minutes: 'It's great, and gives me a feeling of security, and independence.' A lifelong bachelor, Boylin had no close family nearby, but he did have good friends and neighbours. A carer came round two days a week, but Boylin did his own shopping and cooking. Sidney Platt, aged 101, from Havering in east London, also lived alone, but complained that his family, who were worried about him, kept trying to get him to 'sell up'. Lucy d'Abreu, who survived to 113, managed to live on her own until she was 106. Then a bad fall meant she had to move into a nursing home, while Gertrude Baines, at one time the oldest person in the world, kept her independence until she was 107, when she broke her hip. Dina Manfredini from Iowa, who had a two-week reign as the world's oldest person before her death in 2014, did better still, living independently until she was 110, while in 2016, the oldest person in the world, a 116-year-old Italian woman, Emma Morano, was still living alone in the same small apartment that had been her home for 90 years, though she had not been able to go out for the last 25.

So much for individual examples. What do the statistics tell us? Among the admittedly small sample in Marjorie Bucke and Morag Insley's pioneering work, half of the centenarians were still living at home, though they usually had continuous care from a son or a daughter. But one blind 100-year-old lived alone in a group of dwellings looked after by a warden, who brought in meals. Of the researchers' 38 centenarians, two had Meals on Wheels and one a home help. The authors remarked that the centenarians were from 'the self-help generation – all expected to stand on their own feet'. In the *TV Eye* survey, eleven of the 100 centenarians still lived alone, while sixteen were with family members, and the remainder in care homes. A study of 38 Italian centenarians in the Padua region published in 1998 found that 24 were still living at home, though only one lived alone. Half of those questioned needed help with some daily tasks, such as shopping, taking medicine and using the telephone, but only seven were completely dependent on others. As expected, the male centenarians were fewer in number, but a higher proportion of them had stayed out of institutions. Research from Australia from 2001 showed that 27 per cent of centenarian men and 14 per cent of women were still living alone in their own homes, with another 52 per cent of the men and 24 per cent of the women living with a partner or other family member. And according to the u.s. Census Bureau in 2010, 33 per cent of male centenarians and 34 per cent of female ones were still living alone at home. Perhaps even more striking is a survey of 32 supercentenarians by the University of Southern California, which concluded that two in five 'required minimal assistance or were independent', while the remainder were wholly or partially dependent.

Other surveys paint a more dependent picture. Figures from South Korea from 2010 showed that fewer than 10 per cent of centenarians lived alone, most of the others being with their families. From its examination of the lives of centenarians between 1988 and 2009, the Georgia Centenarian Study reported that although about a quarter were 'vibrant and full of life', up to 70 per cent had a disability of some kind, and most were 'completely dependent'. Figures on where English centenarians breathe their last breath do not suggest independence is common, either. In 2014 academics from King's College London examined nearly 36,000 death certificates of centenarians and people in their eighties and nineties from 2001 to 2010. More than 61 per cent of the centenarians had died in care or nursing homes, more than 27 per cent in hospital, and just 9 per cent had passed away at home. The proportion dying in hospital in England was much higher than in the Netherlands and Finland, but in both of those countries the majority of centenarians shuffled off this mortal coil in care homes – 90 per cent in the Netherlands, and 76 per cent in Finland.

Though fewer people reach 100 in developing than in developed countries, there are some studies suggesting that those who do are more likely to be able to live independently. One found that centenarians in three Chinese cities were more active than those in Denmark. Experts from China and the United States who reviewed a large range of surveys speculated the reason might be that because there were fewer facilities to help old people in developing countries, it might force them 'to perform daily activities by themselves, and the frequent exercise may enable them to maintain their physical capacities for a longer time'.

You might expect independence and good health to be closely linked, but a survey of 207 Danish centenarians in 2001 found that the 25 living alone appeared to have just as many illnesses as the rest. The researchers uncovered only one centenarian they considered to be free from any illness or chronic condition; of the remainder, nearly three-quarters had cardiovascular disease, and just over half had arthritis. In addition, 60 per cent had been treated for a serious illness. Analysis of the Georgia centenarian data revealed that those centenarians who had been in poorer health in childhood were most likely to complain of health problems once they passed the century, while poorer health was also likely to be reported by those centenarians who had experienced the most 'negative events', such as the death of a spouse or child. In the Italian study of 1998, all the centenarians were on some kind of medication, and one was taking fifteen different types, while a Portuguese survey of 50 centenarians in the Porto area concluded that just a couple could be considered 'robust', with 30 'frail'. The researchers described the rest as 'pre-frail'.

When it comes to individual centenarians, we know of plenty who seem to have been pretty fit, such as the retired Californian nurse Marge Jetton, who at 104 was still walking a mile a day, riding an exercise bike and lifting weights. Her only afflictions were high blood pressure and 'bad eyes'. Some studies too were more optimistic on health. Bucke and Insley regarded those in their small sample as 'mainly healthy', and in his New England study Tom Perls said the centenarians made fewer calls upon medical services than did people who died in their seventies and eighties. This, he argued, disproved 'the perception that the older you get the sicker you get. Centenarians teach us that the older you get the healthier you have been.' In 2010 a professor of nursing, Tina Koch, and her colleagues interviewed sixteen centenarians across the UK, noting that if their subjects had suffered illness, 'it had predominantly been in the past two years', though a number of the women complained about chronic arthritis, which they had 'learned to self-manage'. But because the centenarians in the sample had to be able to cope with a fairly elaborate interview process, it might be they were not typical, and enjoyed better health than the average 100-year-old.

As we have seen, when it comes to health, some experts divide centenarians into three categories: those who escape the diseases of old age, those who delay them and those who survive them. The American study of 32 supercentenarians found that only two had suffered heart attacks and four had suffered strokes, while eight had suffered from, but survived, cancer. And the King's College study of 36,000 death certificates showed that relatively few centenarians were killed by cancer or heart disease. What they did die of, according to their death certificates, was: 'old age' – 28 per cent; pneumonia or other respiratory diseases – 24 per cent; stroke – 10 per cent; and Alzheimer's disease – 6 per cent. The lead author, Dr Catherine Evans, commented that the centenarians were 'a group living with increasing frailty'. So different studies seem to point to different conclusions, and a broad survey of the available evidence by the UK's International Longevity Centre published in 2011 advised caution, noting that any overall judgment about the health of centenarians was 'compromised by the small sample sizes of many studies, and by a dearth of in-depth research'. The authors were particularly concerned that studies might present too favourable a picture because those with poor mental and physical health were the least likely to be involved.

Centenarians themselves often give quite upbeat assessments of their health. In the Georgia study, nearly 20 per cent rated it as excellent, and more than 52 per cent said it was good. Some commentators suggested that this might not mean centenarians were *actually* healthier, and that perhaps, having outlived so many other people, they felt they *must* be enjoying better health. Or, it might be another indicator of that positive attitude we have heard so much about. 'People who think they are ageing well are not necessarily the healthiest individuals,' said Dilip Jeste, professor of psychiatry and neurosciences at the University of California, San Diego: 'Optimism and effective coping strategies were found to be more important to ageing successfully than traditional measures of health and wellness.' Indeed, the Italian study of 1998 revealed that centenarians had just as many painful conditions as those aged 75 to 85, but they were only half as likely to complain about them. Daniella Jopp, who worked on a survey of 91 centenarians living around Heidelberg in the early years of this century, said they had dealt with ill health by adapting: 'They often have chronic diseases, but they don't seem to suffer as much as younger people do, because they change their attitudes . . . For them, it's a blessing that they can still be alive.' And a study of Chinese centenarians indicated they were more likely to have positive views of their health than were people in their eighties and nineties.

One of people's greatest fears about reaching the age of 100 is dementia. It had certainly not afflicted Mary Padley, who at 104 was known as the 'wonder of Walworth' (the area of south London where she lived) thanks to her spontaneous wit, good memory and agile mind, wrapped up in a four-foot-nine-inch (1.45 m), seven-stone (44 kg) body. Equally, when Lucy Askew was Britain's oldest person at the age of 114, she was described as 'very much with it' right up until the day she died, while the American Besse Cooper, also 114 and for a time the oldest person in the world, was said still to have a very good memory. Among the men, Sir Robert Mayer, who remained chair of the organization Youth and Music until he was 101, felt his mental faculties had not changed in half a century: 'so far as force of thinking goes, it's the same as 50 years ago.' Bucke and Insley said of their subjects, 'their memories were in fact very reliable where it was possible to check,' while Tina Koch said none of her sixteen subjects was 'intellectually frail', though as we have explained, her study might present an untypically optimistic picture. These various encouraging snapshots have led some to theorize that centenarians might be spared Alzheimer's disease and dementia because these conditions tend to kill people before they reach 100.

Unfortunately, some studies have presented a less encouraging picture, and even quite mentally sharp centenarians have admitted that while their remembrance of things long ago remains bright, their short-term memory fades, with Lady McFadyean commenting: 'Memory from today and yesterday, that goes, but one's memory of a long way back gets clearer.' At least half the centenarians in the Georgia and Danish studies had some form of dementia, while Tom Perls said just 13 per cent of the New England centenarians were 'cognitively intact'. In the Heidelberg study, just over half suffered from dementia while a quarter were 'cognitively intact', but these figures might present too favourable a picture because 65 subjects were excluded from the survey owing to dementia or severe health problems, or because they might find the interview too stressful. The authors also recorded that centenarians often suffered a marked decline in mental ability in the six months before they died. (They also noted a tendency to a marked physical decline 21 months before death.)

As with health generally, the picture is far from clear. One review of the statistical evidence in 2010 said the number of centenarians with dementia was 'still being debated', with figures ranging from 27 to 100 per cent. Another review of studies published the following year put the range at 0 to 50 per cent. There is some evidence, though it is not conclusive, that a higher proportion of women centenarians than men suffer from Alzheimer's disease. One reason may be that men tend to die more quickly after developing the condition. But even dementia had its compensations for one centenarian, who was born in Cyprus and then lived in the UK for over half a century without ever learning to speak English. When he moved into a care home, his daughter said he loved it, because he thought he was in a hotel in Cyprus.

As well as loss of mental ability, loss of sight also features in Shakespeare's spine-tingling evocation of what he saw as the seventh, and final, age of man:

Last scene of all,
That ends this strange eventful history,
Is second childishness and mere oblivion;
Sans teeth, sans eyes, sans taste, sans every thing.

Grace Earll, aged 101 and from Sussex, told how she used to love reading and sewing but that her eyes were no longer up to it, lamenting: 'I don't want to do nothing! If I don't do anything, I fall asleep, and I don't want to!' Ella Scotchmer said she did not feel her age until her eyesight went, while Julia Johnson, of the Open University's Centre for Ageing, recounted how her own mother had been determined to live to 100, and that when she reached the landmark, she still had a good appetite and was 'very social', but that her sight began to fail so that 'even eating became difficult'. Johnson remarked that because of their disabilities, 'it's very rare to see a very old person at a family celebration. In many ways the oldest old are invisible.'

In the late 1980s the British sociologists Michael Bury and Anthea Holme studied 93 women and 90 men over the age of 90. They found that 45 per cent reported 'severe' or 'relatively severe' problems with their eyes, but the proportion who said they had difficulty hearing was even higher, at 49 per cent. Bucke and Insley's impression of their centenarians was that poor hearing had a more isolating effect than loss of sight: 'failure of vision did not cut them off from mental stimuli in the way that failure of hearing did.' The importance of hearing was illustrated by Christian Mortensen, who coped with his blindness by listening to the radio, especially when it was covering baseball. On the other hand, among Tina Koch's centenarians it was the loss of sight that seemed to have more impact. Hearing problems, she said, could be combated by modern technology, while 'not being able to read, or to connect with the world outside when vision had deteriorated, was experienced as a great loss.'

So what do centenarians do all day? The wide variety of activities he found among 100-year-olds in New England prompted Tom Perls to write: 'The most vigorous centenarians in our study have not shipwrecked on the shore of their 100th birthdays, but arrived in full sail, taking on new challenges.' Bucke and Insley noted that many of their centenarians liked walking, and speculated that this form of exercise might be related to mental alertness. They quoted even earlier work by the American sociology professor Belle Boone Beard, who noted that many 100-year-olds still walked, if only around their rooms – though one had gone rather further, wedding a 72-year-old woman and taking her on a walking holiday in the Ozark Mountains. Walking was very important, said this centenarian, because 'few people die on their feet.'

In the *TV Eye* survey, reading was the centenarians' most popular pastime, chosen by eleven interviewees. That was followed by seven who picked watching television and chatting, but 36 mentioned no activity. Kamato Hongo from Japan, the world's oldest human at the time of her 115th birthday, celebrated the landmark by sleeping. She completely missed her party because her life followed a pattern of two days spent asleep followed by two days awake, and the big day fell on one of the days allocated to sleep. Even when she was awake, she had trouble hearing and was bedridden, though she could still move her arms to perform a traditional dance. Similarly, when Gertrude Baines passed her 114th birthday, she slept most of the day, while a third holder of the 'oldest human' title, Besse Cooper, was said by her son to spend 80 per cent of her time sleeping. The former London dentist David Arkush, a relative youngster at 100, named sleeping as one of his favourite activities.

But not every centenarian takes things so easy, and plenty seem to make sure they add 'life to years' and not just years to life, as the saying goes. When he was the world's oldest man, the 112-year-old Japanese man Tomoji Tanabe got up early, read his morning newspaper and wrote in his diary each evening. In Britain, a reporter who went to see 105-year-old Edith Robinson recounted that she answered the door herself, walking with a frame and 'beaming excitedly'. She had got married for the first time at the age of 82 and was then widowed two years later. Until a couple of years earlier, she had played the church organ every Sunday. Now she had to be content with writing letters and reading a little, though she could still play the piano, and go to church by taxi on Sundays. At 104, Mary Padley was still making cakes, ironing shirts for a neighbour and doing a spot of gardening.

Among Tina Koch's centenarians, one man was busy enough to have to consult his diary before he could fit in the interview. Another liked going to the theatre while yet another preferred dancing. One woman still went to art exhibitions, another to the pensioners' club with her son, another played bridge, while a sixth had carried on dancing and swimming past her 100th birthday. A seventh was campaigning against the proposed closure of her care home, an eighth against nuclear weapons. Not all activities were enjoyable. One man described himself as a full-time carer for his wife, eight years younger than him, who was blind. 'I am feeling the pressure of it,' he said, 'but I just get on with it.' In the UK, the Department for Work and Pensions team responsible for making sure centenarians get their 100th birthday greeting from the Queen, said they had heard of people celebrating the big day with 'street parties, hot air balloon rides, trips of a lifetime abroad, and even a pool party'.

None of that sounds as strenuous as the walker in the Ozarks, and just pottering around is plainly not good enough for quite a few centenarians. At 103, Ella Scotchmer was working with an Alexander Technique instructor twice a week, and reported that she had got an inch taller since she started doing the exercises. At the age of 101, one of the centenarians in the New England Study, Tom Spear, was said to have won an over-65s golf tournament with a highly respectable round of 86, and could still hit the ball 180 yards (1.65 m). More energetically still, as we have seen, Fauja Singh was running marathons after passing the century, Mieko Nagaoka was swimming record-breaking distances, while Frank Shearer, a retired doctor from Washington state, was waterskiing.

As the Department for Work and Pensions noted, another activity on some centenarian agendas was travel. Among the record-breakers, we saw how, at 110, Charlotte Hughes from Cleveland in the north of England became the world's oldest air passenger. Ella Scotchmer travelled across America on Greyhound buses in her nineties, then visited the Canaries, the Caribbean and Majorca; and went on a Rhine cruise after she passed her century. Aged 100, Ruby Holt from Tennessee travelled 'only' 400 miles, but it allowed her to see the sea for the first time. Holt, who had spent most of her working life picking cotton, had been out of the state of her birth only once previously. Her care home organized the trip with help from a charity, and provided a special motorized wheelchair so she could go on the sand and, assisted by care workers, dip her toes in the ocean.

But for some, mental exercise matters just as much as physical. As we saw with the record-breakers, Mary Moody kept working as chair of a company until her death at 104, and David Henderson ran his farm until he was 107. They were not alone. James Kelly wrote a column for the *Irish Times* until he was 100, while Sir Robert Mayer, who continued as chair of Youth and Music until he was 101, remarked,

'I have by-passed old age. It doesn't worry me. I ignore it.' In Tokyo, Matsu Yamazaki carried on working in her family's grocery shop until she was 103. She also did puzzles to keep her mind active, remarking, 'I just don't want to lose my mind . . . I know lots of people who've lost their memory. They go out and wander around town and can't find their way home.' At the age of 108, in New York, Irving Kahn, one of the few people who saw the 1929 stock market crash coming and made a lot of money out of it, was still going into the offices of his investment firm three days a week. In Somerset, the Rev. Peter Humphry celebrated his 100th birthday by delivering a sermon, and Leila Denmark from Athens, Georgia, was the world's oldest practising doctor when she retired at 103, after 70 years' service. At a pub in Wendover, Buckinghamshire, 100-year-old Dolly Saville was claimed to be the world's oldest barmaid, still pulling pints after her children had retired, saying she would get bored sitting at home all day, and that she preferred to keep her mind active.

Lots of others made sure they carried on exercising their brains outside the workplace. Chelsea Pensioner Joe Britton continued to play bridge, as did Lady McFadyean – for money. Britton also gambled, but for him, that meant gliding around to the bookmaker's on his mobility scooter. At 100, former Lancashire schoolmaster Alan Walsh was still a talented raconteur: 'the voice is strong and the laugh is big,' said one listener. Like Matsu Yamazaki in Tokyo, Winnie Langley of Croydon, south London, kept on doing crosswords and puzzles until her death at 102. Fred Moore from Hampshire was named Britain's oldest student, as he attended art classes until he was 107, while in east London, 100-year-old Sidney Platt carried on with the computer lessons he had started five years earlier to help him manage his investments better. While some continue with existing activities, others break new ground. In Wisconsin in 2015, Marie Hunt finally got her high school diploma at the age of 103. She had had to leave education at sixteen to take care of her eight younger brothers and sisters. The authors of the 1998 Italian study concluded that 'the most well-preserved people are those who remain intellectually stimulated,' as well as 'those who have spent years working in crafts requiring creative skills or who have kept their interests alive', though in addition they emphasized the importance of maintaining 'satisfactory social relationships' and being able to count on the help of family members and other caregivers.

Fauja Singh.

Continuing to look good was important for Fauja Singh. His 'only extravagance', he said, was clothes and shoes, of which he had 50 pairs: 'I like to look dapper.' Other male centenarians clearly enjoy remaining attractive to the opposite sex. For Sidney Platt, one of the perks of his computer classes was being able to impress female students with his knowledge: 'I always get a lovely smile from the ladies,' he said. Leonard 'Rosie' Ross was a trumpeter who carried on playing at a club in Arizona until past his 100th birthday. He used to say to his audience, 'I've always said life begins at 80. It gets better when you reach 90, but, oh when you reach 100!' He was quite a ladies' man, saying, 'there's something about me that girls like', and when he was 90, he had told a friend he still did 'everything I did when I was at college'. Whether interest in the opposite sex was at the root of their decision is not clear, but one gerontologist even told a story about a centenarian couple he knew who chose to get divorced. They said they had 'waited out of consideration for our children', putting it off 'until they all had died'. As we saw earlier, the oldest man ever to speak in the UK Parliament,

Lord Shinwell, admitted, a little reluctantly, that he had lost all sexual desire, and all of the Italian centenarians in the 1998 study said they had completely lost interest in sex, while some in a comparative group aged 86 to 99 still professed some interest.

Often, rather than celebrating the things they are able to do, centenarians lament the things they can no longer enjoy. At the age of 100, former hospital administrator Maud Ford said she used to like going out for coffee with her daughter, 'but I can't go now because of my legs', while for former model Eileen Symonds, 'one of the saddest things is not being able to drive any more. I had a prang at 98. It wasn't my fault but the car was messed up, and that was the end really.' Still, as we saw, nearly 200 centenarians in the UK hold driving licences. Muriel Fieldus from Shoreham, West Sussex, who died aged 106, also felt frustrated: 'I wish I could do more. You can't do the things you want to do. If I could do anything now, I wouldn't be in a care home. I'd like to do a bit of travelling. I've been abroad – one or two places – but I would like to do more. I'd like to go to places like India or China.' Another thing missing for many 100-year-olds is money. An American study from 1999 suggested that 21 per cent of male centenarians and 25 per cent of female ones were living in poverty.

Not surprisingly, loneliness is a problem for many. If we look at the record-breakers, many outlived their spouses, often by considerable margins – Alice Herz-Sommer by 70 years, Jeanne Calment by 55, Jiroemon Kimura by more than 40 years, Henry Allingham for just short of 40, while Harry Patch was widowed twice, and Lord Shinwell three times. Because women tend to live longer than men, they are also more likely to be widowed. An Australian study in 2008 showed that only one centenarian woman in twenty had a living spouse, while for male centenarians the figure was one in five. Among the centenarians in the King's College study, 85 per cent were widowed, while in the Georgia Centenarian Study more than 87 per cent had experienced the loss of a spouse. It is not unusual for centenarians to outlive their children, either, like Henry Allingham, Harry Patch and Alice Herz-Sommer, or their children and grandchildren, like Jeanne Calment. Of the Georgia centenarians, 32 per cent had outlived a child.

Violet Butler lost her husband in the D-Day landings when she was 29. She never remarried, instead devoting herself to bringing up the two children her husband had left her: 'You get lonely sometimes, but I've worked and kept healthy, although now I'm taking too many damn pills.' Maud Ford said, 'The saddest thing about getting old is you gradually lose bits of yourself. Your friends, brothers and sisters. I'm the only one left.' Naomi Mitchison, a former novelist, socialist, feminist and bon vivante, took a similar note, noting tearfully, 'Most of my friends are dead, most of the ones I knew so well are gone.' Among them were Aldous Huxley and E. M. Forster. Mitchison had been married for 50 years, but it was an 'open' relationship, and she had had many lovers: 'I'm afraid I did things everyone thought wrong – and I enjoyed it.' At 100 she complained, 'It's annoying to be too old for a love affair.' Muriel Fieldus also said she had lost all her friends.

That sad refrain, 'all my friends have gone,' was heard a lot from the over-nineties in Bury and Holme's study, with about half saying they no longer had any friends. On the other hand, 60 per cent said they never felt lonely. Perhaps it is down to that positive thinking again. For some centenarians, a care home was an antidote to loneliness, with Bella Storer from Ealing, west London, declaring: 'It's lovely. There's company.' And at the age of 101, in a care home in Sussex, Alf Arnold found romance, marrying an 81-year-old woman whom he met there. Lord Shawcross, the lead British prosecutor at the Nuremberg trials, wanted to get married for a third time when he was 95. He had already been widowed twice. The woman he chose was a long-standing friend, 25 years younger than him. His family opposed the union, so Shawcross and his bride eloped to Gibraltar and tied the knot there, spending six years together until his death at 101.

The Georgia survey showed that the more children a centenarian had, the less lonely they felt and the more active they were likely to be. Tina Koch also told the story of one centenarian in her study who had had no children of her own, but always seemed to be surrounded by great-nephews and great-nieces. For another, friends as well as family were the antidote to loneliness: 'Living to be 100 wasn't my idea. I've just enjoyed life and go on enjoying it. I celebrated my 100th birthday with a big lunch party for friends and family. I've been awfully fortunate with friends and relatives.'

In the *TV Eye* survey, we asked the centenarians if they were glad to have reached 100; 74 said they were, against eighteen who were not. Michael Bury offered the explanation that once you approached the century, 'a special effect takes hold. The increased threat of disability, dependence and death is matched with celebration and a sense of achievement.' Edith Robinson, who was still living alone at 105, enjoyed the fact that other people recognized her achievement: 'It's very nice when you get past 100. I get made more of now than I've ever been in my life.' Bill Proctor, who at the age of sixteen had walked from the Cumbrian coast to the Wirral to find a job, had every right to feel satisfaction. After his epic walk, he fought at the Somme, continuing to have nightmares about it until late in life. His granddaughter said he was proud of being the oldest man in Britain, but also 'amazed he managed to live so long'. Among Tina Koch's interviewees, a 104-year-old woman recalled: 'when I turned 100, that was a lovely feeling. We had all these different events and all the excitement, which was great. I got over 200 cards. We had a party and people came from all over the world.' Mary Padley said that for her, life began at 100: 'I've always been cheerful and never thought much about myself. I have more friends now than I ever had. Life is great . . . And I hope it never stops.' When a reporter asked supercentenarian Ellen Watson, aged 110, whether she liked all the attention her great age brought, she answered, 'Absolutely!' When he left, she kissed his hand. Lady McFadyean thought she had had a 'wonderful life', and her granddaughter summed her up like this: 'she has a curious and enchanting innocence. A hundred years of the world haven't made her cynical . . . She is never cantankerous, testy, or querulous.' Another centenarian still enjoying life was 106-year-old Gwen Lelas. In a Hampshire rest home, she quoted an old radio catchphrase: 'It's being so cheerful as keeps me going,' adding her own philosophical comment: 'Anything that comes along, I'm willing to accept it.'

This ability to handle life's triumphs and disasters impressed Tina Koch. She said the centenarians she and her colleagues interviewed were able 'to accept their losses, grieve and then move on'. A number talked about being able to handle change, 'coping', 'carrying on' or 'getting on with it'. Daniela Jopp from the Heidelberg study said she was struck that the centenarians 'were so happy despite the fact that they've gone through many things, and their lives are pretty much characterized by losses and difficulties'. Some had 'goals and projects that they pursue'; others derived meaning in life from being able to contribute to the happiness of friends and family. The Italian study showed that the older people got, the more satisfied they seemed with life, with the centenarians more content than the 86- to 99-year-olds, and that group happier than the 75- to 85-year-olds.

The journalist who interviewed Edith Robinson spoke to four other centenarians, and said all of them seemed to share that view that once you get past about 80, you stop feeling any older. Minnie Franklin, who lived in a care home near Bristol, told her: 'Eighty, 90, 100. Makes no difference to me. I think I'm young now!' A similar sentiment came from Naomi Mitchison: 'I rather thought I was 77. I don't feel 100.' Across the Atlantic in Baltimore, Emmy Lou Taylor, aged 101, was playing bridge and downing the occasional cocktail. Still not needing to wear glasses and taking few medicines, she reported: 'I don't feel old at all. As long as I can yak and laugh, I'm happy.' The granddaughter of George Francis, who for a time was the oldest man in America, said he never talked about getting old. In the UnitedHealthcare survey of 2015, 60 per cent of the centenarians said they did not feel old; when asked what age they felt, the average answer was 79.

Of course, moods change, and even those who are generally glad to have reached 100 may at times be depressed by their limitations. One 105-year-old woman said, 'The best part of my life actually is now.' But although she could still live in her own home, and get around unaided, she was often frustrated: 'I tire easily now, which rather spoils things. I get cross with myself.' And while Sidney Platt might still enjoy getting compliments from the ladies, he was also irritated because there were so many things that he used to be able to do that he could not do any longer: 'I haven't the strength . . . It's a bit of a tragedy – age really, isn't it?' A 113-year-old woman from Portugal sounded an even more dispiriting note: 'I don't know what to do with my life. I am old. I am very sick. I would like to be younger. Younger is better.' And, as we have seen, centenarians can be heard to grumble about the many things their lives now lack: driving, going out for coffee, travelling; or for others, playing cricket or bowls, climbing or walking, enjoying a garden or the countryside.

So how to sum up what you can expect if you are one of the 'super-survivors' who make it to 100? Can you hang on to your independence? Well, we know of centenarians up to the age of 116 who have managed it, and in the u.s. more than a third of centenarians seem to be still living alone, but most other studies suggest much smaller numbers, with the figure from Padua, for example, being lower than 3 per cent. As for health, we have seen some centenarians who are the picture of health, but many others who have multiple illnesses. Experts in the field warn how difficult it is to draw general conclusions. Back in the 1970s, Bucke and Insley described their 100-year-olds as 'mainly healthy', but the Danish study of 2001 found just one centenarian in 200 who was free from illness, while somewhere in the middle, the Georgia survey said about a quarter were 'vibrant and full of life'. The question of how likely a 100-year-old is to suffer from dementia produces no clearer answers. Again, we have striking stories of individual centenarians remaining sharp after their 100th or 110th birthdays, and in the case of world record-breaker Jeanne Calment, even her 120th. But overall, reviews of the available research put the number of centenarians suffering from dementia at anything between 0 and 100 per cent, which is not very helpful. Perhaps the best indication we have is that the Danish, Georgia and Heidelberg studies all come up with a figure of around 50 per cent. One interesting fact that emerges when we consider independence and health is that what men lose on the swings of quantity, they may gain on the roundabouts of quality. In other words, though fewer of them may live to be 100, those who do may have healthier and more independent lives when they get there.

Looking at individual stories provides a genuinely impressive list of the things centenarians are still able to do – travelling, dancing, running, swimming, campaigning, going to the theatre, going to work, baking, gardening, learning and getting the qualifications they had missed when they were young. But these cannot be seen as typical. In the *TV Eye* survey, more than a third of centenarians did not refer to any favourite activity, and the most popular ones were unspectacular – reading, chatting, watching television. With up to 90 per cent of centenarians having lost a spouse, and more than 30 per cent in the Georgia study having outlived a child, it is not surprising that loneliness was a problem for many, and yet in Bury and Holme's study of over-nineties, 60 per cent said they never felt lonely. But this was just another example of a positive attitude, like centenarians' tendency to complain less about poor health than people much younger. Indeed, their positive outlook is perhaps the most impressive thing about the lives of centenarians, with those glad to have reached 100 outnumbering those who were not by more than five to one in the *TV Eye* survey. Having others see their survival as an achievement was an important element in these positive feelings.

So, finally, what about death? Lord Shinwell made it clear that he was not afraid of it, though he was curious about what, if anything, came afterwards. Pearl Cantrell's daughter said her mother never talked about dying, and one of Tina Koch's centenarians said, 'I don't think of death. I think of living and what I am going to do and what I am going to enjoy.' But the American Walter Breuning, who lived to 114 and was for a time the world's oldest man, stressed that we should not be afraid of dying: 'Some people are scared of dying. Never be afraid to die. Because you're born to die.' Studying the Heidelberg centenarians, Daniella Jopp said they had 'no problem talking about death and dying. They have their last wills and they're fully prepared, but they still want to stick around. They say they enjoy life.' Part of the reason for the absence of fear might be, she thought, that as 'supersurvivors' they had seen the deaths of so many people close to them. At 103, Arthur Boylin from south London said, 'I am very happy, not afraid of death, and know I want to die here,' referring to the flat where he had spent nearly 40 years. Nor was Grace Earll afraid, declaring: 'The time goes faster and faster. I'm prepared for death. I don't fear it . . . I'm ready to go up there, or down there. It doesn't worry me a scrap. I've had my ups and downs. I've done what I can for others.'

Among Bury and Holme's 90-pluses, just 4 per cent said they feared death, but there were other worries. Fourteen per cent were afraid of declining health, and more still – 24 per cent – feared becoming a burden on others. Perhaps that was in Violet Butler's mind when she said, 'If anything goes wrong, I want to die quickly. If I go funny, I don't want to live on.' And other centenarians not only did not fear death, they would have welcomed it; they had had enough. Charlotte Gibson, who was Britain's second-oldest person when she died aged 110, had outlived both her children. Having had to give up her flat six years earlier, her view of her life span was, 'It's a bit too long. I think a hundred is quite sufficient.' But she resigned herself to God's will: 'He doesn't want me up there, so I have to be content down here.' Sir Robert Mayer confessed he was depressed by the state of the world, and Ella Scotchmer had similar feelings, noting sadly, 'I'm ready to go now. There's too much violence in the world, you can't trust anybody. Things are getting worse.' Others, though, were definitely in no hurry. Bucke and Insley's centenarians included a man who had left school at twelve, who said there were so many wonderful things going on in the world that he was keen to stay. If anything, Naomi Mitchison was even more enthusiastic: 'When you wake up, it's rather good to find you're still alive. You feel like that when you wake up in the middle of the night. I'd like to live another hundred years.'

EIGHT

Location, Location!

'My name is Herbert Badgery. I am a hundred and thirty-nine years old and something of a celebrity.' So begins the novel *Illywhacker* (1985) by the Australian writer Peter Carey. In the course of the narrative, we are given information about dates of events and the age of the conman hero at the time they happened, which do not seem to tally with the stupendous longevity he claims. Then, finally, all is made clear. The book ends with him being exhibited in a bizarre human zoo, where he tells us, 'The chart on my door says I am a hundred and thirty-nine years old. It also says I was born in 1886, but there are no complaints. The customers are happy.'

Herbert Badgery is a fictional character, but, as we have seen, some real people have claimed feats of longevity that would knock 122-year-old Jeanne Calment's world record into a cocked hat. In England, in the fifteenth, sixteenth and seventeenth centuries, Thomas Parr was supposed to have lived to 152. But that was nothing compared with Henry Jenkins from North Yorkshire, who was said to have survived to 169. And that is just in England. People in Persia, China, ancient Iraq and so on claimed far more outlandish ages – but that was all a long time ago. Surely, you might think, as we got closer to the present day, claims of extreme longevity would have started to fade away. In fact, legends of incredible age have themselves proved to have extraordinary longevity, along with the idea that there are remote, simple, idyllic corners of the world where primitive folk live to ages we can only dream of.

So it was that in 1929, the *Evening Independent* in St Petersburg, Florida, printed a 'remarkable' story from the 'veracious' Associated

Press about a Chinese man named Li Ching-Yun, born in 1667, who was 'still going strong' at the age of '252'. It reported that the documents on which this claim was based were 'well authenticated', and that the Chinese government had marked his 100th and 200th birthdays. The paper predicted Li Ching-Yun would survive to 300. He had outlived 23 wives, and was now living with his 24th, it said, a spring chicken of 60. The secret of his longevity was that in the mountains of Yunnan, he had discovered 'herbs which prevent the ravages of old age'. There is a touch of the Herbert Badgery about this story. For example, if the figures given by the newspaper were right, Li Ching-Yun would have been 262, not 252. Another source quotes him as having died in 1928, 'aged 250', while still another claimed he lived on until 1933, though that one said he had not been born until 1736, making him 'only' 197.

And even in the modern era, since the Second World War, official bodies have continued to be prepared to endorse highly unlikely sounding feats of longevity. In 1956 the Colombian government issued a postage stamp to commemorate Javier Pereira, who was allegedly 167 – no less than half a century older than the oldest authenticated man. A member of the Zenú tribe, Pereira was said to have been born in 1789 – the year of the French Revolution and of George Washington becoming the United States' first president. He stood four feet four inches (132 cm) tall and weighed less than six stone (38 kg), and he had outlived five wives as well as all his children and grandchildren. The Pereira stamp was spotted by Doug Storer, an American who wrote a newspaper column entitled 'Amazing but True'. Storer recounted that the Colombian's 'great age' was confirmed by 'the authorities of Monteria', the town where he lived. They apparently had 'several written records' plus 'statements by other very ancient Zenu Indians'. In the journalist's view, though, the 'best evidence' was the old man's detailed accounts of events from the early 1800s. As he could not read or write, 'only first-hand experience' could explain this knowledge, Storer maintained.

Still, just to be sure, the writer brought Pereira to New York for ten days of medical tests. When really bizarre events occur, journalists have a saying: 'you couldn't make it up'; Pereira's visit to America would certainly fall into this category. At a news conference, he reportedly behaved like a 'pint-sized volcano'. At one point, he got bored with proceedings and told his interpreter, 'I'm getting the hell out of here.' He was persuaded to stay and sit next to a blonde woman who held his hand 'fervently'. The old man also took exception to this after a while, and aimed a slap at her. A press agent gallantly intervened and took the blow himself. But Pereira had not finished yet: he also took a swing at a photographer, and hit a male journalist, who noted ruefully, 'Believe me, it hurt.'

The tests to determine Pereira's age were done at a New York hospital. Its verdict was: 'Although medical science possesses at present no method of determining the exact age of any adult, non-medical evidence indicates that Mr Pereira is indeed a very old man, and that possibly he may be more than 150 years of age.' The hospital added that 'His skin is like that of an old man, but shows no more of the effects of age than of most men of 70,' while a reporter noted that he had no teeth, but that he was blessed with a 'complete crop of dark hair only interspersed with grey'. The hospital also noted that Pereira could still dance, but that his eyesight was 'slightly impaired'. In view of events at the press conference, it was also interesting that the doctors commented that Pereira was 'gregarious and likes to meet people'. Storer said they told him they were astonished at how fit the old man was, with heart action, arteries and blood pressure like 'those of a healthy 20-year-old'. He was 'mentally alert' with an 'excellent' memory, and 'bones and joints in a condition that many a young man might envy'. Pereira's own recipe for long life was, 'Don't worry, drink lots of coffee, and smoke a good cigar.' Coffee, incidentally, is one of Colombia's main exports. According to Storer, the doctors came up with a similar explanation, minus the plug for coffee and cigars: 'he lived a natural life quite free of stress, his diet was a simple one of rice, vegetables and fruit, and he probably came from a tribe of unusually long-lived people.' An American newsreel endorsed Pereira as 'the oldest of us all', though it admitted even the old man himself was 'not sure about his age' and, of course, he had no birth certificate. Pereira died eighteen months later, with the *Chicago Tribune* noting that 'some persons claim he was 168'.

It is not only for individuals that claims of remarkable longevity are made. As we saw, one of the explanations offered for Javier Pereira's stupendous age was the supposed longevity of his tribe, and in their pioneering work on centenarians, Marjorie Bucke and Morag Insley noted how groups such as the 'Hunzas of "Shangri-La"' were said to live to extraordinary ages. Their remote valley in northern Pakistan, where the local language is not related to any other on earth, was reputed to be the inspiration for the isolated, harmonious land where people live long beyond our normal allotted span, created by the writer James Hilton for his novel *Lost Horizon* (1933). Travellers to the valley told stories of sickness being unknown there, and of people working the fields at the age of 140. Some attributed the Hunzas' longevity to eating the local apricots.

The small Ecuadorian town of Vilcabamba was also supposed to be full of centenarians, and it had another thing in common with the Hunza Valley: it was remote, being high up in the Andes. Scientists who arrived there in 1970 were astonished to find people surviving to more than 140, their ages apparently confirmed by baptismal records. The following year, the provincial authorities conducted a census which indicated that, among its population of 819, the town had nine centenarians. Seven were men, four of them over 120, including one said to be aged 142. If there really were nine centenarians there, that would equate to an astonishing rate of one for every 91 people. At the time, the United States boasted just one in every 33,000. It was also very unusual to have male centenarians outnumbering women – by 3.5 to one. Later researchers in Vilcabamba found even more centenarians, one turning up a total of 23. One 113-year-old climbed a mountain every day to cultivate his plot of land, while a man who announced 'matter-of-factly' that he was 132 not only hiked in the mountains but composed poetry while he did so. The centenarians' prescription for long life was, 'Keep moving, don't stop, now or ever,' and soon outside experts were offering their own theories for Vilcabamba's extraordinary record, such as the absence of stress or the way the inhabitants lived in harmony with nature. Their stories did wonders for tourism to the area, and the Ecuadorian government poured in money to help develop it. A website set up to promote Vilcabamba used the familiar slogan, 'Where years are added to your life . . . and life is added to your years!' It claimed the prodigious longevity its people enjoyed was down to negative ions in the air and the perfect mineral balance of the water, while the fact that Vilcabamba meant 'sacred valley' in the Inca language seemed to give a bit of religious underpinning to the claims.

Economic self-interest provided a motive for the Ecuadorian government to promote claims of extraordinary longevity, but other countries have been motivated more by national or ideological prestige. In ancient Japan, the ages of emperors were sometimes inflated to allow the country's history to be stretched back further. In modern times, the Soviet media advanced claims of super-longevity, especially in the Caucasus, a mountainous region between the Black and Caspian seas which has long been regarded as a place where people lived to miraculous ages. Most of the area was part of the Soviet Union, though some areas belonged to Turkey and Iran. In 1957, the USSR issued a stamp celebrating Mahmud Aivazov, who was allegedly 149 years old and from a village more than 6,000 feet (1.82 km) above sea level in what is now Azerbaijan. According to the Soviet news agency TASS, Aivazov was still riding a horse and working, as he had been for 134 years after starting as a shepherd at the age of fifteen. The agency caught up with him on his first ever visit to Moscow, where he attended an agricultural exhibition. He spent eight hours there every day, running up stairways 'with ease'. Proclaiming that 'age has no terrors for me,' he challenged an 86-year-old to a wrestling match. The younger man beat a hasty retreat. Aivazov's mental state was just as impressive. He liked to crack a joke and had a 'vivid memory', even about events of a century earlier, though he was also keenly interested in current affairs. He boasted 152 descendants, including a 121-year-old daughter. Fortunately, this paragon of healthy ageing was a model Communist. Indeed, he still regarded himself as a 'young Communist' and had helped to set up the collective farm on which he still toiled. He was 'indignant' about any suggestion that he should retire. Aivazov died in 1959, supposedly aged 151. But while Colombia proclaimed Pereira the oldest man on earth, for the Russians, Aivazov was not even the oldest in the Soviet Union – just 'one of the oldest'.

Indeed, the Caucasus was said to be crawling with astonishingly aged people among its 40 ethnic groups, including Georgians, Azerbaijanis and Abkhazians, and it was Azerbaijan, where Aivazov lived, that Soviet statistics pointed to as having the highest concentration of centenarians. Some villages claimed to have half a dozen or more. The daddy of them all was alleged to be another Azerbaijani man, Shirali Muslimov, who died aged 168 in 1973. (Just as in Vilcabamba, the ranks of supposed centenarians in the Caucasus contained an unusually high number of males.) The following year, *Izvestia* carried a report about the 140th birthday celebrations in an Abkhazian village of a woman named Khfaf Lazuria. Just four feet two inches (1.27 m) tall, she could thread a needle without needing glasses, and had taken up smoking at 100. There were supposed to be another dozen centenarians in her family, and party guests included a 120-year-old and a

111-year-old man who had galloped to the event on his horse from his village twenty miles away. Lazuria, of course, was still working, and picking a quota of tea that put many young people to shame. Sadly, she lasted only one more year, succumbing to pneumonia which she caught from swimming in a stream during the winter. Some of the villages in the area became tourist attractions, with one setting up a dance troupe made up entirely of centenarians. The oldest member was said to be 115. The district's growing fame motivated the authorities to build a hotel as well as new houses for many of the inhabitants. As for the Soviet Union as a whole, the census of 1970 reported that out of a total population of 241.72 million, the country had 19,304 centenarians. That was about one centenarian for every 12,500 people, or nearly three times the rate in the United States.

As we saw earlier, the Soviet media were careful to point out that Mahmud Aivazov was a model Communist, and the authorities could not have been blind to the propaganda value of having people living to extraordinary ages. Joseph Stalin was himself a Georgian, and was no doubt gratified by these stories, especially if they implied that he too might expect to live to a very ripe old age. A big American yoghurt company was sufficiently impressed to film a commercial in the Caucasus in 1977, pointing out that yoghurt was an important part of the local diet and featuring a number of people who claimed to be over 100 years old as they worked or rode horses. It was said to be the first American commercial ever filmed in the Soviet Union. But more sceptical American commentators said the Russians were creating a state-sponsored 'Methuselah-cult'.

It was hard for foreign experts to get access to the evidence behind the longevity claims, but in the 1970s a respected Soviet geneticist named Zhores Medvedev defected to the West, and blew the whistle. The first comprehensive Russian census had been carried out in 1897, and it claimed the country had 15,677 centenarians, 4,000 of whom were said to be aged '100'. Medvedev regarded the overall figure as completely unrealistic, and it was also odd that such a high proportion should be exactly 100. He found that in this census, and the first Soviet census of 1926, a disproportionate number of people gave their age as a nice round number, so in 1926, 1.147 million women were said to be 60, while there were just 210,000 aged 59 and 179,000 aged 61. The fact was that most people, particularly in rural areas, did not know how old they were. There were no birth certificates, church records had often been lost, and even in those that survived, people were often registered under different names from those they used at home. Muslims did not register their babies at all, and when Abkhazian women got married, they often changed their first names as well as their surnames. Returns from remote villages had shown some people allegedly aged over 200. Medvedev also pointed out the curious feature that as life expectancy increased, the number of centenarians unearthed by Soviet censuses fell – from 29,000 in 1926 to 21,708 in 1959, and 19,304 in 1970.

Around the same time that Medvedev was pursuing his inquiries, other investigators started examining the claims of centenarians in Abkhazia by asking about their memories of specific events, such as the major migration from the area to Turkey in 1877. This led the researchers to conclude that among 548 alleged centenarians, only 241 had a valid claim, though Medvedev considered this number still far too high. He pointed out that while in 1970, Georgia claimed to have fifteen times as many centenarians per head of population as Latvia and Estonia, Azerbaijan eighteen times and the Karabakh mountain region 38 times, although Latvia and Estonia had much better average life expectancy than any of those areas. Another thing that caught his eye was that centenarians were more than three times as common in rural areas as in urban ones. Soviet scientists in august bodies such as Kiev's Institute of Gerontology or Moscow's Institute of Ethnography offered a variety of explanations for the area's extreme longevity, Medvedev said, including diet, the fact that people there did not retire but kept on working, their settled and stress-free way of life, the altitude of their villages – or perhaps it was something in their genes. But the organizations never cast doubt on the official figures and neglected the most obvious explanation: that extreme longevity claims were closely linked with areas with 'the highest level of illiteracy, with the communities where there were not any birth or marriage registrations'. Medvedev added that they were most common among 'small national minorities which did not have written language'. Or, as another commentator noted, 'cases of extreme old age have nowadays mostly been reported from the countries in which . . . there were no reliable birth registers.' As for Khfaf Lazuria, it emerged after her death that she told different stories to different people – changing her age, the number of husbands she had had, the ages at which her parents had died, and so on – and that there was a tradition in Abkhazia of telling tall tales, especially to outsiders.

Another communist regime also claimed to have the oldest man of all time, though the Cuban Benito Martínez Abrogán was said to be only a modest 120 when he died in 2006. He had been unveiled to the world the previous year as a member of the island's '120 Club', mainly made up of people alleged to be already over 100 and who wanted to live even longer. The club was the brainchild of President Fidel Castro himself, and his government quoted the longevity of Abrogán and his friends as an endorsement of the country's health care system, while Castro's personal physician declared Cuba to be the only country with 'all the conditions people need to live to 120 years'. Until the end, Abrogán was still growing bananas, breeding fighting cocks and dancing with young nurses at the senior citizens' centre. In fact, no one knew how old he was. He had arrived from Haiti in 1925, claiming to be 45. In 2010, Cuba also declared it had a 125-year-old woman citizen, based on a church record from 1885, but outside the country, her claims have been greeted with scepticism.

Vilcabamba went the same way as the Caucasus. In 1971, Dr Alexander Leaf from Harvard Medical School went there and met a man who claimed to be 122. When Leaf returned three years later, the same man said he was now 134. Leaf persuaded two other American scientists, Richard Mazess and Sylvia Forman, to help him take a closer look at the area's claims of extreme longevity. They reported in 1978 that they had not been able to find a single true centenarian in Vilcabamba. The oldest person in the village was 96, and the average age of those claiming to be 100 or over was actually 86. When it came to life span, Vilcabamba was nothing special. So how had the longevity legend come about? It seems that as they grew older, the locals started to exaggerate, and the older they got, the thicker they laid it on. At the age of 61, one man claimed he was 70 – and by the time he was 66, he gave his age as 80. At 87 he said he was 121, and at 91 claimed to be 127. Another supposed centenarian was said to have quoted a date of birth that would have made him five years older than his mother.

The researchers concluded that this had been going on for years, and that the initial motive was probably to gain kudos. Once the international spotlight was shone on Vilcabamba, even more prestige was on offer, so the locals exaggerated even more. What made the myth possible was confusion. It was a small, rather in-bred community, and many people shared the same names, so they often got mixed up with their parents or older relatives. It was true that Vilcabamba had an unusually high percentage of older people, but this was because so many younger ones had left. One encouraging factor the researchers noted, though, was that people there did enjoy a relatively vigorous old age, thanks to a diet low in calories and animal fat. (One Ecuadorian did get to be the world's oldest living person, but María Capovilla, who survived to 116, lived in a big city far from Vilcabamba.)

An American journalist who investigated the Hunza people of Pakistan in 1989 came to similar conclusions. He wrote that their valley was one of the most beautiful places he had ever seen, but the locals suffered from a variety of ailments – bronchitis, tuberculosis, malaria, dysentery, cancer and so on. Life expectancy was in fact in the low fifties, and the secret of the people's longevity turned out to be 'the absence of birth records'. Older people did not actually know their ages, but tended to think of a number and add a decade – or three, as the reporter discovered when he probed their recollection of historical events.

It is not only governments that sometimes have a financial incentive to exaggerate longevity: individuals do, too. In the United States, the Gerontology Research Group unearthed the case of a supposedly 117-year-old woman who many years before had assumed the identity of an aunt 24 years older than her in order to claim a pension. Similarly, an American man thought to be 116 years old when he died in 1999 had secured benefits by adding sixteen years to his age in the 1950s. Another motive has been to avoid military service. This is thought to have happened in the case of a Pole named Paweł Parniak who was said to have been 116 when he died in 2006. That would have meant his mother was fourteen when she gave birth to him. In fact, it is now believed that he inflated his age by five years in an unsuccessful attempt to avoid being conscripted for the Second World War.

Then there is religion. As we saw earlier, the claims of extraordinary age for biblical figures such as Methuselah may simply have been a way to underpin their prestige. More recently, the two-and-a-half century life span claimed for China's Li-Ching Yun was put down by some to his Taoist philosophy. In Tibet in 1978, a Buddhist sage was said to be 142, and to have attained a state in which he was no longer made of flesh but of 'pure light', while there are Hindu swamis claiming to be aged 130 or more. In some societies, village elders are revered, so the older they are, the better. Take a South African woman named Moloko Temo, who in 1988 was given an identity card saying she had been born in 1874. There was no other evidence for her exceptional age, she had no idea of her birthday and some of her children were suspiciously young, but some in the media credited her with being 134 when she died in 2009.

In countries with good records, false claims of extreme longevity can usually be debunked easily. So it was that in the u.s. in 2003, Mattie Owens was found to be 105, not 119, and Macy Bare to be 107, not 115, while in 2004, William Coates turned out to be 92, not 114. But records are not infallible, particularly when they are copied, and this too can result in inflated ages. In France, for example, when she died in 1992, Eva Jourdan was declared to be 112, but in fact someone had miscopied 1890 as 1880, and she was really 102.

Norris McWhirter, co-founder of Guinness World Records, said, 'No single subject is more obscured by vanity, deceit, falsehood and deliberate fraud than the extremes of human longevity.' Organizations such as Guinness and the New England Centenarian Study therefore insist on exhaustive scrutiny. The claimant must have an original birth certificate or a certified copy produced at or close to the event. Sometimes a census report can be accepted, provided it is from a year reasonably close to the claimant's date of birth, but for claims of extreme old age the procedure gets more rigorous, with a complete family reconstruction to ensure there is no danger of confusion with someone of the same or a similar name, and to verify that the claimant's age at key events such as the birth of a child is plausible. (When a Georgian woman named Antisa Khvichava said she was 130, for example, the thing that blew her claim out of the water was that this would have meant her eldest son was born when she was 60.) Registration of births in the uk began in 1837, but of the tens of millions of people recorded, not one has survived beyond 115. No wonder Tom Perls wrote that 98 per cent of ages claimed over 115 are false, and a group of longevity experts who examined claims of extreme old age declared, 'in our experience, claims to age 130 exist only where records do not.' Meanwhile, the gerontologist Dr Robert Young from the New England Centenarian Study, who has investigated many claims, drily remarked, 'Myths of longevity are universal, except in those areas where we have compulsory birth registration.'

But just as those who went to see Herbert Badgery wanted to think he was 139, whatever the evidence, many of us seem to have a need to believe that in faraway lands with a much 'simpler', more old-fashioned

The Hunza valley.

(and, no doubt, poorer) lifestyle than ours, centenarians are found around every corner and live to prodigious ages. And even when it is demonstrated that, for example, the Hunza who live in traditional villages have less chance of reaching 100 than do their neighbours in more modern homes, closer to civilization, it appears to make little difference. And for journalists, 'this is the oldest human who has ever lived' is plainly a more appealing story than 'the person who claims to be 130 probably isn't.' So the debunking of the various Shangri-Las has not killed off claims of extreme longevity, even in official circles.

In 1997 the King of Nepal honoured Bir Narayan Chaudhary for supposedly living to 140. Apparently, he smoked 'regularly' but he had never been in hospital, and he had no birth certificate. Chaudhary died the following year. In 2009, the Turkish authorities agreed that Halime Olcay was 135. She had been confined to her bed for 25 years, though apparently she looked 'great for her age', and enjoyed 'relatively good health'. Having seen no activity in her bank account, and no updates to her documentation in a quarter of a century, the authorities had become suspicious and cancelled her pension, but after visiting her in a little village in the southeast of the country, they agreed to reinstate it. According to Olcay's great-great-grandson, she was not sure about her age; she might in fact be over 150.

Similar claims continued to appear in the most respectable media. In 2000, many newspapers reported that Elizabeth Israel, or 'Ma Pampo', from Dominica was 125 years old – comfortably outstripping Jeanne Calment's record as the oldest human who ever lived – and still going! Even more remarkable, on this relatively poor Caribbean island (which did not even make it into the top 100 of the world's richest countries in 2015), just four doors down the street lived Israel's friend, Rose Peters, who was 117 – making her the world's second-oldest living person. Indeed, Dominica's government claimed the island had at least seventeen centenarians, giving it the highest concentration per thousand inhabitants in the world. Both Israel and Peters had worked well past 100, picking vegetables on a plantation. Though Israel was now, it was admitted, 'frail', her mind was as 'clear as a bell'. She had never touched a drop of liquor, saying, 'It makes you mad,' and she put her longevity down to hard work, which 'never killed anybody. It's laziness that kills.' Peters was still 'full of energy'. She also gave credit to hard work, and to Dominica's water, 'so pure it needs no treatment'.

The women's claims were based on church records, not official birth certificates. And the church records were not originals; those had been destroyed by a hurricane in 1979, so there were only copies available, but the parish priest certified they could not have been 'tampered with'. What guarantee he could give that the copying, or indeed the original records, were accurate is not stated. The waters were further muddied by the fact that for part of her life, Elizabeth Israel was known as Minetta George. She died in 2003, supposedly aged 128, and the Dominican government agitated for her to be named the oldest person who ever lived, but Guinness World Records declined because the paperwork did not meet their exacting standards. Incidentally, it was claimed that her neighbour, Rose Peters, finally died at 118. Tom Perls maintained that the Dominican government, just like the Ecuadorian, supported the claims of people such as Ma Pampo and Rose Peters to promote tourism to their island.

In 2009 the BBC reported that an Uzbek woman named Tuti Yusupova was 'thought to be 128' and perhaps the oldest human who had ever lived, even though the only evidence for her supposed age was a 'birth certificate' issued in 1997. Meanwhile, in the same year, the *Scientific American* reported on the case of a Kazakh nun who also managed to be a mother of ten. Sakhan Dosova was alleged to be 130, based on a passport and an identity card. One of her children was said to be 76, meaning Dosova would have had to be 54 years old when she gave birth to her; indeed, according to some reports she gave birth to several children in her sixties.

The claims of the various Shangri-Las may not survive much scrutiny, but that does not mean that where you live is irrelevant to your chance of surviving to 100. For a long time, the United States has had the highest number of centenarians, but there are indications that it may now have been overtaken by Japan. At the time of the last U.S. national census in 2010 there were 53,364 in a total population of 308.7 million, making one centenarian for every 5,785 people, but the country's Census Bureau estimated that by 2015, the number had grown to nearly 77,000 out of a total population of 321 million, about one for every 4,470. The U.S. spends a bigger share of its national wealth on health care than any other country, but one American in three is obese. In 2011 the Japanese government said there were nearly 48,000 centenarians, but by 2015, the estimated number was 91,000, though its figures have been rather tarnished because of the national scandal over fictitious centenarians. Still, it is generally accepted that, of major countries, Japan has the most hundred-year-olds per head of population, about one in every 1,390 inhabitants if the figure of

Boeri Lake, Dominica.

91,000 is correct. Its spending on health care runs at only about half the rate in the USA, but America has ten times as many obese people per head. Canada's figures are almost as impressive as Japan's, with nearly 24,400 centenarians out of a total 35 million citizens, making about one person in every 1,439. The UK, which spends a similar proportion of its national wealth on health care as Japan does, is reckoned to have nearly 30,000 centenarians out of a population of just over 64 million – about one in every 2,190 people. Of the major European countries, Italy has the highest proportion of centenarians, with more than 38,000 out of a population approaching 62 million, meaning a ratio of one centenarian to 1,605 non-centenarians. Across the world, the country with the highest proportion of centenarians is tiny Monaco, with an estimated 340 out of a total population of just 30,535, about one for every 90 inhabitants. The little principality is one of the richest places on earth, and its centenarian ratio may be skewed by the fact that it is a popular place to retire to, with people aged over 65 making up almost 30 per cent of the population, compared with less than 18 per cent in the UK, for example.

In 2015, the U.S. Census Bureau's estimate for the number of centenarians across the developed world was just over 407,000 out of a total population of around 1.25 billion, giving an average frequency of about one for every 3,090 people. Any residual idea that you have a better chance of reaching 100 if you live simply in a primitive Shangri-La, far from the corrupting comforts of modern life, takes quite a knock if you look at the number of 100-year-olds in the world's poorest countries. In quite a few, a person's chance of reaching the century is literally a million (or more) to one. Chad, for example, has 11.6 million people, and just eleven centenarians. In Angola, the chances are worse still – thirteen people aged over 100 out of 19.6 million. Liberia is worse again, with only two centenarians among nearly 4.2 million people, but worst of all is Afghanistan, with just ten out of a population of almost 32.6 million. Indeed, across the world's poorest countries, there are just over 2,000 centenarians among a total population of almost 1 billion people – about one in every 500,000.

But even if there are no Shangri-Las, there are some genuine centenarian hotspots. As we saw earlier, for a time in the 1980s Swansea boasted Britain's oldest woman and oldest man. At one point, John Evans was also the oldest man in the world, and at another time, Anna Williams the oldest person. So perhaps there was something special in the Swansea air or water? Unfortunately, there is no evidence to suggest that people in Swansea have an especially long life expectancy. Indeed, men in the city can expect to live eighteen months less than the average for the rest of the UK, and women nine months shorter, and the fact that for a time the area was home to the oldest man and woman in Britain is almost certainly nothing more than coincidence.

As we have seen, the Japanese islands of Okinawa have long been famous for longevity. Japan has more 100-year-olds per head than any other major country in the world, and there have been claims that in Okinawa, centenarians are four or five times as common as in the rest of Japan. Probably the most authoritative calculation of longevity in the area comes from a study in 2011 by the Belgian demographer Michel Poulain, which calculated Japan's rate of centenarians at about one for every 3,520 people, while Okinawa managed one in 1,642 – in other words, it had more than twice as many 100-year-olds per capita as the rest of the country. Poulain said some question marks might hover over the data, but concluded that overall Okinawa deserved its reputation for 'exceptional' longevity. That reputation has brought scientists, sociologists and journalists to these beautiful islands to investigate. There are more than 40 of them – sub-tropical, praised for their beaches, climate and relaxed way of life, though ironically, they were the site of one of the bloodiest battles of the Second World War, in which perhaps a third of the population perished. Another striking feature about Okinawa's centenarians is how heavily the women outnumber the men – by nearly eight to one, compared with just over six to one for Japan as a whole.

Harbour and Rock of Monaco.

In 2004 a reporter met one of the men, 103-year-old Seiryu Toguchi, who recounted how he got up at six o'clock every morning and immediately opened the shutters, explaining, 'It's a sign to my neighbours that I am still alive.' Next came a few stretches, then breakfast – whole grain rice and miso soup with vegetables. For two hours Toguchi weeded his field, from which he still sold produce. He also did all his own housework since his wife's death seven years before. His children wanted him to come and live with them, but he turned them down, saying, 'I enjoy my freedom.' Lunch would be stir-fried local vegetables with egg and tofu, followed by a nap and another couple of hours in the field. In the evening, he sang and played a local musical instrument, filled in his diary and took a nip of homemade wine made from aloe, garlic and turmeric, before going to sleep, his head, he said, filled with all the things he wanted to do the next day. Toguchi's doctor considered his health to be excellent, but if ever the centenarian felt ill, he would simply take a taxi to the hospital, even if it was the middle of the night, leaving a note on the shutters for his neighbours.

Three years later, a British television documentary maker found a 100-year-old Okinawan woman named Tsuru who looked about 70, still grew her own vegetables and said she had hardly ever seen a doctor: 'Despite my age, I am fit. I enjoy everything as I have many friends.' She continued to play gateball, which is a bit like croquet, but faster: 'Even now, no one can beat me. I still have lots of energy.' She also ran her own little shop. As for diet, she could eat 'anything'. Pointing out a bag of crisps, she said, 'Snacks like this. This is the right way to eat. Open it up and eat it on the spot.' But a 103-year-old woman who was still living in her own home with the help of her granddaughter was having less fun, complaining, 'I can't hear and my brain is not working.' In 2003 an American writer, Dan Buettner, assembled a team of experts including anthropologists, demographers and epidemiologists, who designated Okinawa a 'Blue Zone' – a special place where people live longer and stay healthier than the rest of us. He described watching a 104-year-old Okinawan make jasmine tea, 'squatting in the corner and pouring hot water over tea leaves as the room filled with a delicate, floral aroma'. Okinawans, in fact, have a traditional brew made from green tea leaves, jasmine flowers and a bit of turmeric. Having studied the lifestyles of many centenarians in Costa Rica, Greece, Italy, Japan and the United States, Buettner's team came to the conclusion that afternoon tea was a crucial component of a longevity diet.

Tsuru was evidently not an exception on Okinawa; Dr Bradley Willcox, one of the leading lights in the Okinawa Centenarian Study, which has been examining the islands' 100-year-olds since 1975, was struck by the way the inhabitants seem to age more slowly than the rest of us: 'The calendar may say they're 70,' he declares, 'but their body says they're 50.' The result for centenarians is that 'a good lot of them are healthy until the very end.' The study found that an 'unusual' number were 'lean, youthful-looking, energetic, and had remarkably low rates of heart disease and cancer'. Speculation as to why this might be has focused on a hormone known as DHEA, which is involved in the production of male and female sex hormones. Its level in our bodies decreases as we get older, but among Okinawans, the decline is much slower. This in turn may be related to Okinawans' eating habits, particularly *hara hachi bun me*, or continuing only until you are 80 per cent full, which, as we saw earlier, was practised by the oldest man who ever lived, the Japanese Jiroemon Kimura. The result is that Okinawans eat about 20 per cent less than most people in the UK. They also consume more tofu and soybean products than anyone else in the world. (Soybeans are rich in flavonoids, which are strongly linked to low rates of cancer.) Their diet is low in fat and salt, and high in fruits and vegetables. It is also high in vitamin E, which

Milk thistle.

seems to protect the brain, and the islanders do have comparatively low levels of dementia.

But the Okinawa Centenarian Study also noticed that, like Seiryu Toguchi and Tsuru, many 100-year-olds there still got plenty of physical and mental exercise, and wondered whether this too was a factor in their longevity. In addition, OCS surveys showed that elderly Okinawans express a high degree of satisfaction with life. According to some, this is because of a strong sense of community, which ensures old people continue to be valued and respected, helping to give them a sense of purpose and belonging. Elderly women, for example, are regarded as the keepers of a family's bond with its ancestors, and are responsible for organizing festivals to honour them. It is said that in the local dialect, there is no word for retirement. All this is seen as presenting quite a contrast with some Western societies. In the UK, for example, a Church of England report in 2015 concluded that many older people felt 'unwanted, unvalued and unnoticed'. Intriguingly, when Okinawans move from the islands, within a generation, their rates of cancers and heart attacks rise, and their life expectancy falls. For 37 years, Okinawa had the highest percentage of centenarians of all Japan's 47 prefectures, but it lost the title in 2009 to Shimane, a mountainous area on the country's main island, Honshu, which has fewer inhabitants than any other prefecture but one.

Another Blue Zone is the Italian island of Sardinia, or, more precisely, a mountainous region about halfway up the island's eastern side, including the province of Ogliastra, the most sparsely populated in Italy. Here, too, they have a local tea. This one is made from milk thistle, a local wild plant said to 'cleanse the liver'. It contains silymarin, which has been investigated by scientists as an antioxidant that might be used to combat cancer. The island became famous when reports appeared of a 'centenarians' road' winding through forests and hills on which lived eight people over 100. Like Okinawa, Sardinia attracted scientists and journalists searching for its secrets.

For a time, the island boasted the world's oldest man – Antonio Todde, who died in 2002, aged 112. He spent nearly all his life working as a shepherd in the mountains to the north of Ogliastra, and had been lucid right up to the end. He had been married for 78 years, and had always lived in the same house. Tea was all very well, but Antonio recommended 'a good glass of red wine every day'. A lot of Sardinian red wine comes from the local Cannonau grape, which is said to be rich in antioxidants. Todde ate pasta and vegetable soup, but also red meat and cheese, though, according to a relative, 'he wasn't greedy.' She also said he lived life 'to the full'. As for his own prescription for longevity, he advocated: 'Just love your brother and . . . take one day after the other.' His father lived to 90, his mother to 99 and one of his sisters past 100. As part of his Blue Zone research, Buettner examined the Sardinians' diet, and reported that their cheese is generally made from sheep's milk, that they eat a moderate amount of carbohydrates, in flat and sourdough bread, and that fava beans and chickpeas often feature. From his study of centenarians in five countries the writer drew up a few practical prescriptions, in addition to afternoon tea, for a long-life diet: do not have a slap-up evening meal – make that the smallest of the day; stop eating when you are four-fifths full; have meat in small portions and only about once a week; concentrate on vegetables, especially beans; and drink one or two glasses of alcohol every day.

Other explanations for the area's longevity include the natural exercise locals get from climbing all those mountains or even the stairs of their tall, narrow traditional houses. Then there is the matter of genetics. Usually, inbreeding is regarded as unhealthy, and for hundreds of years there was plenty of it in the isolated mountain villages of Sardinia, but here some scientists have surmised that it might have helped longevity, as in the village of Ovodda, which boasted five centenarians among its population of 1,700 – one in every 340. (Interestingly, according to Poulain's figures from 2008, Sardinia as a whole actually had fewer centenarians per head than the rest of Italy, and it appears to be only what he describes as the 'central-eastern' mountainous region that has exceptional longevity.) Professor Luca Deiana tested every Sardinian centenarian he could. He said that in Ovodda, almost everyone was descended from just a few of the original settlers, and he believes this may be why a large number of them have what appears to be a faulty gene on the X chromosome which seems to inhibit the production of an enzyme known as G6PD, which plays a role in the processing of carbohydrates – though why this should prolong life is not clear. In a study in 2004, Dr Poulain and other researchers speculated whether low rates of immigration might have contributed to the area's exceptional longevity, and they also noted that in Sardinia's longevity hotspot, female centenarians outnumbered males by only 1.3 to one, compared with an average of nearly six to one across 27 European countries – a figure they describe as 'unique'. These statistics have led to speculation that the genetic mutation Professor Deiana detected may specifically benefit men.

But although there may be a genetic component to the longevity in Sardinia's mountains, others have stressed the importance of lifestyle factors similar to those in Okinawa. The psychologist Susan Pinker, who wrote a book on Sardinian longevity, noted that every centenarian she met 'was supported by kith and kin, visitors who stopped by to chat, bring food and gossip, provide personal care, a kiss on the cheek'. Relatives of all generations took time off work to look after the old. Pinker says, 'it takes a village to raise a centenarian,' arguing that their survival is often made possible because they 'are surrounded and cared for by a circle of extended family, friends, neighbours and people they know well', a situation she contrasts with modern American society. She wrote about a woman in her sixties who cared for her 102-year-old uncle, saying, 'I do it with pleasure. He is my heritage.'

NINE

Is There a Limit to Our Lives?

Back in ancient Roman times, Cicero said: 'as Nature has marked the bounds of everything else, so she has marked the bounds of life.' This idea was further developed by the great eighteenth-century French naturalist Georges-Louis Leclerc, the Comte de Buffon. He maintained that all species have a maximum life span, and that nothing can change what he called 'the fixed laws which regulate the number of years', arriving at this figure by multiplying by six the number of years during which a creature would grow. Humans were no exception: 'the man who does not die of incidental diseases reaches everywhere the age of ninety or one hundred years.' (Buffon thought that humans carried on growing until they reached 'sixteen or eighteen'.) Of course, in his day, most people did die well before reaching 100, but Buffon's idea was that if sickness, war, crime or accident had not accounted for us by then, our light would certainly go out around the century.

We have seen ample evidence that the number of people reaching the age of 100 has increased dramatically over the last century, and that it is still growing. Indeed, the demographer James Vaupel, along with other experts, wrote that if the trend continued, 'most babies born since 2000 in France, Germany, Italy, the UK, the USA, Canada, Japan, and other countries with long life expectancies will celebrate their 100th birthdays.' But whether our *maximum* life span is increasing is more doubtful. Nearly twenty years after her death, Jeanne Calment remains the only human being, out of all the billions who have walked the earth, known to have survived past 120, and her 122 years puts her way out in front – more than three years ahead of the next oldest person, the American Sarah Knauss. She in turn was the only person to have lived past 119, or indeed 118. Next came Lucy Hannah, who survived to 117 years and 248 days, almost five years below Calment's mark. Nor is that record in any immediate danger. The oldest person currently alive is a mere 117 years old. So, does something around 120 – not far off Buffon's limit of six times the years during which we are growing – represent the maximum time we can live, however many of us may get close to it?

As we saw earlier, support for the theory that we have a fixed maximum life span had come from the pioneering statistician Benjamin Gompertz, who back in 1825 worked out that our chance of dying gradually increases as we get older, doubling about every eight years. Gompertz would have had little chance to study what happens after the age of 100, because there were just not enough centenarians around. But in 2005, Leonid Gavrilov and Natalia Gavrilova found that, surprisingly, the death rate begins to level off after age 105, though they recognized that the small numbers of people left at that point might mean there was some doubt about how much confidence we could have in this conclusion. Assuming the effect was real, they wondered whether it might be because centenarians live in a more protected environment, and they pointed out that what became known as 'mortality deceleration' had already been noted in the final stages of the lives of rats, mice, shrimps, our old friend the fruit fly, nematode worms and other species. Startlingly, the Gavrilovs concluded it might mean there was 'no fixed upper limit for individual lifespan'.

Another factor seeming to support the conclusion that maximum life span will increase is the fact that until the mid-1970s, the number of validated supercentenarians was fewer than ten. Now it is 80, and the Gerontology Research Group reckons the true number may be approaching 450. So, according to the law of averages, surely the more of us get past 110, the greater the likelihood that one of us will be really exceptional and break Jeanne Calment's record. We should also be able to count on receiving a helping hand from continuing medical advances and other general technological and environmental improvements that make our lives easier and safer. In the science fiction film *The Day the Earth Stood Still* (1951), the visiting alien, who has the thankless task of trying to teach humans peace and wisdom, is anatomically identical to us but has a life expectancy of 130, because of his planet's superior medical knowledge. Some evidence, however, seems to point in the opposite direction. In 2010, one demographer calculated that the average age of the oldest person alive had been increasing more slowly than overall average life span, suggesting that perhaps we are approaching an upper limit.

Some flatly disagree with this. In 1987 Malcolm Johnson, Professor of Health and Social Welfare at the UK's Open University, said that by the middle of this century, we might have a life expectancy of 130, thanks to a healthier environment, less danger in the workplace, changing lifestyles and further medical advances, though he added caveats: 'New environmental hazards may arise, some stages of the ageing process may prove hard to alleviate.' Around the same time, Professor Sydney Shall, a biochemist at Sussex University, opined, 'It's my belief that a life span of 150 years – that is, of vigorous, active life, is probably, in quotes, the "natural life span" of humans.' He thought this might be achieved over a century, on the basis that life expectancy had doubled in many countries to about 75 over the previous century, so that if it carried on at a similar rate, it would reach 150 by the 2080s. But an extension of human life span to 130 or even 150 would not have Dr Aubrey de Grey, a 53-year-old Cambridge computer scientist turned self-taught bio-gerontologist, reaching for the champagne. He wants to see us living to 1,000, declaring:

> Given sufficient funding we have a 50–50 chance of completely stopping people from dying of old age within about 25 or 30 years from now. I think we have enough detail now about how we would go about doing that that we have a good chance of putting it all together and making it work.

Resolving the question of whether the limit to our lives is fixed at about 120 or whether we could significantly extend it is made more difficult by the fact that we have not yet properly fathomed the process of ageing. As the French demographer and gerontologist Jean-Marie Robine observed in 2007, 'It is still not understood why man gets older and is incapable of maintaining his body in good working order.' And by 2015, things seemed to have got no clearer, with Dr Eric Karran from the charity Alzheimer's Research UK declaring, 'One of the biggest questions in human biology is how we age.' Still, when you consider how rare really old people were before the longevity explosion of the past few decades, it is perhaps not surprising that gerontology – the

Dr Aubrey de Grey, author of *Ending Aging*.

study of old age – is still pretty young, going back as a distinct science only to the 1940s.

The outward signs of ageing are all too easy to spot. Our skin wrinkles because of the thinning of the superficial epidermis, the deterioration of our skin glands and damage to connective tissue fibres. The hair turns grey. The eyes, the lungs, the kidneys and other organs begin to perform less efficiently. Nerve cells get slower at transmitting messages. We become more susceptible to disease and infection. Andrew Goldsworthy from Imperial College London's Department of Pure and

Applied Biology described ageing as 'an apparently irreversible process which goes on in all or nearly all the cells of the body and which gradually reduces their capacity to perform their normal functions'. On one level, it does not seem so hard to understand. Everything wears out in the end – why should we be different?

Ageing and death seem to be the lot of all creatures. After two weeks of adult life, the wings of houseflies start to fray and they can no longer fly. As octopuses get older, they lose the ability to grow new tentacles to replace those they lose. Young rats swim well; old rats swim badly, and often sink. Most species die earlier than humans do. The small house mouse is old at three. Gorillas may live to 40, a few horses can make it to 50 and the odd elephant into its seventies. A few creatures last longer than we do, such as the giant tortoise, which can live on until 150; the bowhead whale, which can last to 200; or the female Greenland shark found (dead) in 2016, which scientists said was probably about 400 years old. But even these animals are getting only a stay of execution; they will, like all creatures, eventually die. But then if it is all down to gradual deterioration, why do the life spans of different species vary so much?

Nor is it quite true to say that all creatures will eventually die. Some, like sea anemones, freshwater worms and single-celled amoebae,

Bowhead whale.

which multiply simply by splitting into halves, are potentially immortal. An unpleasant occurrence, such as being attacked by an enemy or a poison, can wipe them out, but they do not age and decay as we do. The same is true of bacteria. Ageing, or 'senescence', as scientists have started to call it, seems to happen only in creatures like us, in which the young begin life as eggs. The 'wear and tear' theory of ageing lost favour, partly because of the existence of potentially immortal creatures, because of the different rates at which different mortal creatures age, and partly because, as one scientist calculated, if we were able to keep the same ability to handle stress, injury and disease that we have at the age of ten, throughout our lives, we could go on for something like 700 years.

The gerontologist Professor Tom Kirkwood devised another explanation for ageing: the 'disposable soma' theory. The idea is that we are made up of two sorts of cells: the germ cells that form eggs and sperm and carry our genes on to the next generation when we have children, and the rest – the soma. In the early days of life on earth, and with simple organisms like bacteria and amoeba today, all cells had the job of generating new individuals. But as more complex creatures began to evolve, cells started to specialize – having particular functions in the blood, nerves, brain and so on. In the process, they were relieved of the responsibility for reproduction. They became soma cells, and all beings which have a distinction between germ and soma cells are susceptible to ageing. The DNA of germ cells has to be protected at all costs, as they will be passed on to the next generation and the next and so on, but there is no such need to protect soma cells; as long as they keep us viable for long enough to pass on our germ cells – job done! Our soma, in other words, is disposable, and we age as faults gradually build up in it.

So, if the 'what' of ageing is still a bit problematic, are we any clearer on the 'how'? A number of theories have been advanced. Some say it is associated with low-level chronic inflammation of many of the body's tissues. Or perhaps it is the running down of our ability to produce a crucial enzyme that turns food into the energy our cells need to function. Others point to a double whammy from our immune system: it grows less effective at fighting infection, and becomes more likely to attack our own bodies, causing autoimmune disorders. Dr Robert Kane, director of the Center on Aging at the University of Minnesota, said the questions remain 'profound'. He described ageing as 'a loss of coping mechanism, a failure to be able to maintain internal control and balance'. When we die of 'old age', is that some kind of multiple system failure, as all our organs fail at more or less the same time? And if so, is it down to a single cause, or are multiple factors at work?

In 1965, at the Wistar Institute in Philadelphia, a scientist named Leonard Hayflick, who would later become president of the Gerontological Society of America, demonstrated that in a test tube, human cells would divide at most about 50 times, then stop. This became known as the Hayflick limit. Beyond it, cells are reduced to an inactive state called cellular senescence. Hayflick says it took him fifteen years to persuade the scientific community he was right, overturning the prevailing orthodoxy that cells in a test tube could go on dividing forever. The American also discovered that cells taken from older people will divide fewer times, while if younger cells were frozen after, say, twenty divisions, and then thawed out, they would carry on from where they left off and still 'remember' to stop at their Hayflick limit. The limit for cells of people with Werner's syndrome, which causes premature ageing, is half that for the rest of us, and they usually die in their forties. When other creatures were examined, it was found that the Hayflick limits of those with shorter life spans were lower, so that for a mouse, for example, the number of divisions is fifteen or fewer. And an experiment on mice in 2011 by scientists at the famous Mayo Clinic in Minnesota suggested that cells that have reached their Hayflick limit can adversely affect otherwise healthy cells around them.

But how do our cells know that time is up, and that they need to stop dividing? It was not until another couple of decades after the discovery of the Hayflick limit that an answer appeared. In the nuclei of our cells, at the end of each chromosome are long sequences of repetitive DNA called telomeres that protect them from being damaged. Every time a cell divides, these telomeres get shorter. When they get too short, the cell stops dividing. As we saw earlier, a study in Denmark in 2009 showed that people with longer telomeres looked younger, while five years earlier, Elissa Epel, a researcher at the University of California in San Francisco, found that the telomeres of women suffering from chronic stress (they were caring for chronically ill children) were shorter than those of less stressed women. In 2014, Epel discovered that excessive consumption of sweet fizzy drinks seemed to be linked with shorter telomeres, and there is also evidence that people who are obese suffer from premature shortening of their telomeres.

According to a multidisciplinary team at the University of Michigan in 2015, poorer people too had shorter telomeres. All this seems to fit in well with evidence that poverty, obesity and stress can shorten our lives. Incidentally, research at the University of California in 2011 suggested that reducing stress could promote repair of telomeres, and losing weight has been shown to have similar effects, while a study at Harvard Medical School in 2013 suggested that women who meditated had longer telomeres than those who did not.

Some of us, of course, will die before we reach our Hayflick limit, but its discovery did appear to establish dramatic proof that human life span has a finite limit that cannot be extended. Hayflick, now aged 88 and whose mother lived to be 106, was a strong supporter of the 'limit to life' view, saying the idea that we can keep increasing life expectancy at the current rate is as absurd as thinking that because the world record for running a mile keeps being improved on, we will eventually be able to do it in one second. He castigated the business of peddling ways to increase longevity as 'the world's second oldest profession, or maybe even the first. Individuals are going to the bank at this moment with enormous sums of money gained by persuading people that they've found either a way to extend your life or to make you immortal.'

But does the Hayflick limit actually represent a limit to life? Not subject to it are stem cells, which are found in embryos and can develop into many different kinds of cell during our early life and which are also seen later in organs like the gut and in the bone marrow, where they can work as an internal repair system. Some scientists have also questioned whether the limit applies to all non-stem cells. Human cells contain an enzyme called telomerase. In most cells it is inactive, but in embryonic stem cells and some adult cells such as male sperm cells, it is active, and can replace the bits of telomeres lost as cells divide. Epel reported that in women subject to chronic stress, telomerase was less active, while in 2009, researchers at Albert Einstein College of Medicine in New York City found that among Ashkenazi Jews, centenarians and their offspring had higher levels of telomerase and longer telomeres than normal. Yousin Suh, Associate Professor of Medicine and Genetic, said their findings suggested these factors might be combining 'to help people live very long lives, perhaps by protecting them from the diseases of old age'. Perhaps even more intriguingly, it was shown that if telomerase was inserted and then made active in

Peter Medawar.

normal cells in a test tube, they were able to defy the Hayflick limit, and keep on dividing.

Unfortunately, cancer cells are also rich in telomerase, which enables them to leapfrog the Hayflick limit, and continue dividing, so that tumours continue to grow. So even if the Hayflick limit is the crucial obstacle to extending our life span – and not everyone is convinced – and even if we were to find a way of picking its lock with telomerase, it looks as though we might just end up with cancerous cells. Besides, there are many cells that never divide during adult life, such as the neurons of the brain. Turning on telomerase will not affect the ageing of those cells. And there are still plenty of unanswered questions about telomeres and telomerase. Elizabeth Blackburn shared the Nobel Prize in 2009 for her work in this field, but six years later she said she still did not really know how telomeres worked, adding that they were 'extraordinarily dynamic . . . complex little ecosystems'.

So we are still struggling with the 'what' and the 'how' of ageing, but what about the 'why'? For some scientists, the answer can be delivered in one word: evolution. It is said that once upon a time, a tour guide, reproached over the deaths of a number of people in his care, shrugged his shoulders and replied, 'Life is dangerous. No one has yet survived it.' In 1952, Peter Medawar, who later won the Nobel Prize for Medicine, advanced something similar as a scientific theory of why we grow old and die. Even a group of potentially immortal creatures, he said, will be whittled away by accidents, predators, disease, starvation or other nasty events until eventually none are left. And certainly, if we look at centenarians like Henry Allingham, Harry Patch, Irving Berlin, Herbert Brown or Alice Herz-Sommer, we see that they came within an ace of having their lives snuffed out long before they reached their grand old age. From an evolutionary point of view, therefore, it makes sense for our bodies to invest their precious limited supplies of energy in ensuring that we are effective at reproducing, rather than in repairing our bodies when we are no longer capable of passing on our genes. According to the 'selfish gene' theory, proposed by Richard Dawkins in 1976, the gene is the crucial unit and our bodies are simply 'survival machines' – vessels constructed by the genes to ferry them further down the river of time. Vessels that can be discarded once they have done their job of enabling us to reproduce.

But how would this work in practice? In the late nineteenth century, one of the pioneers of the evolutionary theory of ageing, August Weismann, suggested that we have some kind of internal 'death mechanism' that starts to kill us off once we have reproduced, arguing, 'there is no reason to expect life to be prolonged beyond the reproductive period.' Or, as the old saying goes, 'Nature with its frugal eye asks only that we mate and die.' And suppose it was a 'death' gene or genes that blew the whistle and told our bodies to start switching off vital functions once we have completed the task of reproducing: it would probably not be weeded out by natural selection, provided it did not interfere with our ability to have young. In 2005, Professor Michael Rose, an evolutionary biologist, said he thought it would not be as

Richard Dawkins.

simple as having a 'single death gene'; most genes have more than one effect. But suppose there is one that generates lots of testosterone. It might encourage a man to indulge in risky behaviour early in life, helping him to be quite successful in the competition with other males to reproduce and pass on his genes. Even though these same high levels of testosterone could lead to a greater likelihood of death from a depressed immune system once the man passes his prime, natural selection would probably not weed it out.

Evolution's prioritization of reproduction over longevity might also work in another way, through what became known as the 'mutation accumulation' theory. As we grow older, harmful mutations appear in our DNA, but putting them right consumes a lot of energy, so a proportion go unrepaired. Over time, these gradually accumulate, making our bodies less efficient. Either this or the multifaceted gene mechanism could limit human lifespan, or it could be that both play a part. There might also be a Darwinian explanation for why our bodily systems all seem to fail at the same time. If one system packs up too early, it means the energy put into maintaining all the others has been wasted, while if one is still operating perfectly when all the others have failed then it has been over-engineered, and the effort the body has invested in it has been squandered. This also accounts for why species have typical life spans. It used to be thought that smaller animals tended to die earlier because of their more rapid metabolisms – that the light that burns brightly will not last, like the candle the poet Edna St Vincent Millay burns at both ends, or the life of Rutger Hauer's replicant character in *Blade Runner*: that live fast meant die young. So small creatures, such as mice, burned out early, while bigger ones smouldered more slowly. But not all small creatures die young. Take the Leach's storm petrel, a little seabird about the size of a robin. It has a high body temperature and a fast metabolism, but can live to 40. Or take the little brown bat, found mainly in North America, which can survive into its thirties. It may be significant that, while mice have several litters a year, bats give birth to only one or two offspring every twelve months. It was also discovered in the 1970s that cells in long-lived species were better at repairing DNA than those in shorter-lived.

Discussion then shifted to the notion that the crucial factor determining longevity is the degree of danger from predators and other hazards. The idea is that the more likely it is that a creature will die early in life, the more sense it makes to invest bodily resources in reproduction rather than repair and maintenance, and the less likely it is that genes that do damage later in life will be selected out. In this respect, the evidence about the Leach's storm petrel is not very clear. In many places where they nest, they are free from mammal predators, but they are vulnerable to other birds, such as gulls. They try to combat this by going out only at night. These storm petrels, incidentally, do have unusually long telomeres, which sometimes even seem to get longer as the birds get older. As for little brown bats, there are plenty of predators that would like to eat them, like rats, birds and snakes, but it is thought that their habit of heading for night roosts after they have fed in the evening may protect them.

As we saw, there is an oddity about the evolutionary theory of life span and ageing. Women lose their ability to reproduce during the menopause, while men can go on ferrying their genes down that river of time until much, much later in life. And yet it is women who generally live longer. The explanation offered for this is that women are needed to stick around longer than men because of the more important role they play in child-rearing, while men's ability to reproduce into old age tends to be more theoretical than actual. Indeed, the idea used to be that if you added a woman's age at the menopause to the years needed to bring up her last remaining child, it would give you the natural female life span – which worked all right when that was around 70, but over the last few decades, it has gone up by leaps and bounds. Perhaps grandmothers are now playing a more important role in child-rearing? Certainly, there seems to be evidence of that kind from other species. Apparently, among dolphins, females too old to reproduce have been observed providing milk for the offspring of younger females while they are out searching for prey, and males of grandparent age have been seen doing guard duty while parents are away. While with elephants, older females are said to take on a kind of chief executive's role in the herd. To add to the confusion, it has been pointed out that medflies lay few eggs beyond their first month of life, and yet some survive for many more months.

But for humans, even if it was necessary to have a limited life span for evolutionary reasons back in the days when we were at the mercy of so many predators and life was 'nasty, brutish and short', surely things have now moved on? Life today is much safer, so can we reset evolutionary priorities to favour longevity? That was the question Michael Rose tried to answer in the 1980s, with experiments on fruit flies, or *Drosophila*. These flies are much favoured by scientists because they get through generations in double-quick time, breeding like, well, flies. Rose prevented the *Drosophila* from reproducing early in life, so removing the advantage of those who traded in longevity for success in breeding early. Nature responded by evolving flies in which the ageing process was postponed, so that after fifteen generations, they were living up to 50 per cent longer. This was, of course, in laboratory conditions. The problem was that the longer-lived flies flew less well and produced fewer offspring, and would never have been able to hack it in the wild, underlining why evolution prefers early reproduction over late repair. Still the experiment seemed to show that if the dangers of the insect's natural environment were removed, it was possible to get evolution to favour increased life span. Eventually, Rose was able to double the life span of the flies, leading him to remark in 1992 that there was 'nothing deeply problematic about doubling the human life span'.

Among humans, too, there are signs that delaying reproduction may prolong life. As we saw earlier, the oldest ever member of the British royal family, Princess Alice, gave birth to her last child when she was 43, and Tom Perls and his colleagues found that women who had children after the age of 40 were more likely to live to 100, arguing that the genes that made them fertile later in life also predisposed them to longevity. In Britain, the gerontologist Tom Kirkwood went further back in time, analysing the genealogies of 33,000 European aristocrats, starting in the eighth century. He found that those with the fewest children tended to live longest. Of course, this might be a reflection of the dangers of childbirth, though there is also the possibility that women with highly active immune systems might be better at fighting off disease, but also more likely to reject embryos in the womb.

Nowadays, of course, we are in many ways more like the fruit flies in Rose's laboratory than those in the wild, well protected from many external hazards. And in 1997, for the first time, the average age at which a mother in the UK gave birth to her first child passed 30. Maybe, like those *Drosophila*, we are gradually responding to a safer environment by reducing our need to reproduce early, and perhaps this will lead to the lengthening of our life spans. The trouble is that we are much more complicated than fruit flies and reproduce much more slowly, so even if delaying reproduction works, increasing our life span to 150 or 200 might take hundreds of years.

So, could we do something a bit less long-term? For thousands of years, humans have been exploring ideas for extending our life span. In ancient Rome, aged spectators would totter into the arena to drink the blood of dying gladiators, while Pope Innocent III was said to have downed the blood of boys, and the North Korean dictator Kim Jong-il was alleged to have had himself injected with the blood of virgins. Medieval alchemists recommended using gold, the withered flesh of mummies, or viper meat, while the great physicians Galen and Herman Boerhaave suggested inhaling the breath of virgins.

A better idea might be underfeeding. For many years, there has been evidence that it can lengthen the life of laboratory animals. In 1941, two eminent American nutritionists, Clive McCay and Leonard Maynard at Cornell University, reported that male rats restricted to about 60 per cent of their usual calorie intake lived for an average of

1,025 days, compared with 896 days for those on a normal diet, while for females the figures were 1,320 days against 985. In the 1960s and '70s at Philadelphia's Institute for Cancer Research, Morris Ross used underfeeding to increase the maximum life span of his laboratory rats by no less than 60 per cent. A Californian doctor and guru on extending life span, Roy Walford, tried a similar approach on mice. He said it worked even if the mice did not start their restricted diet until they were well into adulthood. Restricting calorie intake also seems to be effective for nematode worms and fruit flies, but more interesting for us humans are probably the results achieved by Dr Richard Weindruch and his team at the University of Wisconsin in 2009 with rhesus monkeys. For twenty years, one group of 38 monkeys had eaten a normal diet, while another 38 had their rations cut in stages by 30 per cent. At the end of this time, fourteen of the monkeys on a normal diet – but only five of the underfed group – had died of age-related diseases such as type 2 diabetes, cancer and heart disease. The downside of these experiments was that some scientists reported that the rats and mice on smaller rations were less fertile, and could be more depressed than those fed normally, though other researchers reported their rodents as being physically younger than their well-fed equivalents.

As to why underfeeding should extend life, some scientists think it may cause animals to pass into a biological state normally reserved for dealing with the threat of starvation. This reverses the normal priorities of evolution, and the precious resources an animal would normally invest in reproduction are instead diverted to basic body maintenance, so that they can still be around to reproduce if better times return at some later date. When it comes to the mechanics of how underfeeding works, there are a number of theories, but some scientists think it may slow down the speed at which cells divide, meaning it takes longer to reach the Hayflick limit.

Now, underfeeding may sound familiar from the story of the oldest man who ever lived, the Japanese Jiroemon Kimura, who made sure he always rose from the table when he was only four-fifths full, as do many Okinawans. But they were getting a few extra years, while the underfed rats, mice, fruit flies and monkeys were getting the equivalent of extra decades. So could calorie restriction significantly extend our maximum life span? Roy Walford decided to try the theory out, saying if humans could emulate rats and mice, we could live to 150 or even 180. Some scientists had said that extending the life span of laboratory animals

Tom Kirkwood.

had involved taking them to the edge of malnutrition, but Walford responded that for humans, he was advocating 'not malnutrition, but high quality nutrition', as he recommended a gradual lowering of calorie intake to about 1,500 a day, supplemented by vitamins and minerals, against the normal male intake of 2,500 a day. The doctor theorized that our diet still owed too much to that of primitive humans in those nasty, brutish and short days when the most important thing was to make us big, swift and strong as quickly as possible. He fasted for two days a week, and ate his supplemented diet the other five days, though he later relaxed these limits. (Walford pointed out that there was nothing good about just being thin, quoting a study of 750,000 people by the American Cancer Society which showed that people who were more than 10 per cent lighter than average actually had lower life expectancy. Similarly, rats that were allowed to eat whatever they liked, but remained underweight, tended to survive less well.) Walford himself died of motor neurone disease, aged 79.

The rationale for why underfeeding might enable us humans to live longer is the same as for animals. The body is being conned into thinking a famine is on the way, and so goes into maintenance-first mode. It also has a similar downside: women may stop ovulating. And Michael Rae, a man who had been subjecting himself to calorie restriction for three years, confided to a television programme in 2006 that 'My libido is lower than it was,' but added, 'there seems to be an enhancement of staying power.' With an estimated 100,000 people across the world today said to be cutting their calorie intake by up to 40 per cent, we may get a better idea of how far underfeeding works for humans over the coming decades, though according to one team of scientists from the United States' National Institute on Aging, because of the difficulty of setting up experimental studies, 'we will never know for sure.'

Another explanation offered for why underfeeding can increase life span is that it reduces production of free radicals. When the mitochondria – the biological power stations inside our cells – burn oxygen to provide the energy the cells need to work, this process releases free radicals, which are highly reactive chemicals that oxidize and damage our DNA, our telomeres and other molecules in the body. One of the founders of scientific gerontology, Dr Bruce Ames, calculated that each cell's DNA gets bombarded by 100,000 free radicals every day. He reckoned that accumulated damage can reduce a cell's power supply by up to 80 per cent, impairing the functions of vital organs such as the heart, liver and brain, and that this loss of power may also be a factor in stroke and diseases such as Alzheimer's and Parkinson's. As we saw, repair is costly, and Ames calculated that in rats about 1 per cent of the damage does not get put right. Professor Rajindar Sohal from the Southern Methodist University, Dallas, has said it is this accumulation of irreversible damage that kills us: 'We are oxidised to death.' And just as stress depresses the activity of telomerase, Elissa Epel found it also seemed to increase the damage from oxidation to cells in the immune system.

The free radical theory of ageing was first proposed in the 1950s by Denham Harman, an American professor of bio-gerontology. He showed that giving laboratory mice high doses of industrial anti-oxidants extended their lives by up to a quarter, though some have suggested that the real reason for the increased longevity was that it put the animals off their food. Later, Bruce Ames found that feeding elderly rats chemicals to combat oxidation damage could pep up their mitochondria, making them more vigorous and improving their memory. In 1990, Thomas Johnson of the University of Colorado said he had found the first gene specifically associated with ageing in nematode worms, and that it appeared to be involved in neutralizing free radicals. Johnson found he could make the nematodes live 70 per cent longer than normal by stimulating production of two enzymes that performed this task. There is also evidence that a similar process seems to work in fruit flies, and those long-lived storm petrels also produce extra supplies of antioxidants. So, could these chemicals help to extend human life?

You would hope so, as the shelves of so many health food shops groan with teas, tablets, capsules and supplements that are rich in them. Fruits and vegetables are also good sources, while green tea contains antioxidants called catechins. Then there are those long-lived Okinawans: as we saw, they are champion consumers of tofu and other soybean products, which are rich in antioxidants known as flavonoids, and there is indeed evidence that elderly Okinawans have unusually low levels of free radicals in their blood. A study of sixteen centenarians in Poland in 2000 found that they too had high levels of antioxidants. Unfortunately, there is no conclusive evidence yet that dosing with antioxidants will help extend human life span, with some scientists believing that supplements will just disperse through the body, having little impact on what happens in individual cells. Ames was more optimistic, but felt that any gains from taking antioxidants would result in improving average, not maximum, life span.

In recent years, though, the idea that antioxidants can help us live longer has come under more fundamental attack. In 2008, scientists from University College London genetically manipulated a group of nematode worms so that they were more efficient at mopping up free radicals, but the worms failed to live any longer than the unmodified variety. Then, in 2014, a team led by Siegfried Hekimi at McGill University in Canada found that free radicals could actually reinforce the defence mechanisms of nematode cells. Dr Hekimi said the team had demonstrated that the free radical theory of ageing was 'incorrect' and that free radicals 'actually combat – not cause – aging', though not everyone agrees.

So what about pharmaceutical drugs? In the soil of remote Easter Island in the 1970s, scientists discovered a substance called rapamycin. Doctors started using it to prevent patients rejecting transplanted organs. In 2009, however, u.s. scientists found it could extend the lives of mice by nearly 40 per cent, even though they did not start receiving the drug until they were twenty months old – equivalent to about aged 60 in a human. The researchers were excited. One, Dr Arlan Richardson, said, 'I never thought we would find an anti-ageing pill for people in my lifetime; however, rapamycin shows a great deal of promise to do just that.' Again, though, a note of caution was sounded, with Dr Lynne Cox, an expert in ageing at the University of Oxford, noting that rapamycin was used to suppress the immune system, and that although this might not be a major problem for laboratory mice, it would be for humans trying to live a normal life.

One theory as to why rapamycin prolonged the life of the mice was that it mimicked the effects of calorie restriction. Such an approach certainly sounded appealing: if we humans could somehow get our bodies to believe we are eating less without our actually having to do anything quite so tiresome, what a clever wheeze that would be! David Sinclair of Harvard Medical School even founded a company to explore proteins called sirtuins, which seem to be able to perform this trick, helping to prolong life in simple species like worms and yeast, and perhaps in more complex ones – such as the French. One of the peculiarities about our neighbours across the Channel is that although they love red meat and other quite fatty foods, they have very good life expectancy. Some researchers think this is to do with their taste for red wine, which contains resveratrol, which in turn activates sirtuins.

Other potential life-prolonging drugs have been explored, too. Might we be able to find something that stimulates production of telomerase or lengthens telomeres? Though that could increase the danger of cancer, unless we are able to find a way of just switching on the telomerase for a short time. So far, the jury is out. In 2008 Dr Robert Kane, director of the Center on Aging at the University of Minnesota in Minneapolis, said, 'There are a lot of nostrums out there. None of them has credibility . . . Every time anyone has studied them with any degree of rigour, they do not pan out.'

Might another route to extended life span be hormone treatment? Doctors at so-called 'life extension centres' in America can be found prescribing human growth hormone, also known as somatotropin, to middle-aged men, claiming that it can preserve lean body mass, boost the immune system and improve heart and kidney function. Unfortunately, it can also cause diabetes and the abnormal enlargement of the internal organs. Then as we saw from Okinawa, there is also DHEA, another hormone that occurs naturally in our bodies. High levels are linked with good health and a strong immune system, and low levels with infirmity and death, but as we get older, our bodies make less and less of it. DHEA is supposed to prevent cancer and heart disease, restore sexual vigour, improve brain function and stop middle-aged spread, but not a great deal is known about it, and Professor George Fink of the Medical Research Council's Brain Metabolism Unit in Edinburgh warned, 'It does have some effects on the brain. Until we know more, I don't think it would be wise to use it.' At Northwestern University, Illinois, of sixteen rats fed DHEA, fourteen developed liver cancer.

All right then, what about gene manipulation? As we have seen, scientists have used this to enable yeast, worms and fruit flies to live longer, sometimes to the equivalent of 150 years old in a human, and we have also discovered that there appears to be something in the genes of centenarians that helps explain their long life. So, is there a way of messing with our genes to increase our life span? The launch of the Human Genome Project in 1990, and its final mapping in 2003, seemed to offer real opportunities. In 2008 scientists at the University of Washington reported that fifteen genes that regulated life span in yeast and worms were similar to human genes, but humans are a lot more complex, and Jan Vijg from the Albert Einstein College of Medicine warned, 'We seem to know a lot about longevity in worms, but we don't know if any of it is relevant for humans.'

The simplest thing of all would be to discover a special longevity gene, but progress has been rather stop-start. French researchers did find a gene that was more common in centenarians, but it actually made people more prone to coronary heart disease, though perhaps it has other less apparent beneficial effects. In 2008 Nir Barzilai, also from Albert Einstein College, said a quarter of Ashkenazi centenarians carried a variant in the CETP gene that helped control cholesterol levels and reduce blood pressure, heart problems and memory loss. Six years later, researchers at Stanford University, California, tried studying the DNA of seventeen supercentenarians, but they found nothing. 'We were pretty disappointed,' said Professor Stuart Kim. A few months later, though, scientists at Brown University in Rhode Island had another success with mice. They said that by switching off a single gene known as Myc, they had been able to extend the lives of the mice by 15 per cent. The gene plays a role in the division and death of cells, and when it is overactive, it can cause cancer. Not only did the mice live longer, but they were generally fitter, their immune systems and brains performed better, and they avoided age-related diseases such as osteoporosis. The only downside was that they were a bit smaller than average. John Sedivy, Professor of Medical Science at Brown, said he was confident the findings could be used to help extend human life span. Also delving deep inside the cells of mice, researchers working with David Sinclair at Harvard turned up another possibility, when they found that DNA in the nucleus and in the mitochondria of the cells of two-year-olds had stopped communicating effectively. The team discovered this was down to shortage of a protein known as NAD. Within a week of increasing its levels, the mice had the body tissue of a six-month-old. 'In human years, this would be like a 60-year-old converting to a 20-year-old in these specific areas,' said Sinclair.

Yet another idea raises the question of whether those ancient Romans who drank the blood of dying gladiators had really got it so wrong. Scientists at Harvard's Department of Stem Cell and Regenerative Biology uncovered a protein known as GDF11 in the blood of young mice which petered out as they aged. They found that when they gave GDF11 to older mice, it improved the function of every organ in their bodies. Around the same time, researchers at Stanford University discovered that if they injected blood from a three-month-old mouse into an eighteen-month-old, the brain performance of the older one improved. These developments sound encouraging, but there are up to 8,000 different genes involved in the human ageing process, and a single cell can contain up to 2,500 different types of protein. At the Wellcome Collection in London, you can view the map of the human genome in a collection of books that stretches from floor to ceiling, each one packed with page after page of close type. Identifying the nuggets in them that might lengthen human life span looks like a daunting task.

It all seems so unfair. There is a tiny Caribbean jellyfish known as *Turritopsis nutricula*, which is just one-fifth of an inch (1/2 cm) long, that can turn back its biological clock and revert to a younger version of itself each time it mates, making it effectively immortal. If some minuscule jellyfish can savour the joys of everlasting life, why should we humans have to settle for a measly 120 years? As we saw, the Cambridge computer scientist Aubrey de Grey wants us to survive for centuries more. In 2003 he co-founded the Methuselah Foundation (bankrolled by one of the founders of PayPal) to 'find ways to extend healthy life' – but not, presumably, by calorie restriction. A television documentary from 2006 reported that by ten to ten in the morning, de Grey was already on his third pint of beer, though a medical examination indicated he was in great shape. Frustrated by the slowness of progress on life span extension, in 2009 de Grey brought 200 scientists to Cambridge for what he called the SENS (Strategies for Engineered Negligible Senescence) conference. He proclaimed that thanks to 'conventional' medical progress, 'a child born today can expect to live 120 to 150 years,' but he reckoned that 'If we make the right breakthroughs in the next 25 years, then there is a 50:50 chance that people alive today could live to be 1,000 years old.' That would depend on us reaching what he calls 'human longevity escape velocity', getting to the point at which life expectancy increases more quickly than time passes; in other words, that in a calendar year, life expectancy goes up by more than a year. As we have seen, life expectancy has been increasing by perhaps three months each year, so would it be out of the question to accelerate that to, say, thirteen months a year? If this could be achieved, unlimited life span would, in principle, beckon, as our knowledge of science kept getting better and better. But although de Grey hopes the breakthroughs could be achieved within 25 years, he cautions that there is a 10 per cent chance we will not make them for another 100.

To achieve longevity escape velocity, de Grey identified 'seven deadly assassins' we need to conquer: mutations to the mitochondria inside our cells, which then disrupt our energy supply; the death of cells in areas like the heart and the brain; the growth of unwanted cells, like the fat cells that can lead to diabetes; protein cross-links that cause loss of elasticity in tissues such as artery walls; the build-up of 'junk' proteins within cells, which can cause heart disease; the accumulation of 'junk' proteins outside cells, which can cause diseases such as Alzheimer's; and the chromosomal mutations that cause cancer. The former computer scientist believed all seven should be 'fixable in principle and forseeably'. Gene therapy could protect our mitochondria, while stem cell therapy could replace the cells we do not want to die. We could trick unwanted cells into destroying themselves. In theory, drugs could break down the protein cross-links, while genes or enzymes could be developed to digest the junk, and for cancer a radical bio-engineering therapy known as WILT (whole-body interdiction of lengthening of telomeres) could destroy the ability of vulnerable cells to replicate before they can become cancer cells and replace them every ten years or so with billions of new stem cells. De Grey said that his strategy was based not on discovering some magic-bullet elixir of life, but instead on adopting 'what you might think of as an ongoing maintenance approach. In the same way that it's possible to keep a car or a house going indefinitely if you put enough maintenance in.' Using this piecemeal renewal of damaged, malfunctioning or worn-out bits, 'it should in principle be possible to keep the body going . . . And that's forever.' Once successful therapies had been developed, patients would simply need to drop into hospital for a couple of months, and emerge rejuvenated, so that a 60-year-old would be re-equipped with a 30-year-old body. And this process could be repeated whenever necessary. It would have the curious side effect that a parent who had undergone the treatment would emerge biologically younger than a child who had not.

Unlimited life span, though, does not mean immortality. Remember the warning of Peter Medawar: even *Turritopsis nutricula*, like any other potentially immortal being, will eventually be wiped out by a nasty accident, disease, violence or other mishap. And the concept of 'mortality substitution': if you do not die of one thing, you will die from something else. An actuary calculated in 2012 that a 'medical immortal' human would last an average of 6,000 years before being killed off by some unpleasant event. Still, that is a lot longer than 120.

Not only are some of de Grey's ideas controversial – so are his methods, such as offering cash prizes for scientists who could beat the world longevity record for a mouse. He argued it was good that he came from outside the world of gerontology, because outsiders are not shackled by conventional wisdom and can contribute radical ideas. And ideas he is certainly never short of. One remedy of which he sang the praises was a microorganism discovered in a mass graveyard that can digest lipofuscin, some of the 'junk' that builds up in vital organs like the heart, liver and kidneys and impairs their functioning. De Grey has also confided that he has made arrangements to have his head preserved in liquid nitrogen when he dies, so that, assuming science progresses as he hopes, it could one day be resuscitated, though he concedes, 'a lot of people think that I'm completely crazy.'

Not everyone, though. Professor Mark Pepys, a biomedical researcher at University College London who spoke at the 2009 SENS conference declared, 'Aubrey de Grey is not crazy. He's got serious hard-core scientists working for him that are doing great work on ageing.' Those who thought like de Grey got dubbed 'immortalists'. They see conquering ageing as essentially an engineering problem, and the way to beat it as the replacement of worn-out or defective body parts. At the British Anti-ageing Conference in 2011, gerontologist Dr Marios Kyriazis, chairman of the British Longevity Society, declared that our maximum life span will go on increasing, until 'before long, it's reasonable to say that we'll be living for 500 years.' People will 'still die from diseases, or in car crashes or being shot by a terrorist. But they will not die of old age.' Incidentally, a journalist reported that Dr Kyriazis looked a good deal older than his 55 years.

But de Grey certainly does have his opponents. In 2006, 28 scientists including Professor Richard Miller, associate director of the Geriatrics Center at the University of Michigan, dismissed his SENS agenda as wildly over-optimistic, saying it was 'so far from plausible that it commands no respect at all from within the scientific community'. A couple of years later, S. Jay Olshansky, a demographer from the University of Illinois, together with another 50 of the world's top longevity experts, gave a stern warning on the immortalist agenda: 'Our language on this matter must be unambiguous. There are no lifestyle changes, surgical procedures, vitamins, antioxidants, hormones, or techniques of genetic engineering available today that have been demonstrated to influence the processes of aging.' He added, 'The only control we have over the duration of our life is to shorten it, and we do that all the time.' The distinguished geneticist Robin Holliday also rejected the idea that we could dramatically extend our maximum life span, saying such claims were 'breathtakingly arrogant', that the anti-ageing 'movement' had degenerated into 'science fiction' and that something like 125 was the maximum human life span.

In between enthusiasts and opponents are another group of scientists, who do not believe humans can start living for hundreds of years, but do not accept either that 120 or so represents the limit to our life span. They can point to history. In the 1950s it was believed that the maximum human life span was probably 110, and limited by 'clock genes' or 'death hormones' that kill us off at the appropriate time. Twenty years later, another demographer raised the figure to

117, a barrier that has been beaten by a select few. Then in 2007 the French demographer and gerontologist Jean-Marie Robine declared, 'human longevity has no limits in terms of age and there are no biologically-controlled limits.' Professor of demography John Wilmoth concluded that two developments suggest 'a finite human life-span limit is not presently within sight': first, the slowing of the death rate in extreme old age, observed by the Gavrilovs, and second, the way that average life expectancy keeps increasing. Wilmoth argued that 'If we were close to observing a biological maximum, intuition suggests that this trend would show some sign of deceleration.' In fact, 'none is evident'. Jim Oeppen from the Cambridge Group for the History of Population and Social Structure acknowledged there had been an assumption that eventually, life expectancy would 'reach a ceiling it cannot go through', but he pointed out that people had been saying that 'since the 1920s and it hasn't proved to be the case'. Nonetheless, he believed there was a ceiling, 'but we don't know where it is. We haven't got there yet.'

James Vaupel thought that we might be more hopeful about the human evolutionary priorities that concentrate on making sure we can reproduce when we are young and do not bother very much about our ability to survive later in life. He compared the human body to a fly-by space probe sent to investigate a planet in the solar system: the priority of the designers is to engineer a probe that can do this job, but often those probes go on functioning long after they have passed their target, even though no specific features have been built in to enable them to do this. Vaupel contended that a similar thing might be happening with the human body. Although no particular features may have been provided to allow us to survive in old age, perhaps they are nevertheless there incidentally, because of their value earlier in our lives. So evolution may have accidentally given us a good start on the task of solving the problems of ageing. But he did warn against over-optimism, noting that 'even the simplest bacterium is vastly more complicated than the most elaborate machinery.'

More hopeful was Professor Valter Longo, who set a world record for life span extension in any organism at the University of Southern California in 2008, when he helped create a strain of yeast that could live ten times longer than normal. He achieved it by putting the yeast on a calorie-controlled diet and by deleting two genes that promote ageing from its genome. Longo said that, in principle, 'If we can find out how the longevity mechanism works, it can be applied to every cell in every living organism.' Like Aubrey de Grey, he thought it would be possible for humans to survive for hundreds of years: 'at a certain point I think it will be possible to get people to live to 800. I don't think there is an upper limit to the life of any organism.' But the timescale required to achieve this he saw rather differently: we are still 'very, very far' from it.

Tom Kirkwood, originator of the disposable soma theory, has spent much of his life thinking about these issues. Delivering the BBC's Reith Lectures in 2001 on 'The End of Age', he said, 'our bodies are not programmed with some unavoidable sell-by date; we are not programmed to die.' Ageing is 'neither inevitable nor necessary'. He endorsed the evolutionary view: that ageing happens through the gradual build-up of unrepaired faults in our cells and tissues because our genes prioritize reproduction over repair and maintenance. 'If we can discover the nature of these faults,' Kirkwood said, 'we can hope to slow their accumulation.' He was confident that we have not yet reached the limits of human life span: 'It may be some time before Jeanne Calment's record is broken, but broken it will be.' On the other hand, he dismissed talk of a life span of 200 or more as 'fanciful'. 'Ageing', he pointed out, 'is a complicated process with multiple changes affecting every organ,' and added a reminder about how frustratingly slow we have been to find effective solutions to fight illnesses such as cancer, stroke and heart disease. There would be no 'quick fix', he said, but then added intriguingly, 'equally, there is no limit.'

'Never make forecasts,' Sam Goldwyn is supposed to have said, 'especially about the future.' But we have seen some developments that suggest Aubrey de Grey's care and maintenance approach may show results. Spare-part surgery began with transplanted organs from human donors. Then, scientists began to grow body parts, such as ears, and by 2009, 300,000 people were said to have been fitted with them. In regenerative medicine, stem cells can be injected into damaged areas such as the heart to help repair them, and scientists are also working on treatments that could mobilize the body's own stem cells and get them to migrate to the areas that need attention. Professor Chris Mason, a biomedical researcher at King's College London, said we can already regenerate some bits of our bodies, such as the liver and the tongue, and that in future we should be able to grow other parts too, like arms and legs.

Not every bright idea works, of course. Take the drug Bapineuzumab, which looked as though it might be able to break up the amyloid plaques in the brain – some of Aubrey de Grey's 'junk' – that are thought to be a cause of Alzheimer's disease. In 2012, Bapineuzumab failed to produce significant cognitive improvement in patients in two clinical trials. It was this kind of disappointment that led scientists such as Professor Martin Raff from University College London to point to Aubrey de Grey's inexperience in experimental science, saying that he was very well informed, but naive, not realizing 'how difficult it is, how long things take, and how often things don't work'. Raff quoted his own efforts at testing an enzyme that might prevent Alzheimer's. After seven years' work, he still did not know whether it would break down one of 10,000 proteins in the nerve cell. Medicine is full of similar examples. In stem cell research, Tom Kirkwood quoted the example of Parkinson's disease. It was hoped that transplanting foetal cells might cure it, but the idea was abandoned when two clinical trials exhibited no benefits (though now there is renewed interest in the treatment). He explained that embryo stem cells go through a series of complex processes to form the cells of the adult. If we put early stem cells into adult tissue, were we sure we could replicate all these processes? On the other hand if we used adult stem cells, we ran the risk that these might have been damaged. As for gene therapy, he pointed out that we have not even been able to conquer diseases caused by a single gene, such as cystic fibrosis: 'we have long known what we want to do. Would that we could do it.'

Peter Medawar may have warned about the fate of potentially immortal beings, but he also said something more encouraging for the immortalists: 'anything which is possible in principle – which does not flout a bedrock law of physics – can be done if the intention to do it is sufficiently resolute and long sustained.' In 2011, the anti-ageing business was said to be worth $88 billion in the United States alone, and plenty of effort has been going into it, for quite a while. In the 1980s, film stars, politicians and even popes were said to have gone to Lake Geneva to be injected with cells from unborn lambs. In Bavaria, you could indulge in a serum supposed to have been developed to try to keep Joseph Stalin young, and in Mexico there was an injection that would allegedly 'wash' your blood. Now, though, much more mainstream business people are involved, like Bill Maris, president of Google Ventures, a fund which has invested nearly $2 billion in the life sciences, and who says, 'If you ask me today, is it possible to live to be 500? The answer is yes.' Then there is Larry Ellison, co-founder of American software giant Oracle, who has called mortality 'incomprehensible'; or Google co-founder Sergey Brin, who hopes one day to 'cure death'; or Russian entrepreneur Dmitry Itskov, who says he plans to live to 10,000.

So, which is it to be: maximum life span, stuck somewhere around Jeanne Calment's age of 122; a gradual push beyond that by incremental steps; or a big bang that sees us measuring our time in centuries? Aubrey de Grey now tends to talk more about healthy ageing than extending life span, telling a journalist, 'What we want to do is keep people healthy and we have to do this as quickly as possible, and the longevity is purely a side effect.' He points to the fact that 'about 100,000 people – 30 World Trade Centers – every day die of ageing,' noting, 'The main problem about ageing is not just that it kills you, but that it kills you really horribly.' His Methuselah Foundation says it has dispensed more than $4 million in grants for funding regenerative medicine, which it says will 'transform' health care this century. It wants to ensure everyone enjoys 'a vibrant and productive life, not just in their early years, but into their 70s, 80s, and 90s' and that by 2030, '90 year olds can be as healthy as 50 year olds are today.' Promotion of healthier old age tends to be less controversial than searching for longer life, but Kirkwood argues that we should not see the two as different objectives; they are probably interlinked: 'If we can assure greater quality of life in old age, it may be that we can slip in some extra years as well.'

Deciding who is right in this argument is not easy. After all, the *Technology Review*, which offered a prize for anyone who could prove that Aubrey de Grey's SENS approach was 'so wrong that it was unworthy of learned debate', decided neither side had won. The SENS Research Foundation itself admits that 'no currently-available medical intervention or lifestyle choice has been shown to affect the basic human aging process,' but its supporters, of course, would argue this just emphasizes the need for more research.

But should we even be trying to extend our life span into centuries? Some people argue the idea is just plain wrong. A couple of millennia ago Cicero proclaimed: 'It is desirable for a man to be blotted out at his proper time.' More recently, Professor Allan Pacey, former chair of the British Fertility Society, said: 'I think humans have a good innings on the whole and we should try and be content with that.' Others, like Leonard Hayflick, say that trying dramatically to extend life span goes against nature – that age is not a disease to be cured and that those who try to stave it off are disturbing a process as natural as the development of a child.

On the other hand, one of the fathers of modern science, Francis Bacon, argued at its dawn in the sixteenth century that its 'true aim' was 'the discovery of all operations and all possibilities of operations from immortality (if it were possible) to the meanest mechanical practice'. Modern supporters of extending life span argue that if there were an illness, or a dictator, killing people by the million, we would be up in arms and desperate to do something about it; but when the killer is ageing, we just shrug our shoulders. The immortalist Marios Kyriazis certainly has no misgivings:

> It's nonsensical to believe nature, God, whatever, created life only to allow it to end after a set period of time. A living being, once created, should be allowed to live indefinitely, or – put it another way – should not be allowed to die. Otherwise, what was the point of creating it in the first place?

He thinks it is terrible that we humans, who can go to the moon (well, a few of us, anyway), should become fodder for worms.

Another argument advanced against dramatically extending life span is that we would all get terribly bored. Certainly not, says Aubrey de Grey: 'People with a good education and the time to use it never get bored today and can't imagine ever running out of new things they'd like to do.' Roy Walford offered a similar opinion:

> a person's allotted span of life is simply too short to permit a satisfying exploration of the world's outer wonders and the realms of inner experience. We are cut off in the midst of our pleasures, separated too soon from our loved ones, shelved at the mere beginning of our understanding.

While the poet, philosopher and neuroscientist Raymond Tallis said that from an individual's point of view, death, however long it is delayed, 'will always be premature – at least for the one who is dying. A late death is never late enough.' And suppose some centuries-old humans did find they were so fed up they could not stand it any longer: they could always kill themselves. Even the immortalists do not think actual immortality is on offer.

One thing we can be sure of is that any means of dramatically extending life span will not come cheaply, especially at first. So only the rich are likely to be able to afford them. We have seen that poorer people already have a considerably shorter life expectancy than rich folk. What if that discrepancy started to be measured in centuries? Would that be morally repugnant? And if longevity treatments eventually became widespread, and we had an army of 'medical immortals', would they all be on pensions? And if so, how would we pay for them – or would one of the downsides of living for centuries be that you would also have to work for centuries? Kyriazis's reply is: 'We wouldn't retire, but we would change careers. We'd take big chunks of time off, we'd learn to do things like play the piano.' As for how we would pay for this: 'A manual labourer could start a restaurant or a bed and breakfast. He could sell oranges in the marketplace. The point is, people won't be stuck building walls or digging up the street until they're 50 and retire.'

Then there is the question of overpopulation. In 1950 there were 2.5 billion people in the world; by 2017 there were more than 7.5 billion. If large numbers of us start living for centuries, will the world's population not go through the roof? De Grey acknowledges that this presents a 'problem', but he points out that new technologies might mean we will inflict less environmental damage on the planet (and if we knew we were going to be around for centuries, perhaps we would also care more about it). De Grey, who has no children, says that 'women are already having fewer children and later in life.' If we start living for centuries, it 'might mean they delay having children even longer'. Kyriazis has tried to enlist the anti-immortalists' 'it's against nature' argument in the immortalists' cause: 'nature is telling us we don't need to have so many children. We should achieve intelligence and complexity through ourselves, rather than through our offspring.' He theorized that one reason we have seen 'such an emergence of homosexuality in recent years' is that 'nature knows that we no longer need to populate the planet'. De Grey argues that whatever the rights and wrongs of the population issue are, it would be immoral to stop exploring ways of fighting ageing, because that would be to deny humanity the choice of whether to adopt them. If we were to discover them, we would have a decision to make about whether to use these therapies and stop ourselves from ageing, stop ourselves from dying – and therefore have to cut down very sharply on the numbers of kids we have, or alternatively, maintain the birth rate as it is, and cope with the over-population problem by simply not using these therapies.

He adds: 'humanity has the right to make those choices for itself. If we were to hold back and not develop these therapies, we would be making that choice on behalf of the humanity of the future – imposing our values on them – and I think we have a duty not to do that.'

Finally, there is our old friend evolution. Tom Kirkwood dismissed as a 'misconception' the idea that 'we are programmed to die because this is necessary to make way for the next generation.' But imagine if human adults were immortal: they would be bigger, stronger, more knowledgeable and experienced than – and would compete unfairly with – smaller, younger newcomers, who might actually be improved versions of humanity. So if we were to slow down ageing, we might be slowing down evolution, too. The British biologist and scientific philosopher C. H. Waddington said that death and old age may be necessary 'to make room for the maturation of a new generation in which new genetic combinations can be tried out for their fitness'. This is essential so that we can adapt to changes in our environment. Steve Jobs once described death as 'very likely the single best invention of life . . . it clears out the old to make way for the new.'

Aubrey de Grey believes that once promising approaches to combatting ageing start to appear, opposition to the idea will melt away:

Our doubts about it are a coping strategy, to put it out of our minds because ageing is currently inevitable. When we realise it isn't inevitable, we'll wake up out of this pro-ageing trance we're in, realise that ageing is the one unsolved problem for mankind, and we'll get on and fix it.

Perhaps it is a coping strategy, but misgivings about immortality seem to lie very deep inside us. A Greek myth dating back 3,000 years or more tells the story of Tithonus, the handsome brother of Priam, king of Troy at the time of the Trojan War. Eos, the goddess of dawn, fell in love with him, and carried him off to be her lover. They had two children, and even though Eos had flings with other mortals, Tithonus was her great love, so she asked Zeus, king of the gods, to grant him immortal life. But, unfortunately, she forgot also to request eternal youth, and Zeus granted her request to the letter. So Tithonus got older and older and more and more decrepit. In Alfred, Lord Tennyson's telling of the story, Tithonus is reduced to begging to be allowed to die: 'Let me go: take back thy gift.' In one version of the myth, he becomes so wizened that Eos, out of pity, turns him into a cicada – but he still croaks out his wish to be allowed to die.

The elixir of life that features in the 1920s opera *The Makropulos Affair* by the Czech composer Leoš Janáček does provide enduring youth as well as extended lifespan. It is swallowed by the beautiful Elina Makropulos, who over three centuries attracts an endless string of lovers. But by the time she reaches her 320s, she is thoroughly bored, has completely gone off sex and is happy when the elixir finally wears off and she can die. Said to have been inspired by Janáček's unrequited love for a much younger woman, the opera is often seen as an expression of the view that it is only the acceptance of death that gives meaning to life.

Far from losing interest in sex, the immortal 'struldbrugs' in Jonathan Swift's classic fantasy *Gulliver's Travels* (1726) become consumed with envy at those who can still indulge in 'the vices of the younger sort'. Gulliver not only travels to lands of giants and of tiny Lilliputians; he goes to the kingdom of Luggnagg, where every so often a child is born with a red spot over its left eyebrow – a sign that it will live forever. Our hero is elated, imagining what joyful lives these children will live, freed from the constant fear of death, what endless achievements they will be able to accomplish, what changes they will be able to witness. The other inhabitants soon put him right. Unfortunately, as with Tithonus, for the struldbrugs everlasting life does not come with the added feature of everlasting youth. Gulliver learns that until the age of 30, most are reasonably happy; after that they start to become 'melancholy and dejected' and dominated by 'envy and impotent desires'. They are incapable of friendship or affection. At 90 they are still prone to disease and lose their teeth, their hair and their memory. It does not help that when the struldbrugs reach 80, the normal age for death in Luggnagg, they are stripped of their possessions and given just a small pittance to live on. No wonder that 'whenever they see a funeral, they lament that others are gone to a harbour of rest to which they themselves can never hope to arrive.' The traveller gets to meet a few struldbrugs, who exhibit not the slightest interest in him or his adventures and just want to beg from him. 'They were the most mortifying sight I ever beheld,' concludes Gulliver, 'no tyrant could invent a death into which I would not run with pleasure, from such a life.'

Everlasting life brings no more happiness to the hero of 'The Immortal', a short story written in 1947 by the Argentinian writer Jorge Luis Borges. It tells of a Roman soldier who sets off to find a river, the water of which can bestow eternal life. He drinks from it, and finds the Immortals, who built a great city but who now live as troglodytes, having decided that 'all undertakings are in vain'. They are sad people and 'invulnerable to pity'. One falls into a hole, and though he cannot die, he suffers terribly from thirst, but it is 70 years before any of the others bothers to throw him a rope. The fact that the Immortals live forever has robbed everything of value: 'Nothing can happen only once. Nothing is preciously precarious.' The soldier is thrilled when he happens to drink from another river, making him mortal again.

Contemporary authors do not seem any more cheerful. In his science fiction novel *The End Specialist* (2011), the American writer Drew Magary describes how, in 2019, science discovers how to make people 'post-mortal' through a course of injections. It leads not to paradise but to an overpopulated dystopia, while in their personal lives, the post-mortals find that things like marriage and ambition lose their meaning. But – remember Peter Medawar – the post-mortals are not immortal. Only ageing has been cured; they can still die of disease or unpleasant occurrences of various kinds, and overpopulation is sorted out by such means as nuclear weapons. Magary was 34 years old when he wrote the book. Perhaps it is easier to be hostile towards the wish to cure ageing when you are young.

Where does this leave us, then? Barring some natural or man-made catastrophe, most forecasters expect our average life expectancy to go on increasing, but the prospect of dramatically extending humans' maximum life span appears far more uncertain. Perhaps we are fortunate that, for the moment, it seems unlikely that we will have to take decisions on the awesome question of whether we humans should seek to live for centuries. The scientific problems are just too complex. We may see maximum life span pushed upwards by incremental steps – though even beating Jeanne Calment's record appears tough enough at present – but a big bang of the kind hoped for by Aubrey de Grey and those who think like him seems well beyond our horizons for the foreseeable future. Is there a limit to our lives? For the moment, yes.

BIBLIOGRAPHY

BOOKS

Arthur, Max, *Last Post* (London, 2005)

Borges, Jorge Luis, 'The Immortal', in *Labyrinths* (London, 1970)

Bury, Michael, and Anthea Holme, *Life After Ninety* (London, 1991)

Carey, Peter, *Illywhacker* (London, 1985)

Jeune, Bernard, and James Vaupel, *Validation of Exceptional Longevity* (Odense, 1999), Monographs of Population Aging, 6, www.demogr.mpg.de

Jonasson, Jonas, *The Hundred-year-old Man Who Climbed Out of the Window and Disappeared* (London, 2014)

Lancaster, H. O., *Expectations of Life: A Study in the Demography, Statistics, and History of World Mortality* (New York, 1990)

Laslett, Peter, *The World We Have Lost: Further Explored* (London, 1983)

Magary, Drew, *The End Specialist* (London, 2011)

Robine, Jean-Marie, ed., *Human Longevity, Individual Life Duration, and the Growth of the Oldest-old Population* (Heidelberg, 2007)

Rogers, Richard G., and Eileen M. Crimmins, eds, *International Handbook of Adult Mortality* (Heidelberg, 2011)

Swift, Jonathan, *Gulliver's Travels* (London, 1726)

Thoms, W. J., *Human Longevity: Its Facts and Its Fictions* (London, 1873)

Wachter, Kenneth W., and Caleb E. Finch, eds, *Between Zeus and the Salmon: The Biodemography of Longevity* (Washington, DC, 1997)

Walford, Roy L., *Maximum Life Span* (New York, 1983)

Willcox, Donald Craig, Bradley J. Willcox, and Leonard W. Pool, eds, *Centenarian Studies: Important Contributors to Our Understanding of the Aging Process and Longevity* (London, 2010)

ARTICLES

Abrams, Mark, 'A Longitudinal Study of Ageing: First Report' (September 1981)

Adler, Lynn Peters, '7 Life Secrets of Centenarians', www.nextavenue.org, 14 August 2013

'Albert Hofmann', *The Economist*, 10 May 2008

Andersen-Ranberg, Karen, 'Healthy Centenarians Do Not Exist, But Autonomous Centenarians Do', *Journal of the American Geriatrics Society* (July 2001)

'Antioxidants "Cannot Slow Ageing"', www.bbc.co.uk/news, 1 December 2008

Arnold, Jonathan, et al., 'Predicting Successful Aging in a Population-based Sample of Georgia Centenarians', *Centenarian Studies: Important Contributors to Our Understanding of the Aging Process and Longevity* (2010), doi:10.1155/2010/989315

Arthur, George, 'Why Self-pity is Bad for Your Health', *The Independent*,
    26 August 1997
'Auschwitz Survivor is World's Oldest Man – Guinness World Records',
    www.bbc.co.uk, 11 March 2016
Barclay, Eliza, 'Tea Tuesdays: Tea-drinking Tips for a Longer Life', www.npr.org,
    28 April 2015
Batrinos, Menelaos L., 'The Length of Life and Eugeria in Classical Greece',
    www.hormones.gr, 5 December 2007
Beck, Melinda, 'Boys Face More Danger Than Girls in Womb', www.wsj.com,
    14 November 2013
Berger, Marilyn, 'Irving Berlin, Nation's Songwriter, Dies', www.nytimes.com,
    23 September 1989
Bingham, John, 'Queen's "Birthday Card Team" Expands to Cope with Surge
    of 100-year-olds', www.telegraph.co.uk, 25 September 2014
'Biological Process Linked to Early Aging, Death Among Poor in Detroit',
    www.ns.umich.edu, 9 June 2015
Bland, Martin, and Doug Altman, 'Do the Left-handed Die Young?',
    www.onlinelibrary.wiley.com, 30 November 2005.
'The Bob Hope Story', www.dailymail.co.uk, accessed 20 December 2016
Briggs, Helen, 'Biological Clue to Why Women Live Longer Than Men',
    www.bbc.co.uk, 15 May 2013
—, 'DNA Sequenced of Woman Who Lived to 115', www.bbc.co.uk, 15 October
    2011
Brindle, David, 'Terminally Ill "Put Off Death" for a Festival', *The Guardian*,
    23 September 1988
'Britain: "The Fat Man of Europe"', www.nhs.uk, 6 November 2013
Bucke, M., and M. L. Insley, 'Centenarians are Healthy, but They Need Mental
    and Emotional Care', *Modern Geriatrics*, VI/2 (1976), pp. 24–8
—, 'Living to One Hundred – Chance or Achievement?', *Age Concern Today*, 21
    (Spring 1977)
Bury, Michael, and Anthea Holme, 'Quality of Life and Social Support in the
    Very Old', *Journal of Aging Studies*, IV/4 (1990), pp. 345–57
Caba, Justin, 'Centenarian Populations are Growing, Calling for Better End-of-
    life Care to Accommodate Longevity', www.medicaldaily.com, 3 June 2014
Campbell, Denis, 'Cancer Risk Higher among People Who Eat More Processed
    Meat, Study Finds', www.theguardian.com, 7 March 2013
College of Public Health, Institute of Gerontology, 'Phase I and Phase II of
    the Georgia Centenarian Study', www.publichealth.uga.edu, accessed
    20 December 2016
Connor, Steve, 'Leading with Your Left May Shorten Your Life',
    The Independent, 3 March 1991
Corliss, Richard, and Michael D. Lemonick, 'How to Live to Be 100',
    www.time.com, 30 August 2004
Dello Buono, Marriosa, et al., 'Quality of Life and Longevity: A Study of
    Centenarians', www.ageing.oxfordjournals.org, 1998
Deluty, Jennifer A., et al., 'The Influence of Gender on Inheritance of
    Exceptional Longevity', www.ageing-us.com, 22 June 2015
Deshpande, Rina, 'The Science of Meditation's Effects on Aging',
    www.huffingtonpost.com, 21 August 2015

Desjardins, B., 'Validation of Extreme Longevity Cases in the Past: The French-Canadian Experience', in *Validation of Exceptional Longevity* (Odense, 1999), ed. B. Jeune and J. W. Vaupel, Monographs of Population Aging, 6, www.demogr.mpg.de

Doheny, Kathleen, 'Planet Talk: Centenarian Expert Tom Perls', www.seniorplanet.org, 25 March 2013

Donnelly, Laura, and Gallagher, Sarah, 'Britain's Binge Drinking Levels are Among the Highest in the World', www.telegraph.co.uk, 13 May 2014

Duarte, N., 'Frailty Phenotype Criteria in Centenarians: Findings from the Oporto Centenarian Study', www.europeangeriatricmedicine.com, December 2014

Edge, Simon, 'The Secret to a Long Life?', www.express.co.uk, 18 April 2014

Evans, Catherine J., et al., 'Place and Cause of Death in Centenarians: A Population-based Observational Study in England, 2001 to 2010', *PloS Med* (2014), doi:10.1371/journal.pmed.1001653

Faig, Kenneth, Jr, 'Living to 100 and Beyond: Survival at Advanced Ages, Session 7: Mortality at Oldest Ages Session – Part 1. Author reply' available at www.soa.org/library/.../living-to-100/2002/mono-2002-m-li-02-1-faig-reply.pdf

'Family Link to Long Life', www.bbc.co.uk, 10 June 2002

Fernandez, Colin, 'Men Who Live to 100 Healthier Than Women', www.dailymail.co.uk, 22 June 2015

'Five Score and 12', *The Guardian*, 11 June 1990

'For Ever and Ever', *The Economist*, 28 April 2012

'Forever Young?', *The Economist*, 5 November 2011

Forman, Jonathan Barry, 'What Do We Know about the Oldest Old?', *In the Public Interest*, 9 (January 2014), pp. 9–13

'Forward to Methuselah', *The Economist*, 7 January 1995

Fowler, Rebecca, 'Brandy for Breakfast Keeps Spirit Alive for Britain's Oldest Woman – Charlotte Hughes', *Sunday Times*, 2 August 1992

Fraser, Gary, 'Adventist Health Studies Indicate a Long, Healthy Life is No Accident', www.news.adventist.org, 18 May 2011

Gallagher, James, 'Short People's "DNA Linked to Increased Heart Risk"', www.bbc.co.uk, 9 April 2015

Gavrilov, Leonid A., and Natalia S. Gavrilova, 'Mortality of Centenarians: A Study Based on the Social Security Administration Death Master File', paper accepted for presentation at the 2005 Annual Meeting of the Population Association of America, Philadelphia, 31 March–2 April 2005, http://paa2005.princeton.edu

—, 'Physical and Socioeconomic Characteristics at Young Age as Predictors of Survival to 100', presented at the Living to 100 and Beyond Symposium, Orlando, Florida, 7–9 January 2008, www.soa.org

—, 'Search for Predictors of Exceptional Human Longevity', *North American Actuarial Journal*, x/1 (January 2007)

Gerontology Research Group, 'Current Validated Living Supercentenarians', www.grg.org, 1 January 2015

Gillie, Oliver, 'Secrets of the Oldest Man in the World', *Sunday Times*, 23 June 1985

'Golden Oldies! Grandparents were a Rare Breed until 30,000 Years Ago . . . When Life Expectancy Grew', www.dailymail.co.uk, 20 July 2011

Gove, Walter R., 'Sex, Marital Status, and Mortality', *American Journal of Sociology*, LXXIX/1 (July 1973), pp. 49–67

'GP Explains Life Expectancy Gap', www.bbc.co.uk/news, 28 August 2008

'Grandma Moses Is Dead at 101; Primitive Artist "Just Wore Out"', www.nytimes.com, 14 December 1961

Griffiths, Sarah, 'Scientists Search for the Secret to Long Life', www.dailymail.co.uk, 12 November 2014

Guner, Nezih, et al., 'Does Marriage Make You Healthier?', http://pareto.uab.es, October 2014

Hadfield, Joe, 'Stayin' Alive: That's What Friends are For', http://news.byu.edu, 27 July 2010

Haiken, Melanie, 'Height Linked to Women's Cancer Risk? New Study Suggests Yes', www.forbes.com, 25 July 2013

Harris, Richard, 'Why are More Baby Boys Born Than Girls?', www.npr.org, 30 March 2015

Hellmich, Nanci, 'Study: Being Even a Little Overweight May Shorten Life', www.usatoday.com, 23 August 2006

Hodgson, Godfrey, 'Obituary: Rose Kennedy', *The Independent*, 24 January 1995, www.web.archive.org

Hope, Jenny, 'Why Women Live Longer Than Men', www.dailymail.co.uk, 2 May 2015

Hotz, Robert Lee, 'Secrets of the "Wellderly"', www.wsj.com, 19 September 2008

'How to Live Forever', *The Economist*, 5 January 2008

Hubbard, Sylvia Booth, 'Survey Reveals Simple Habits that Could Help You Live to 100', www.newsmax.com, 30 April 2015

Hunt, Liz, 'The Age Old Problem', *The Independent*, 2 February 1997

'If the Cap Fits', *The Economist*, 4 December 2004

Ingram, Donald K., 'The Potential for Dietary Restriction to Increase Longevity in Humans: Extrapolation from Monkey Studies', www.springerlink.com, 27 May 2006

'It's in Our Genes: Why Women Outlive Men', Monash University, www.monash.edu, 3 August 2012

'Japanese Expert Debunks Idea of "Village of 100-year-olds"', www.supercentenarian.com, 6 April 1987

'Japan's Oldest Twin Dies', www.bbc.co.uk, 28 February 2001

Juncosa, Barbara, 'Is 100 the New 80?', www.scientificamerican.com, 28 October 2008

Kaplan, Lawrence, 'Human Life Span', www.britannica.com, 2016

Kaufman, Marc, 'Cigarettes Cut about 10 Years Off Life, 50-year Study Shows', www.washingtonpost.com, 23 June 2004

'Keys to Long Life', www.newsroom.ucr.edu, 11 March 2011

Kirkwood, Tom, 'Sex and Death', www.bbc.co.uk, 2001

Kłapcińska, Barbara, et al., 'Antioxidant Defense in Centenarians (A Preliminary Study)', *Acta Biochimica Polonia*, XLVII/2, www.actabp.pl, 31 January 2000

Klimaski, Joanna, 'Living Past 100, and Living Well', http://legacy.fordham.edu, 16 July 2012

Knapton, Sarah, 'Ageing Reversed as Scientists Discover How to Turn Clock Back in Mammals', www.telegraph.co.uk, 20 December 2013

—, 'Could Switching Off Single Gene Extend Life by 12 Years?', www.telegraph.co.uk, 22 January 2015.

—, '"Vampire Therapy" Could Reverse Ageing, Scientists Find', www.telegraph.co.uk, 4 May 2014

Koch, Tina, et al., 'Storytelling Reveals the Active, Positive Lives of Centenarians', *Nursing Older People*, XXII/8 (October 2010), doi:10.7748/nop2010.10.22.8.31.c7995

Kwak, Chung Shil, 'Discovery of Novel Sources of Vitamin B12 in Traditional Korean Foods from Nutritional Surveys of Centenarians', *Current Gerontology and Geriatrics Research* (2010), doi:10.1155/2010/374897

Langreth, Robert, 'How to Live to 100', www.forbes.com, 4 August 2009

'Longevity Facts Revealed in 50-year Study of Men Who Made It to 100', www.seniorjournal.com, 5 May 2015

Longevity Science Panel, 'Life Expectancy: Past and Future Variations by Gender in England and Wales', Longevity Science Advisory Panel Paper 2, 2012, www.longevitypanel.co.uk

'Love and Death', *The Economist*, 13 June 1998

'Marriage Makes People Live Longer', www.bbc.co.uk/news, 10 August 2006

Marx, Arthur, 'The Ultimate Cigar Aficionado', www.cigaraficionado.com, Winter 1994–5

Matsuyama, Kanoko, and Terje Langeland, 'Oldest Man in History Dies at Age 116', *Sydney Morning Herald*, 12 June 2013, www.smh.com.au

Medvedev, Z. A., 'Age Structure of the Soviet Population of the Caucasus', National Institute for Medical Research (London, 1985)

'Men's Genes "May Limit Lifespan"', www.bbc.co.uk/news, 2 December 2009

Meyer, Julie, 'Centenarians: 2010', United States Census Bureau (Washington, DC, 2012)

Middleton, Christopher, 'Why Do Women Live Longer Than Men?', www.newsweek.com, 1 August 2014

Mihill, Chris, 'Marriage is the Key to Long, Healthy, Relatively Stress-free Life, Says Report', *The Guardian*, 18 July 1995

'Mind and Body', *The Economist*, 26 February 2011

Minton, Torri, 'One of World's Oldest Dies in His Sleep', www.sfgate.com, 28 April 1998

Mitchell, Braxton D., et al., 'Living the Good Life? Mortality and Hospital Utilization Patterns in the Old Order Amish', www.journals.plos.org, 19 December 2012, doi:10.1371/journal.pone.0051560

Montagu, J. D., 'Length of Life in the Ancient World: A Controlled Study', *Journal of the Royal Society of Medicine*, LXXXVII (January 1994), pp. 25–6

Moore, Lucy, 'A Wicked Twinkle and a Streak of Steel', www.theguardian.com, 31 March 2002

'Mr Muscle', *The Economist*, 29 August 2009

'Mutant Genes "Key to Long Life"', www.bbc.co.uk/news, 15 November 2009

Norris, Jeffrey, 'Sugared Soda Consumption: Cell Aging Associated in New Study', www.ucsf.edu, 16 October 2014

'Of Mice and Monkeys', *The Economist*, 11 July 2009

'Okinawa Centenarian Study', www.okicent.org, 2017

'Pacific Health Research Institute/Kuakini Medical Center Releases First Ever Long-term Human Study Showing Link between Decreased Calorie Intake and Longevity', www.businesswire.com, 30 August 2004

Park, S. C., et al., 'Environment and Gender Influences on the Nutritional and Health Status of Korean Centenarians', *Asian Journal of Gerontology and Geriatrics*, III/2 (August 2008), pp. 75–83

Parker-Pope, Tara, 'Is Marriage Good for Your Health?', www.nytimes.com, 14 April 2010

Pedoe, Arthur, 'Further Perspectives about Longevity', *The Actuary*, III/2 (February 1969)

'Pensioners Who Retire from Life', *New Society*, 5 June 1987

'People Who Look Young for Their Age "Live Longer"', www.bbc.co.uk/news, 14 December 2009

Perls, Thomas, and Ruth Fretts, 'Why Women Live Longer than Men', www.cmu.edu, June 1998

Perls, Thomas T., et al., 'Middle-aged Mothers Live Longer', www.nature.com, 11 September 1997

Pinker, Susan, 'Why Face-to-face Contact Matters in Our Digital Age', www.guardian.com, 20 March 2015

Polidori, M. C., et al., 'Different Antioxidant Profiles in Italian Centenarians: The Sardinian Peculiarity', www.nature.com, 17 January 2007

Poulain, Michel, 'Exceptional Longevity in Okinawa', www.demographic-research.org, 21 July 2011

—, et al., 'Identification of a Geographic Area Characterized by Extreme Longevity in the Sardinia Island: The AKEA study', www.sciencedirect.com, 9 August 2004

Preidt, Robert, 'Centenarians a Happy Lot, Survey Says', http://consumer.healthday.com, 2 May 2013

Richmond, Robyn L., 'The Changing Face of the Australian Population: Growth in Centenarians', *Medical Journal of Australia*, CLXXXVIII/12 (2008), pp. 720–23

Riding, Alan, 'Leni Riefenstahl, Film Innovator Tied to Hitler, Dies at 101', *New York Times*, 10 September 2003, www.writing.upenn.edu

Robine, J.-M., and M. Allard, 'Jeanne Calment: Validation of the Duration of Her Life', in *Validation of Exceptional Longevity* (Odense, 1999), ed. B. Jeune and J. W. Vaupel, Monographs of Population Aging, 6, www.demogr.mpg.de

Schoenhofen, Emily A., et al., 'Characteristics of 32 Supercentenarians', *Journal of the American Geriatrics Society*, LIV/8 (August 2006), doi:10.1111/j.1532-5415.2006.00826.x

'Secrets to Longevity: It's Not All about Broccoli', www.npr.org, 24 March 2011

Serra, Valentina, et al., 'Living Beyond 100: A Report on Centenarians,' www.ilcuk.org.uk, November 2011

Shafy, Samiha, 'The Secrets of the Supercentenarians', www.spiegel.de, 20 September 2010

'Single Men "Die Younger"', www.bbc.co.uk/news, 23 August 2001

'A Slow-burning Fuse', *The Economist*, 27 June 2009

Smith, George Davey, et al., 'Sex and Death: Are They Related? Findings from the Caerphilly Cohort Study', *British Medical Journal*, cccxv (20 December 1997), pp. 1641–4

Spickernell, Sarah, 'Living Near a Noisy London Road Could Shorten Your Life', www.cityam.com, 24 June 2015

'The Stronger Sex', *The Economist*, 15 January 2005

Tafaro, L., et al., 'Smoking and Longevity: An Incompatible Binomial?', www.ncbi.nlm.nih.gov, 2004

Templer, Robert, 'General Vo Nguyen Giap Obituary', www.theguardian.com, 4 October 2013

'Tests Raise Life Extension Hopes', www.bbc.co.uk/news, 8 July 2009

Thatcher, Roger, 'The Demography of Centenarians in England and Wales', Population Trends 96, Office for National Statistics, Summer 1999, www.ons.gov.uk

—, 'The Growth of High Ages in England and Wales, 1635–2106', in Heiner Maier, Jutta Gampe, Bernard Jeune, Jean-Marie Robine and James W. Vaupel, eds, *Supercentenarians* (Berlin, 2010)

Thean, Tara, 'Even the Long-lived Smoke, Drink and Don't Exercise', TIME, 5 August 2011, www.time.com/health

Tierney, John, 'The Optimists are Right', www.nytimes.com, 29 September 1996

Trimingham, Robin W., 'Is Life after Retirement the Same for Men and Women?', www.olderhood.com, 22 May 2013

Vasto, Sonya, et al., 'Centenarians and Diet: What They Eat in the Western Part of Sicily', *Immunity and Ageing* (23 April 2012), doi:10.1186/1742-4933-9-10

'Vilcabamba: The Town of Very Old People', www.hoaxes.org, accessed 20 December 2016

Whiteman, Honor, 'Free Radicals "Do Not Cause Aging, They Combat It," Study Suggests', www.medicalnewstoday.com, 11 May 2014

Wilmoth, John, et al., 'The Oldest Man Ever? A Case Study of Exceptional Longevity', *The Gerontologist*, xxxvi/6 (December 1996), pp. 783–8

Winterman, Denise, 'The Towns Where People Live the Longest', www.bbc.co.uk/news, 19 February 2008

'Women "Fight Off Disease Better"', www.bbc.co.uk/news, 13 May 2009

The Work Foundation, Lancaster University, 'Unemployment is Bad for your Health', 11 June 2014, www.theworkfoundation.com

United Nations, 'World Population Ageing: 2009', www.un.org, 19 December 2009

Young, Robert D., et al., 'Typologies of Extreme Longevity Myths', www.hindawi.com, 28 December 2010

Zeng, Yi, and Ke Shen, 'Resilience Significantly Contributes to Exceptional Longevity', *Centenarian Studies: Important Contributors to Our Understanding of the Aging Process and Longevity* (2010), doi:10.1155/2010/525693

ACKNOWLEDGEMENTS

I would like to thank my wife, as always, for her unfailing support and encouragement.

PHOTO ACKNOWLEDGEMENTS

The author and the publishers wish to express their thanks to the below sources of illustrative material and/or permission to reproduce it.

Alamy: p. 83 (Reuters); Bering Land Bridge National Preserve: p. 208; Roman Bonnefoy: p. 94; Centraal Museum, Utrecht: p. 16; Charlottea: p. 196; Dutch National Archives, The Hague: p. 135; Eric Gaba: p. 133; Getty Images: pp. 30 (Topical Press Agency), 64 (John G. Mabanglo/AFP), 74 (Peter Macdiarmid), 78 (Shula Kopershtouk), 88 (photo by The Asahi Shimbun via Getty Images), 90 (Jiji Press/AFP); HiraV: p. 177; Steve Jurvetson: p. 214; Johnrabe: p. 143; Library of Congress, Washington, DC: pp. 119, 128, 140; National Archives and Records Administration (NARA), Washington, DC: pp. 109, 151; National Portrait Gallery, London: p. 21; Bengt Oberger: p. 219; Prado Museum: p. 19; Robert Scarth: p. 13; REX Shutterstock: pp. 51 (Excel Media), 61 (Sipa Press), 77 (Daily Mail), 89 (Michael Fresco), 93 (ANL), 95 (Michael Bowles), 106 (Tim Rooke), 124 (Fresco/ANL), 207 (Tom E White); Saqibmahayı: p. 194; Thomas Schmidt: p. 132 top; Ricardo Stuckert (PR/ABr/Brazil): p. 131; SuperJew: p. 200; Tobi 87: p. 198; Alan Warren: pp. 104, 114; Wellcome Library, London: pp. 20, 23, 117.

INDEX